Battle Orders • 17

US Army Infantry
Divisions 1942–43

John J Sayen Jr

Consultant Editor Dr Duncan Anderson • *Series editors* Marcus Cowper and Nikolai Bogdanovic

First published in Great Britain in 2006 by Osprey Publishing,
West Way, Botley, Oxford OX2 0PH, United Kingdom.
443 Park Avenue South, New York, NY 10016, USA

Email: info@ospreypublishing.com

ISBN 1 84176 952 5

Editorial by Ilios Publishing, Oxford, UK (www.iliospublishing.com)

Design: Bounford.com
Index by Glyn Sutcliffe
Originated by The Electronic Page Company, Cwmbran, UK

06 07 08 09 10   10 9 8 7 6 5 4 3 2 1

A CIP catalog record for this book is available from the British Library.

For a catalog of all books published by Osprey Military and Aviation please contact:

Osprey Direct, C/o Random House Distribution Center, 400 Hahn Road,
Westminster, MD 21157
info@ospreydirect.com

Osprey Direct UK, P.O. Box 140, Wellingborough, Northants, NN8 2FA, UK
E-mail: info@ospreydirect.co.uk
www.ospreypublishing.com

Image credits and author's note

Unless otherwise indicated, the photographic images that appear
in this work are from the US Army Signal Corps collection. In the
tree diagrams and maps in this volume, the units and movements
of national forces are depicted in the following colors:

US Army units	Olive Drab
US Marine Corps units	Navy Blue
Japanese units	Red
German Army units	Gray
British Army units	Brown
Australian Army units	Orange

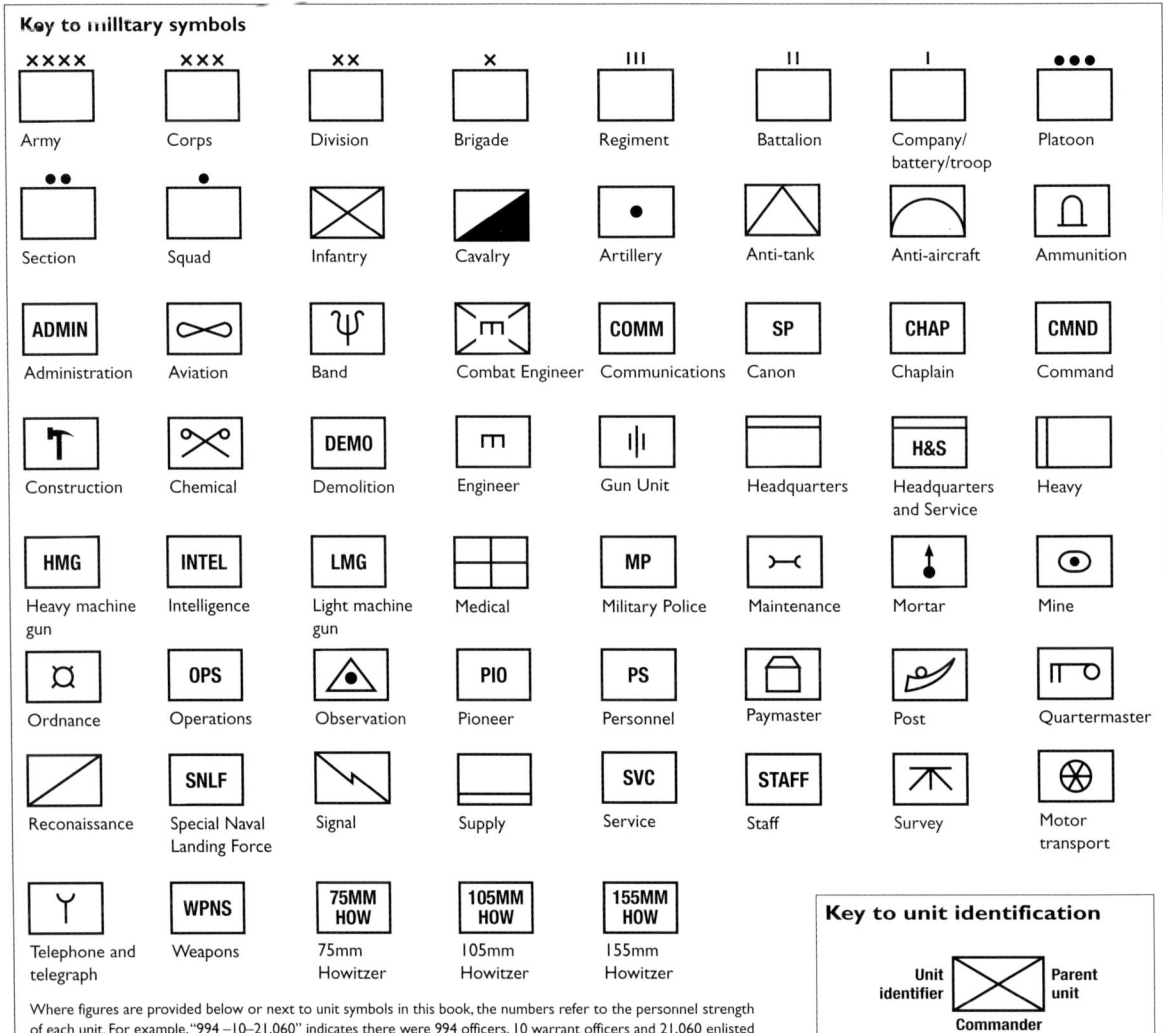

Key to military symbols

Army · Corps · Division · Brigade · Regiment · Battalion · Company/battery/troop · Platoon

Section · Squad · Infantry · Cavalry · Artillery · Anti-tank · Anti-aircraft · Ammunition

Administration · Aviation · Band · Combat Engineer · Communications · Canon · Chaplain · Command

Construction · Chemical · Demolition · Engineer · Gun Unit · Headquarters · Headquarters and Service · Heavy

Heavy machine gun · Intelligence · Light machine gun · Medical · Military Police · Maintenance · Mortar · Mine

Ordnance · Operations · Observation · Pioneer · Personnel · Paymaster · Post · Quartermaster

Reconaissance · Special Naval Landing Force · Signal · Supply · Service · Staff · Survey · Motor transport

Telephone and telegraph · Weapons · 75mm Howitzer · 105mm Howitzer · 155mm Howitzer

Where figures are provided below or next to unit symbols in this book, the numbers refer to the personnel strength
of each unit. For example, "994–10–21,060" indicates there were 994 officers, 10 warrant officers and 21,060 enlisted
men. Where only two figures are provided, for example "72–1,608," they indicate the number of officers and enlisted
men only (the unit had no warrant officers.)

Key to unit identification

Unit identifier — Parent unit
Commander
(+) with added elements   (-) less elements

Contents

Introduction

Notwithstanding the power of American industry, the real fighting strength of the US Army during World War II lay in its infantry divisions. In this respect, the US Army did not differ from any other army of World War II, notwithstanding the headline-grabbing successes of Germany's Panzers and even, later in the war, of the US Army's own armored divisions. Though US infantry divisions were relatively manpower-intensive, they were far easier to ship overseas than armored divisions. In addition, the infantry divisions were the only type of large fighting unit that literally could go anywhere and fight anyone, while in nearly all situations enjoying combat power at least equal to and usually greater than that of their opponents.

This volume covers the history and development of these infantry divisions up until the end of 1943. At that time, two-thirds of the US Army's ground forces had not yet left the United States. Of those units that had, many were still awaiting their first combat. However, by the same time most of the decisive battles of the war had already been fought. Stalingrad, Kursk, and the limited success of the U-Boat war had left Germany permanently on the defensive. The Japanese, following their disasters at Midway and Guadalcanal, were well on their way towards eventual defeat.

Troops of H Co, 179th Infantry, 45th Division bypass a demolished bridge near Faicchio (vicinity of Naples) Italy 18 October, 1943.

Combat mission and preparation for war

The infantry division had been the key component of the US Army's combat power ever since the Army organized its first permanent divisions in 1914. By 1918, when the American Expeditionary Force (AEF) first experienced a major European war, its standard infantry division was probably the largest formation of its kind ever fielded. With an authorized strength of over 28,000 officers and men, it was nearly twice the size of a French or German division. It was a "square" division, meaning that its main fighting element consisted of four infantry regiments (grouped under two brigades). In Europe in 1914 square divisions had been the rule, but heavy losses and the tactical unwieldiness of their square divisions, had caused the French and German armies to switch to smaller but more mobile and efficient "triangular" divisions. The main fighting element of a triangular division was only three infantry regiments.

Townsfolk cheer as a CCKW-353 (long wheel base) with hard-top cab but no winch carries troops from the 180th Infantry, 45th Division, through Lioni, Italy, September 26, 1943.

In battle, despite their great size and heavy firepower, the AEF square divisions were a disappointment. Their command and control structures were inadequate and they lacked qualified commanders and staff officers. Shortages of draft animals and a consequent over-reliance on primitive and underpowered trucks that could only operate on the few available roads made logistics a constant problem. Heavy casualties and a poorly thought out personnel replacement and training system ensured that the AEF divisions were chronically under strength especially in their infantry regiments.

After the war, General John J. Pershing, the former AEF commander, pressed for a triangular division of 16,875, but encountered considerable opposition. Pershing eventually conceded that a square division of less than 20,000 might still meet the requirements of a future war. In 1921 the Army issued organizational tables for a division of 19,997. Although they were barely within Pershing's upper limit (and later expanded to over 22,000), the War Department approved them as the US Army's official war-strength division.

Soldiers of the 143d Infantry, 36th Division land at Paestum (south of Salerno), Italy, on September 9, 1943. The 143d was in reserve during the actual assault so its landing was largely unopposed.

The switch to triangular divisions

During the 1920s and 1930s the Army constantly experimented with alternative combat unit organizations of its own while observing those of foreign armies. As time went on, the triangular division concept gained a great deal of approval. As a result, on August 13, 1936 the Secretary of War approved for field-testing a set of tables for a triangular division of 13,552 officers and men. The 2d Infantry Division would be the test bed. Testing eventually resulted in a March 1938 report recommending a very austere triangular infantry division of 10,275.

In light of the deteriorating world situation and the resultant willingness of Congress to pass larger military appropriations and even a peacetime draft, the War Department believed that it could afford to organize its combat formations more on a basis of

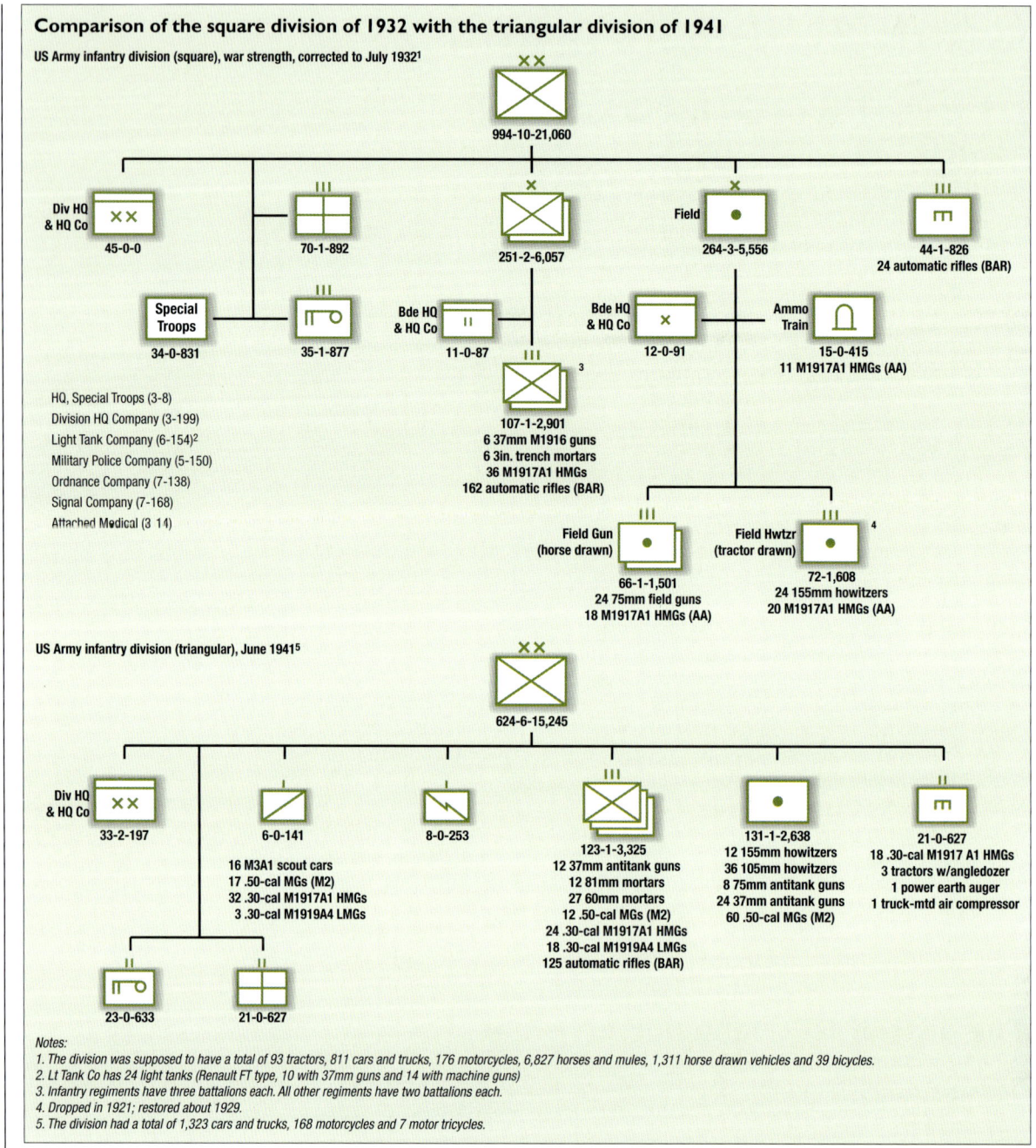

Comparison of the square division of 1932 with the triangular division of 1941

US Army infantry division (square), war strength, corrected to July 1932[1]

994-10-21,060

Div HQ & HQ Co
45-0-0

70-1-892

251-2-6,057

Field
264-3-5,556

44-1-826
24 automatic rifles (BAR)

Special Troops
34-0-831

35-1-877

Bde HQ & HQ Co
11-0-87

Bde HQ & HQ Co
12-0-91

Ammo Train
15-0-415
11 M1917A1 HMGs (AA)

HQ, Special Troops (3-8)
Division HQ Company (3-199)
Light Tank Company (6-154)[2]
Military Police Company (5-150)
Ordnance Company (7-138)
Signal Company (7-168)
Attached Medical (3-14)

107-1-2,901 [3]
6 37mm M1916 guns
6 3in. trench mortars
36 M1917A1 HMGs
162 automatic rifles (BAR)

Field Gun (horse drawn)
66-1-1,501
24 75mm field guns
18 M1917A1 HMGs (AA)

Field Hwtzr (tractor drawn) [4]
72-1,608
24 155mm howitzers
20 M1917A1 HMGs (AA)

US Army infantry division (triangular), June 1941[5]

624-6-15,245

Div HQ & HQ Co
33-2-197

6-0-141
16 M3A1 scout cars
17 .50-cal MGs (M2)
32 .30-cal M1917A1 HMGs
3 .30-cal M1919A4 LMGs

8-0-253

123-1-3,325
12 37mm antitank guns
12 81mm mortars
27 60mm mortars
12 .50-cal MGs (M2)
24 .30-cal M1917A1 HMGs
18 .30-cal M1919A4 LMGs
125 automatic rifles (BAR)

131-1-2,638
12 155mm howitzers
36 105mm howitzers
8 75mm antitank guns
24 37mm antitank guns
60 .50-cal MGs (M2)

21-0-627
18 .30-cal M1917 A1 HMGs
3 tractors w/angledozer
1 power earth auger
1 truck-mtd air compressor

23-0-633

21-0-627

Notes:
1. The division was supposed to have a total of 93 tractors, 811 cars and trucks, 176 motorcycles, 6,827 horses and mules, 1,311 horse drawn vehicles and 39 bicycles.
2. Lt Tank Co has 24 light tanks (Renault FT type, 10 with 37mm guns and 14 with machine guns)
3. Infantry regiments have three battalions each. All other regiments have two battalions each.
4. Dropped in 1921; restored about 1929.
5. The division had a total of 1,323 cars and trucks, 168 motorcycles and 7 motor tricycles.

what was desirable than what was affordable. In this vein the War Department issued new organization tables for a division of about 12,000. It first published these new tables in December 1938 and (with subsequent updates) they officially replaced the old square tables for the Regular Army divisions. National Guard divisions did not become triangular until 1941–42. By 1941 the total authorized strength of a triangular infantry division had increased to more than 15,000.

Mobilization, 1939–42

The US Army mobilization for World War II began in October 1939, well before the United States officially entered the war. The first step was to create new

Soldiers from the 32d Division (probably the 128th Infantry) walk along the beach at Cape Endaiadere, New Guinea, December 21, 1942. They have just reduced a Japanese bunker complex, some of which is barely visible to the left.

divisions to augment the 1st, 2d and 3d Infantry divisions (which had existed since 1917). Using newly activated regiments and regiments made surplus by the triangular reorganization, the Army had created five new divisions (numbers 4 through 8) by August 1940. The addition of two Hawaiian National Guard infantry divisions to the still square 11th (Hawaiian) Division enabled its reorganization as the 24th and 25th Infantry divisions.

The second step was the mobilization of the National Guard. Public Resolution No. 96, passed by Congress on August 27, 1940 (in a partial response to the fall of France) empowered the President to order the National Guard into Federal service for 12 months. In fact, the President had actually started to federalize the National Guard as early as February. It took more than a year to mobilize the 18 National Guard infantry divisions. In 1917, the Army mobilized 17 National Guard divisions within three months, but these divisions were urgently needed in France. The 1917 mobilization began in mid summer and this allowed the troops to live in tents. The World War II mobilization was more in response to a training emergency than a combat emergency. Newly mobilized units would not be going overseas anytime soon

Troops of Company "A," 186th Infantry, 41st Division arrive at Strip #4, Dobodura, New Guinea from Port Moresby to relieve troops of the 32d Division, February 4, 1943.

and they would need permanent shelter. Thus, the War Department mobilized the National Guard divisions no faster than it could build barracks for them.

The third step in the Army's mobilization was the implementation of the first peacetime draft in American history. Congress authorized it on September 16, 1940 but for 12 months only. It could be renewed after that (and it was). Regular Army divisions were already being stripped to provide cadres for new units so draftee manpower was sorely needed to refill them. When they deployed overseas they were composed mainly of draftees. National Guard divisions were under-strength to begin with and lost many men to transfers or discharges after activation. Even though a triangular division required only two-thirds as many men as a square division, by the time the National Guard divisions deployed overseas one-half of their men were draftees.

The conversion of the National Guard divisions from square to triangular began in late 1941 but most of it was only accomplished during the first quarter of 1942. Typically, a division would drop an infantry regiment and both its infantry brigade headquarters; convert its artillery brigade from three regiments to four separate battalions; and convert its engineer, quartermaster, and medical regiments into battalions. Some divisions dropped two infantry regiments and replaced one of them either with another National Guard regiment (often from another state) or a newly raised draftee regiment.

With only a few exceptions, the separate regiments made surplus by the reorganization of the National Guard divisions were not used to form new divisions. Some served as garrisons, usually far away from any combat. A few served in the combat theaters, mostly on rear security missions. Most of the others served inside CONUS as depot or training units. (A future proposed Battle Orders title will carry more information on these regiments.)

Despite the draft, no new infantry divisions could be created before March 1942 or after August 1943. The existing force structure alone consumed all the available manpower. The new divisions would organize from scratch using draftees with a Regular Army cadre.

The infantry division of April 1942

The new division continued, generally speaking, to conform to the basic principles established in 1938 but the numerous additions of personnel and equipment (mainly of trucks) that had occurred since 1938 were certainly a mixed blessing. Although the extra trucks improved tactical mobility, they actually reduced the division's strategic mobility by making it harder to ship overseas. Given the limited amount of shipping available, this was a major consideration. Manpower was also a problem. Air and naval forces were claiming a much larger share of it than they ever had in 1917–18, and the ground forces were already feeling the pinch. More men per division would mean that fewer divisions could be organized.

Three infantry regiments formed the division combat element. Combat support came mainly from the artillery and engineer battalions. The quartermaster battalion (soon to be replaced by separate quartermaster and ordnance companies) and a medical battalion offered limited service support. The division headquarters and its signal company provided command and control.

In a combat theater two to five divisions usually operated under a corps headquarters though there were occasions when divisions operated independently. Two or more corps would fall under an army headquarters. These higher headquarters also controlled supporting troops that could operate in support of or attached to the infantry divisions and equip them for the task at hand. The US Army used far more of these troops, relative to its size, than any other army in the world. That was another reason why (for its size) it fielded very few divisions. Non-divisional organizations included combat units, such as tank and tank destroyer battalions, armored cavalry groups and a few infantry regiments or separate battalions. Far more numerous were the combat

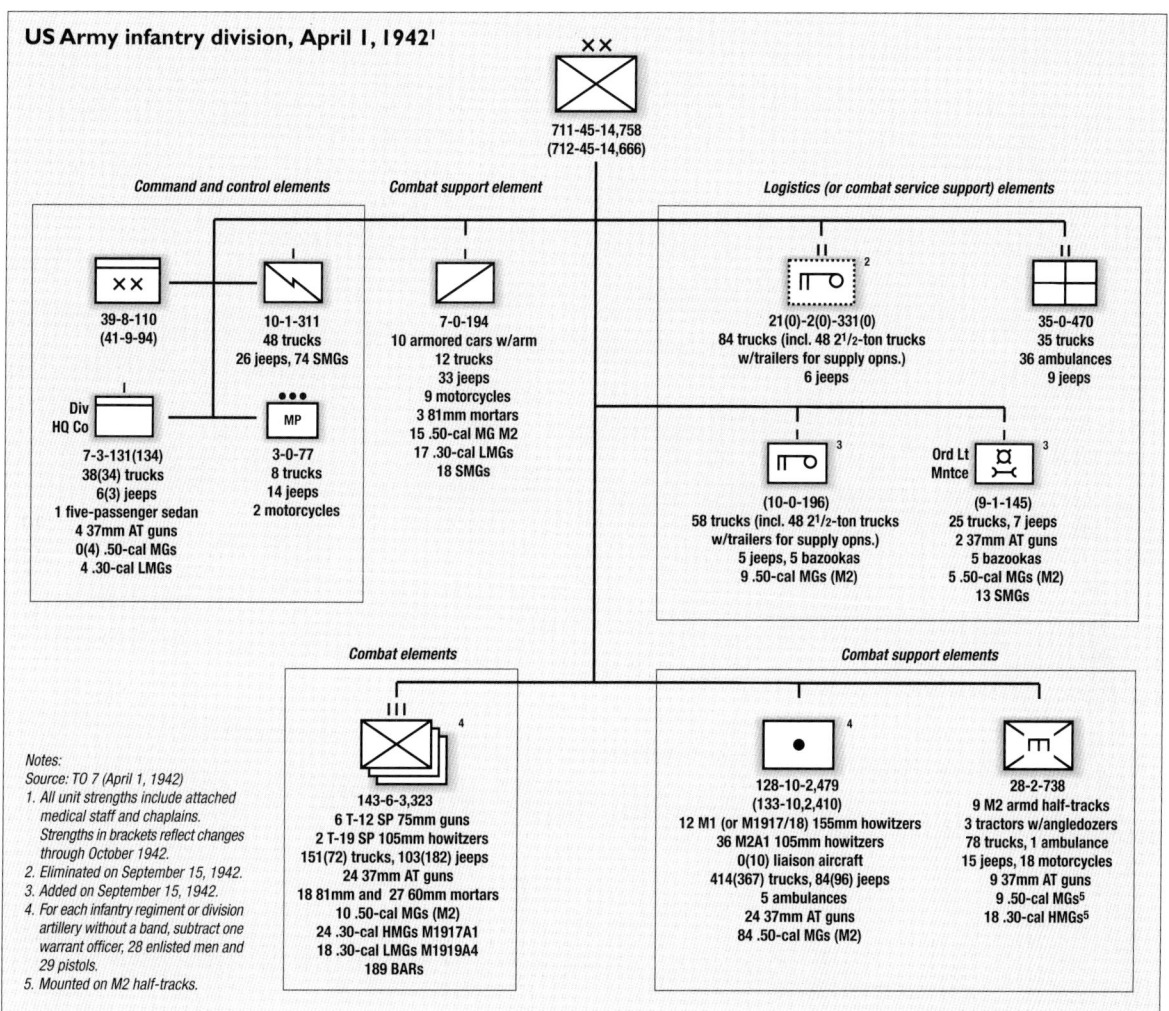

US Army infantry division, April 1, 1942[1]

711-45-14,758
(712-45-14,666)

Command and control elements

×× 39-8-110
(41-9-94)

10-1-311
48 trucks
26 jeeps, 74 SMGs

Div HQ Co
7-3-131(134)
38(34) trucks
6(3) jeeps
1 five-passenger sedan
4 37mm AT guns
0(4) .50-cal MGs
4 .30-cal LMGs

MP
3-0-77
8 trucks
14 jeeps
2 motorcycles

Combat support element

7-0-194
10 armored cars w/arm
12 trucks
33 jeeps
9 motorcycles
3 81mm mortars
15 .50-cal MG M2
17 .30-cal LMGs
18 SMGs

Logistics (or combat service support) elements

21(0)-2(0)-331(0) [2]
84 trucks (incl. 48 2½-ton trucks
w/trailers for supply opns.)
6 jeeps

35-0-470
35 trucks
36 ambulances
9 jeeps

(10-0-196) [3]
58 trucks (incl. 48 2½-ton trucks
w/trailers for supply opns.)
5 jeeps, 5 bazookas
9 .50-cal MGs (M2)

Ord Lt Mntce [3]
(9-1-145)
25 trucks, 7 jeeps
2 37mm AT guns
5 bazookas
5 .50-cal MGs (M2)
13 SMGs

Combat elements

143-6-3,323 [4]
6 T-12 SP 75mm guns
2 T-19 SP 105mm howitzers
151(72) trucks, 103(182) jeeps
24 37mm AT guns
18 81mm and 27 60mm mortars
10 .50-cal MGs (M2)
24 .30-cal HMGs M1917A1
18 .30-cal LMGs M1919A4
189 BARs

Combat support elements

128-10-2,479 [4]
(133-10,2,410)
12 M1 (or M1917/18) 155mm howitzers
36 M2A1 105mm howitzers
0(10) liaison aircraft
414(367) trucks, 84(96) jeeps
5 ambulances
24 37mm AT guns
84 .50-cal MGs (M2)

28-2-738
9 M2 armd half-tracks
3 tractors w/angledozers
78 trucks, 1 ambulance
15 jeeps, 18 motorcycles
9 37mm AT guns
9 .50-cal MGs[5]
18 .30-cal HMGs[5]

Notes:
Source: TO 7 (April 1, 1942)
1. All unit strengths include attached medical staff and chaplains. Strengths in brackets reflect changes through October 1942.
2. Eliminated on September 15, 1942.
3. Added on September 15, 1942.
4. For each infantry regiment or division artillery without a band, subtract one warrant officer, 28 enlisted men and 29 pistols.
5. Mounted on M2 half-tracks.

support units. These included huge numbers of field and antiaircraft artillery of all calibers plus equally large numbers of combat engineers. There would be three to six battalions of each of these for every infantry division. The AGF only controlled those combat service support units that operated in forward areas but these were still quite numerous and included such colorless but essential elements as Quartermaster Corps truck companies, Ordnance Corps maintenance companies, plus signal, medical and military police. The infantry divisions themselves were only the tip of this iceberg. Although relatively few non-divisional units were actually attached to infantry divisions, they worked tirelessly in support of them and the infantry divisions could not have fought effectively without them.

Unit organization

Table 1: Infantry division officer rank abbreviations (1942–43)	
Rank	Abbreviation
Major General	MG
Brigadier General	BG
Colonel	COL
Lieutenant Colonel	LTC
Major	MAJ
Captain	CPT
First Lieutenant	1LT
Second Lieutenant	2LT
Warrant Officer	WO

Table 2: Infantry division enlisted ranks (1942–43)

Pay grade	"Hard stripe" rank	Technician rank	Notes
1	Master Sergeant (MSgt)	T-1	*Technician ranks:* To create a career path for enlisted men with technical skills beyond the basic requirements of their branch but for whom there were no leadership positions, the War Department initiated a system of "technician" ranks in 1921. Technicians received the pay and wore the rank insignia (with a letter "T") of non-commissioned officers (NCO) of the same grade but only had the authority of (and were listed as) senior privates. They could occupy any of the five higher enlisted grades but most were T-4 or T-5. An infantry division had no T-1 or T-2 technicians and only about 20 T-3. Technicians typically served as mechanics, radio operators, telephone and switchboard operators, clerks, stenographers, draftsmen, and senior truck drivers. In a rifle or weapons company the only technicians were the cooks and the armorers (small-arms repairmen) but in division headquarters nearly every enlisted man who was not an NCO had a technician's rating.
2	Technical Sergeant (TSgt)	T-2	
3	Staff Sergeant (SSgt)	T-3	
4	Sergeant (Sgt)	T-4	
5	Corporal (Cpl)	T-5	
6	Private 1st Class (PFC /Pvt.)	None	*Privates/PFC:* In most units 40 percent of the privates without technician rank were PFC.
7	Private (Pvt.)	None	
None	Sergeant Major (SgtMaj)	None	*Sergeant Major:* Not a rank but a title given to the senior enlisted man in a battalion or larger unit. He was usually assigned to the operations and training (S-3) section.
None	First Sergeant (1stSgt)	None	*First Sergeant:* A title given to the senior enlisted man in a company. He usually served at company headquarters, overseeing administrative matters. Like a sergeant major his actual rank might be as low as staff sergeant.

Basic privates: Most organizations within the division included a number of "basic" privates equal to seven to 10 percent of their enlisted strength. They were called "basic" because they had only received basic training for their service branch. They acted as "live-in" replacements, becoming familiar with the unit and performing odd jobs until they were needed to fill a vacancy. The need for them was constant. Even out of combat there was significant personnel attrition from disease, accidents, absences, etc. Basic privates allowed a unit to fill vacancies immediately while awaiting the replacement or return of absent or unfit personnel.

The rifle squad

Until the late 1950s, the rifle squad was the smallest and most basic element in the US Army's infantry above the individual soldier. Since December 1936 the rifle squad had consisted of 12 men. Its purpose was to exploit the effectiveness of the new semi-automatic M1 Garand rifle and initially all its members were riflemen. By 1942, however, only 10 were riflemen (including the squad leader and assistant squad leader). One was an automatic rifleman, armed with an improved version of the Browning Automatic Rifle (BAR), and another was a rifle grenadier. The grenadier carried the older bolt-action M1903 Springfield rifle with an M1 grenade launcher because no grenade launcher was as yet available for the M1 rifle. The grenade launcher could fire the new shaped charge antitank rifle grenades as well more conventional fragmentation grenades. The grenadier also gave the squad a weapon that could attack enemies in below-ground positions such as trenches and fighting holes where the flat trajectory rifles and BAR carried by other squad members could not reach.

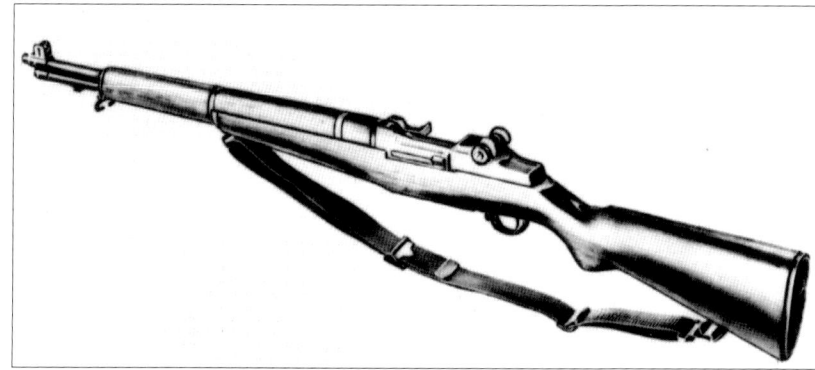

The M1 semi-automatic rifle, a weapon that revolutionized US Army tactical doctrine and was once described by General George Patton as "the best battle implement ever devised."

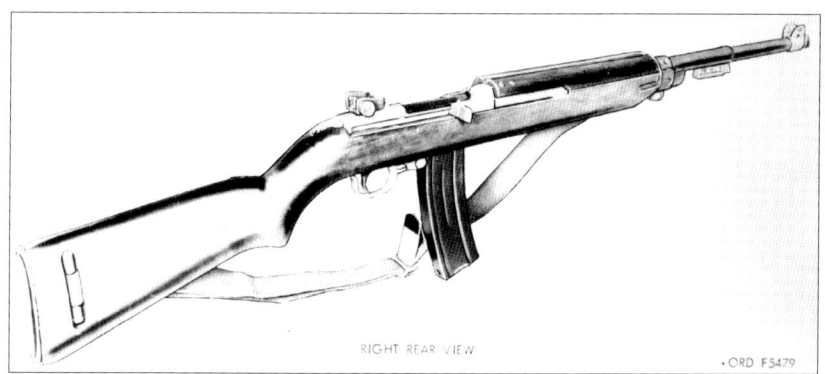

RIGHT REAR VIEW

· ORD F5479

An M1 carbine, fitted with the new (late war) 30-round magazine. First introduced as a pistol substitute, the carbine was light and fun to shoot, but it was underpowered and suffered from poor reliability at extreme temperatures.

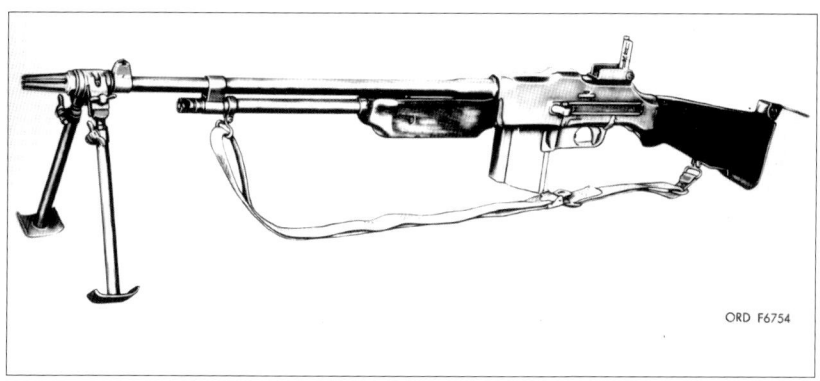

ORD F6754

The improved M1918A2 BAR was the US Army's standard squad-level automatic weapon throughout World War II and the Korean War. In the infantry regiment, up until late 1943, the BAR was also used to protect vehicles from air attack. The far more effective M2 .50-cal machine gun later replaced it in that role.

The rifle platoon and company

There were three rifle squads in a rifle platoon and there were three rifle platoons in a rifle company; from 1939, the rifle company also included a weapons platoon. This enabled the rifle company to displace the battalion as the infantry's smallest fighting unit with its own base of fire. The weapons platoon employed the M2 60mm mortar and the "light" air-cooled Browning M1919A4. John Browning designed the M1919 during World War I to serve as a tank machine gun, but the Army developed it into a weapon intermediate between the heavy M1917A1 Browning and the much lighter BAR. Because it could fire only from its tripod, it could not replace the BAR, even though it could deliver about twice the firepower.

The infantry battalion

A headquarters and headquarters company, three rifle companies, and a heavy weapons company made up an infantry battalion. The heavy weapons company was for the battalion what the weapons platoon was for the company. Its 81mm mortar platoon used the M1 mortar, which, like the 60mm, was a licenced copy of a Hotchkiss-Brandt design. Its two heavy machine gun (HMG) platoons used the World War I-era, water-cooled M1917A1 Browning. Despite its age and weight it was both popular and effective. The machine guns

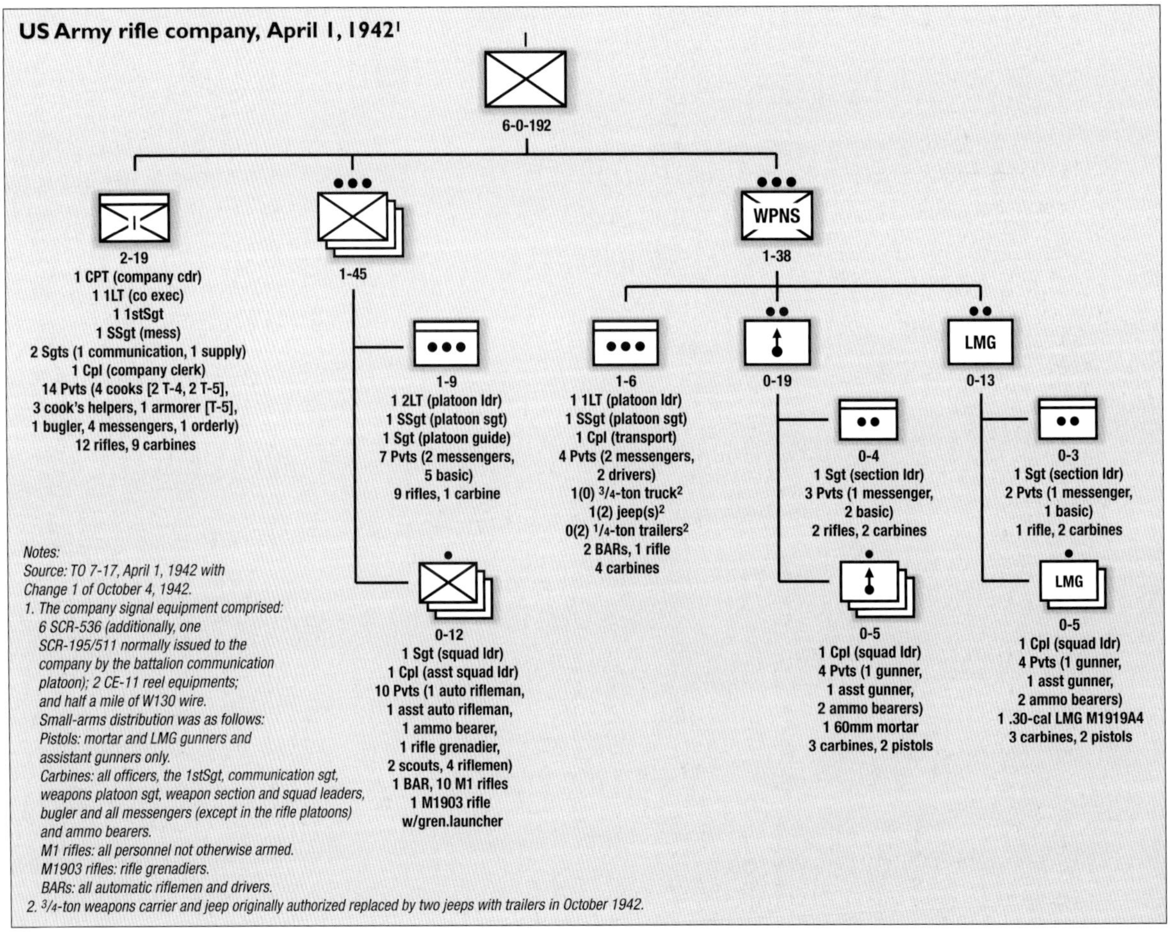

Members of the 397th Infantry, 100th Division firing the 60mm mortar during training maneuvers at Ft Jackson, SC, April 28, 1943.

US Army rifle company, April 1, 1942[1]

6-0-192

2-19
1 CPT (company cdr)
1 1LT (co exec)
1 1stSgt
1 SSgt (mess)
2 Sgts (1 communication, 1 supply)
1 Cpl (company clerk)
14 Pvts (4 cooks [2 T-4, 2 T-5],
3 cook's helpers, 1 armorer [T-5],
1 bugler, 4 messengers, 1 orderly)
12 rifles, 9 carbines

1-45

WPNS
1-38

1-9
1 2LT (platoon ldr)
1 SSgt (platoon sgt)
1 Sgt (platoon guide)
7 Pvts (2 messengers,
5 basic)
9 rifles, 1 carbine

1-6
1 1LT (platoon ldr)
1 SSgt (platoon sgt)
1 Cpl (transport)
4 Pvts (2 messengers,
2 drivers)
1(0) 3/4-ton truck[2]
1(2) jeep(s)[2]
0(2) 1/4-ton trailers[2]
2 BARs, 1 rifle
4 carbines

0-19

0-4
1 Sgt (section ldr)
3 Pvts (1 messenger,
2 basic)
2 rifles, 2 carbines

LMG
0-13

0-3
1 Sgt (section ldr)
2 Pvts (1 messenger,
1 basic)
1 rifle, 2 carbines

0-12
1 Sgt (squad ldr)
1 Cpl (asst squad ldr)
10 Pvts (1 auto rifleman,
1 asst auto rifleman,
1 ammo bearer,
1 rifle grenadier,
2 scouts, 4 riflemen)
1 BAR, 10 M1 rifles
1 M1903 rifle
w/gren.launcher

0-5
1 Cpl (squad ldr)
4 Pvts (1 gunner,
1 asst gunner,
2 ammo bearers)
1 60mm mortar
3 carbines, 2 pistols

0-5
1 Cpl (squad ldr)
4 Pvts (1 gunner,
1 asst gunner,
2 ammo bearers)
1 .30-cal LMG M1919A4
3 carbines, 2 pistols

Notes:
Source: TO 7-17, April 1, 1942 with
Change 1 of October 4, 1942.
1. The company signal equipment comprised:
6 SCR-536 (additionally, one
SCR-195/511 normally issued to the
company by the battalion communication
platoon); 2 CE-11 reel equipments;
and half a mile of W130 wire.
Small-arms distribution was as follows:
Pistols: mortar and LMG gunners and
assistant gunners only.
Carbines: all officers, the 1stSgt, communication sgt,
weapons platoon sgt, weapon section and squad leaders,
bugler and all messengers (except in the rifle platoons)
and ammo bearers.
M1 rifles: all personnel not otherwise armed.
M1903 rifles: rifle grenadiers.
BARs: all automatic riflemen and drivers.
2. 3/4-ton weapons carrier and jeep originally authorized replaced by two jeeps with trailers in October 1942.

and mortars traveled in ³/₄-ton trucks until October 1942 when the Army replaced most of them with jeeps with trailers. This permitted considerable savings in rubber, fuel, and shipping space.

The infantry battalion headquarters company provided battalion-level command and control (see *Command, Control, Communications, and Intelligence*) plus its pioneer platoon provided limited logistical and engineer support (see *Logistics*). From 1942 it also included the battalion antitank platoon.

The battalion communication platoon was loosely divided into (1) a message center and (2) radio and field telephone sections. Its men belonged to the infantry, not the Signal Corps. This made the unit a "communication" rather than a "signal" platoon.

The battalion antitank platoon had been moved from the weapons company to the headquarters company in 1942, so that it could serve as a security force for battalion headquarters. Its 37mm M3 or M3A1 towed guns were unlicenced versions of the German Pak 35/36. As tank killers in the European and Mediterranean theaters, they had nearly become obsolete even before US forces entered combat. However, in the Pacific Theater, these guns remained effective against the poorly armored Japanese tanks until the end of the war.

American soldiers occupying a field position near Oran, November 10, 1942. They are manning a Browning M1919A4 air-cooled LMG.

US Army infantry heavy weapons company, April 1, 1942[1]

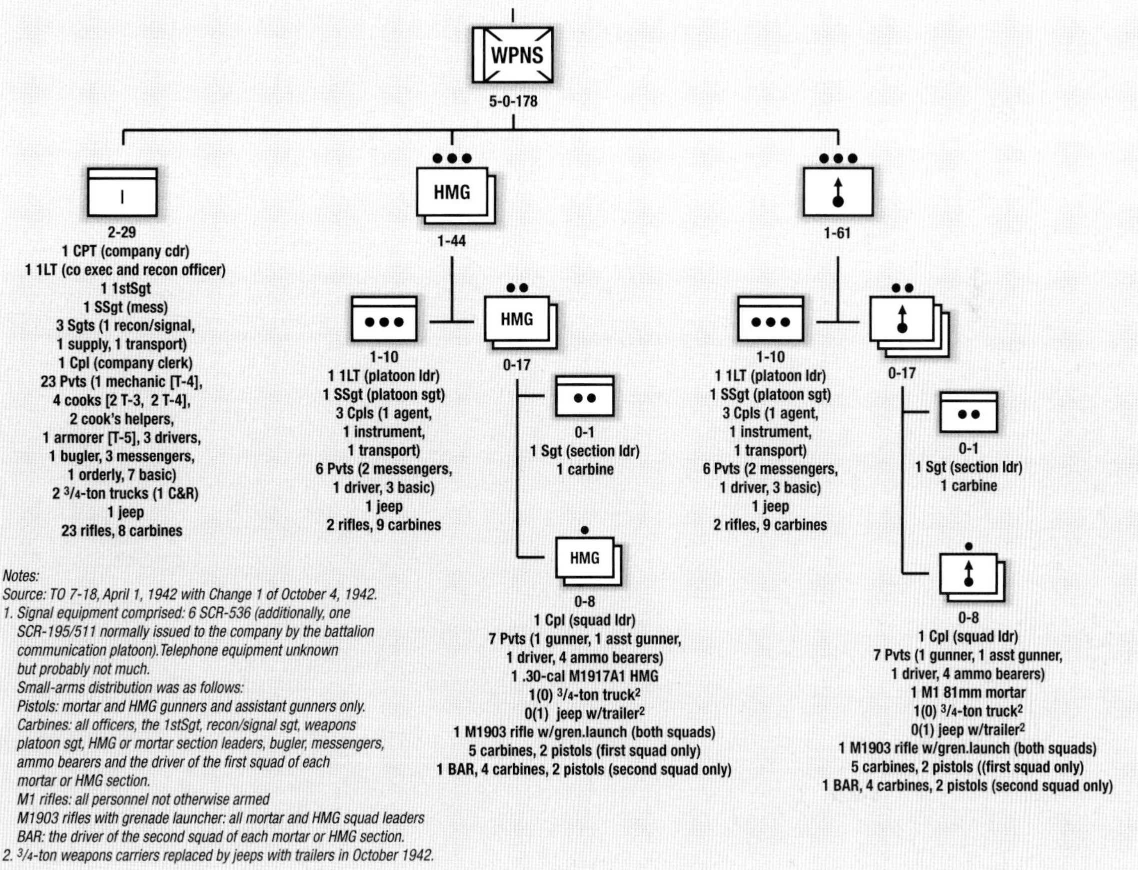

WPNS
5-0-178

[Company HQ]
2-29
1 CPT (company cdr)
1 1LT (co exec and recon officer)
1 1stSgt
1 SSgt (mess)
3 Sgts (1 recon/signal, 1 supply, 1 transport)
1 Cpl (company clerk)
23 Pvts (1 mechanic [T-4], 4 cooks [2 T-3, 2 T-4], 2 cook's helpers, 1 armorer [T-5], 3 drivers, 1 bugler, 3 messengers, 1 orderly, 7 basic)
2 ³/₄-ton trucks (1 C&R)
1 jeep
23 rifles, 8 carbines

HMG
1-44

[HMG platoon HQ]
1-10
1 1LT (platoon ldr)
1 SSgt (platoon sgt)
3 Cpls (1 agent, 1 instrument, 1 transport)
6 Pvts (2 messengers, 1 driver, 3 basic)
1 jeep
2 rifles, 9 carbines

HMG
0-17

[HMG section HQ]
0-1
1 Sgt (section ldr)
1 carbine

HMG
0-8
1 Cpl (squad ldr)
7 Pvts (1 gunner, 1 asst gunner, 1 driver, 4 ammo bearers)
1 .30-cal M1917A1 HMG
1(0) ³/₄-ton truck[2]
0(1) jeep w/trailer[2]
1 M1903 rifle w/gren.launch (both squads)
5 carbines, 2 pistols (first squad only)
1 BAR, 4 carbines, 2 pistols (second squad only)

[Mortar]
1-61

[Mortar platoon HQ]
1-10
1 1LT (platoon ldr)
1 SSgt (platoon sgt)
3 Cpls (1 agent, 1 instrument, 1 transport)
6 Pvts (2 messengers, 1 driver, 3 basic)
1 jeep
2 rifles, 9 carbines

[Mortar section]
0-17

[Mortar section HQ]
0-1
1 Sgt (section ldr)
1 carbine

[Mortar squad]
0-8
1 Cpl (squad ldr)
7 Pvts (1 gunner, 1 asst gunner, 1 driver, 4 ammo bearers)
1 M1 81mm mortar
1(0) ³/₄-ton truck[2]
0(1) jeep w/trailer[2]
1 M1903 rifle w/gren.launch (both squads)
5 carbines, 2 pistols ((first squad only)
1 BAR, 4 carbines, 2 pistols (second squad only)

Notes:
Source: TO 7-18, April 1, 1942 with Change 1 of October 4, 1942.
1. *Signal equipment comprised: 6 SCR-536 (additionally, one SCR-195/511 normally issued to the company by the battalion communication platoon).Telephone equipment unknown but probably not much.*
   Small-arms distribution was as follows:
   Pistols: mortar and HMG gunners and assistant gunners only.
   Carbines: all officers, the 1stSgt, recon/signal sgt, weapons platoon sgt, HMG or mortar section leaders, bugler, messengers, ammo bearers and the driver of the first squad of each mortar or HMG section.
   M1 rifles: all personnel not otherwise armed
   M1903 rifles with grenade launcher: all mortar and HMG squad leaders
   BAR: the driver of the second squad of each mortar or HMG section.
2. *³/₄-ton weapons carriers replaced by jeeps with trailers in October 1942.*

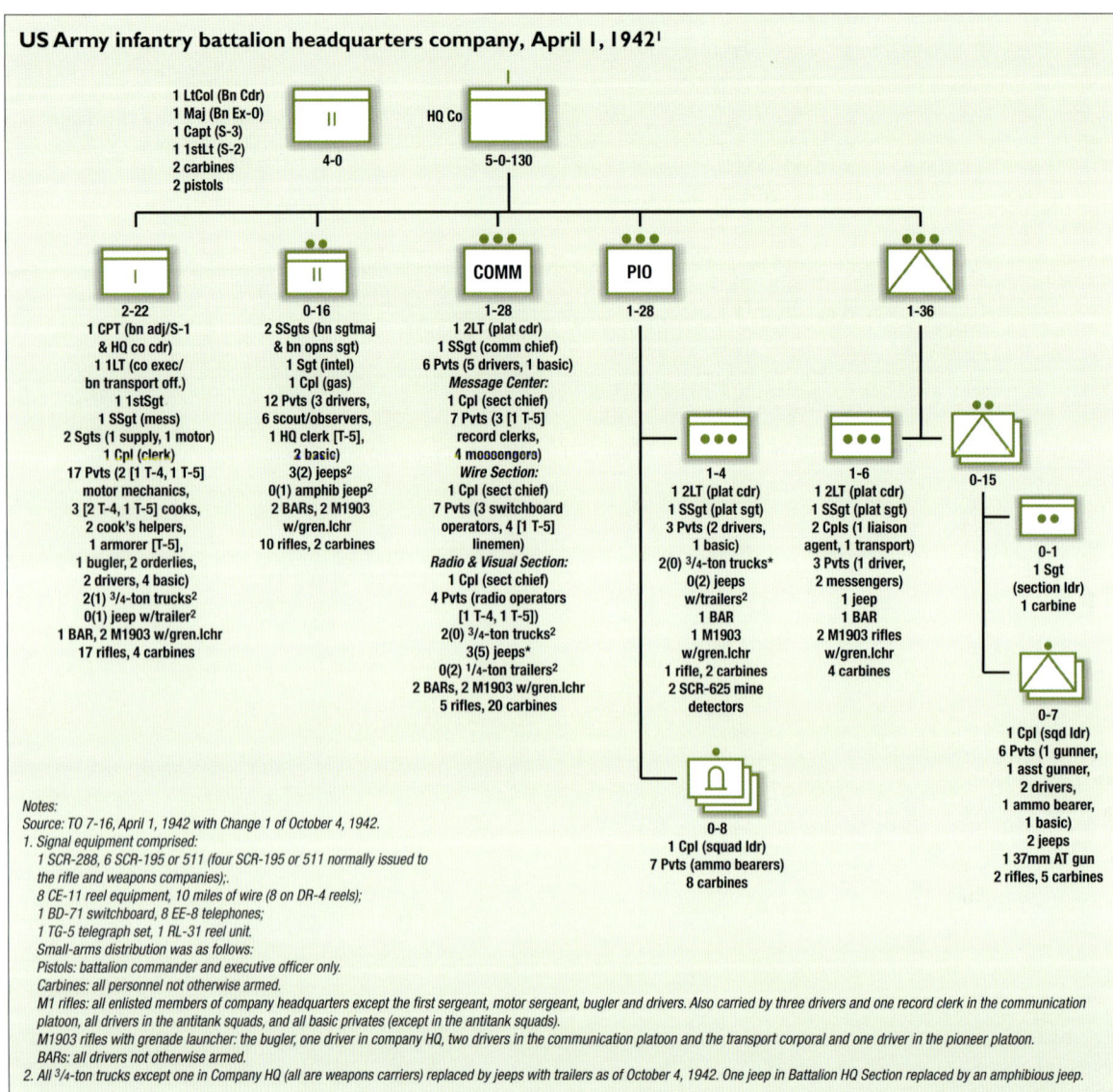

US Army infantry battalion headquarters company, April 1, 1942[1]

Battalion HQ (II) 4-0
1 LtCol (Bn Cdr)
1 Maj (Bn Ex-O)
1 Capt (S-3)
1 1stLt (S-2)
2 carbines
2 pistols

HQ Co 5-0-130

Company HQ (I) 2-22
1 CPT (bn adj/S-1 & HQ co cdr)
1 1LT (co exec/ bn transport off.)
1 1stSgt
1 SSgt (mess)
2 Sgts (1 supply, 1 motor)
1 Cpl (clerk)
17 Pvts (2 [1 T-4, 1 T-5] motor mechanics,
3 [2 T-4, 1 T-5] cooks,
2 cook's helpers,
1 armorer [T-5],
1 bugler, 2 orderlies,
2 drivers, 4 basic)
2(1) 3/4-ton trucks[2]
0(1) jeep w/trailer[2]
1 BAR, 2 M1903 w/gren.lchr
17 rifles, 4 carbines

Battalion HQ Section (II) 0-16
2 SSgts (bn sgtmaj & bn opns sgt)
1 Sgt (intel)
1 Cpl (gas)
12 Pvts (3 drivers, 6 scout/observers,
1 HQ clerk [T-5],
2 basic)
3(2) jeeps[2]
0(1) amphib jeep[2]
2 BARs, 2 M1903 w/gren.lchr
10 rifles, 2 carbines

COMM 1-28
1 2LT (plat cdr)
1 SSgt (comm chief)
6 Pvts (5 drivers, 1 basic)
Message Center:
1 Cpl (sect chief)
7 Pvts (3 [1 T-5] record clerks,
4 messengers)
Wire Section:
1 Cpl (sect chief)
7 Pvts (3 switchboard operators, 4 [1 T-5] linemen)
Radio & Visual Section:
1 Cpl (sect chief)
4 Pvts (radio operators [1 T-4, 1 T-5])
2(0) 3/4-ton trucks[2]
3(5) jeeps*
0(2) 1/4-ton trailers[2]
2 BARs, 2 M1903 w/gren.lchr
5 rifles, 20 carbines

PIO 1-28

Antitank Platoon HQ 1-4
1 2LT (plat cdr)
1 SSgt (plat sgt)
3 Pvts (2 drivers, 1 basic)
2(0) 3/4-ton trucks*
0(2) jeeps w/trailers[2]
1 BAR
1 M1903 w/gren.lchr
1 rifle, 2 carbines
2 SCR-625 mine detectors

(squad) 0-8
1 Cpl (squad ldr)
7 Pvts (ammo bearers)
8 carbines

Pioneer Platoon 1-6
1 2LT (plat cdr)
1 SSgt (plat sgt)
2 Cpls (1 liaison agent, 1 transport)
3 Pvts (1 driver, 2 messengers)
1 jeep
1 BAR
2 M1903 rifles w/gren.lchr
4 carbines

(machine-gun platoon) 1-36

0-15

(section) 0-1
1 Sgt (section ldr)
1 carbine

(squad) 0-7
1 Cpl (sqd ldr)
6 Pvts (1 gunner,
1 asst gunner,
2 drivers,
1 ammo bearer,
1 basic)
2 jeeps
1 37mm AT gun
2 rifles, 5 carbines

Notes:
Source: TO 7-16, April 1, 1942 with Change 1 of October 4, 1942.

1. Signal equipment comprised:
   1 SCR-288, 6 SCR-195 or 511 (four SCR-195 or 511 normally issued to the rifle and weapons companies);
   8 CE-11 reel equipment, 10 miles of wire (8 on DR-4 reels);
   1 BD-71 switchboard, 8 EE-8 telephones;
   1 TG-5 telegraph set, 1 RL-31 reel unit.
   Small-arms distribution was as follows:
   Pistols: battalion commander and executive officer only.
   Carbines: all personnel not otherwise armed.
   M1 rifles: all enlisted members of company headquarters except the first sergeant, motor sergeant, bugler and drivers. Also carried by three drivers and one record clerk in the communication platoon, all drivers in the antitank squads, and all basic privates (except in the antitank squads).
   M1903 rifles with grenade launcher: the bugler, one driver in company HQ, two drivers in the communication platoon and the transport corporal and one driver in the pioneer platoon.
   BARs: all drivers not otherwise armed.

2. All 3/4-ton trucks except one in Company HQ (all are weapons carriers) replaced by jeeps with trailers as of October 4, 1942. One jeep in Battalion HQ Section replaced by an amphibious jeep.

An identification photo of the water-cooled Browning M1917A1 HMG without its tripod. It was standard issue to infantry battalion machine-gun platoons.

ORD F7144

14

An 81mm mortar squad leader uses his field glasses to adjust his mortar's fire (probably as part of a training exercise), in North Africa, 1943. Note his M1903 Springfield rifle issued for launching rifle grenades.

The infantry regiment

An infantry regiment resembled a miniature division. It had its own maneuver elements (the infantry battalions) and its own artillery and logistics units. The regimental headquarters company gave the regimental commander both his communication and reconnaissance assets. The regimental service company provided administration and logistics (see *Command, Control, Communications, and Intelligence*). Its transportation platoon was equipped with the new 6x6 2^1/$_2$-ton cargo trucks and furnished most of the regiment's trains.

Unlike the antitank squads in the battalion antitank platoons, those in the regimental antitank company used ^{3}/$_4$-ton weapons carriers rather than jeeps as their prime movers. Since only one ^{3}/$_4$-ton truck was enough to tow the gun and carry its crew and ammunition, one vehicle and driver per squad could be eliminated. On the other hand, the ^{3}/$_4$-tonners were larger and more conspicuous than jeeps, and were at greater risk in the frontline. The Army had originally intended that the regimental antitank company use the M6 self-propelled antitank gun. The M6 was a ^{3}/$_4$-ton truck with a 37mm gun on a rotating mount anchored permanently to the cargo bed. It had no armor except for the gun shield. A few M6s actually reached North Africa, but they saw little use and were soon discarded. None served with an infantry regiment.

The antitank company's antitank mine platoon was a purely defensive organization that deployed hand-buried mines to canalize enemy tanks into concentrations of antitank guns.

First authorized for the infantry regiment in 1942, the cannon company had been a controversial issue within the Army. The concept of a cannon company had originated during World War I. In that conflict, poor communications made it difficult or impossible for the artillery to respond to infantry calls for fire, or even to alter its scheduled fire to conform to unexpected changes in the tactical situation. Of course, there were no portable field radios in 1918, and broken cables often rendered field telephone systems useless. According to its concept the cannon company should use specially designed guns that traded range and caliber for lightness, an ability to be manhandled, and a low profile. This allowed a cannon company to follow the infantry as it advanced, and deliver direct supporting fire whether communication worked or not. Cannon company personnel could see for themselves what was going on and direct

(continues on page 18)

US Army infantry regiment, April 1, 1942[1]

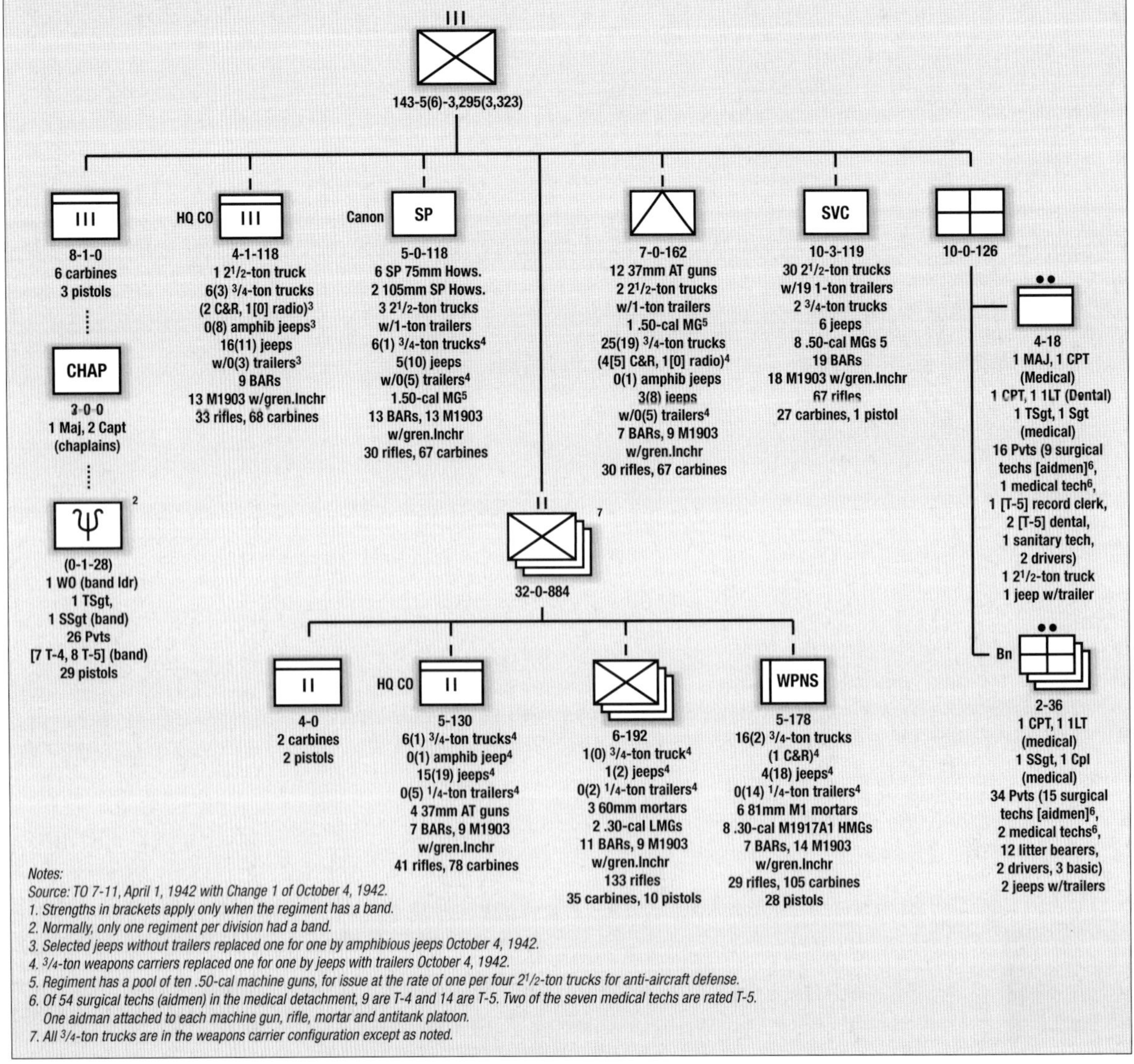

III
143-5(6)-3,295(3,323)

III
8-1-0
6 carbines
3 pistols

⋮

CHAP
3-0-0
1 Maj, 2 Capt
(chaplains)

⋮

ψ [2]
(0-1-28)
1 WO (band ldr)
1 TSgt,
1 SSgt (band)
26 Pvts
[7 T-4, 8 T-5] (band)
29 pistols

HQ CO III
4-1-118
1 2½-ton truck
6(3) ¾-ton trucks
(2 C&R, 1[0] radio)[3]
0(8) amphib jeeps[3]
16(11) jeeps
w/0(3) trailers[3]
9 BARs
13 M1903 w/gren.lnchr
33 rifles, 68 carbines

Canon SP
5-0-118
6 SP 75mm Hows.
2 105mm SP Hows.
3 2½-ton trucks
w/1-ton trailers
6(1) ¾-ton trucks[4]
5(10) jeeps
w/0(5) trailers[4]
1.50-cal MG[5]
13 BARs, 13 M1903
w/gren.lnchr
30 rifles, 67 carbines

SP (AT gun)
7-0-162
12 37mm AT guns
2 2½-ton trucks
w/1-ton trailers
1 .50-cal MG[5]
25(19) ¾-ton trucks
(4[5] C&R, 1[0] radio)[4]
0(1) amphib jeeps
3(8) jeeps
w/0(5) trailers[4]
7 BARs, 9 M1903
w/gren.lnchr
30 rifles, 67 carbines

SVC
10-3-119
30 2½-ton trucks
w/19 1-ton trailers
2 ¾-ton trucks
6 jeeps
8 .50-cal MGs 5
19 BARs
18 M1903 w/gren.lnchr
67 rifles
27 carbines, 1 pistol

10-0-126

(Medical)
4-18
1 MAJ, 1 CPT
(Medical)
1 CPT, 1 1LT (Dental)
1 TSgt, 1 Sgt
(medical)
16 Pvts (9 surgical
techs [aidmen][6],
1 medical tech[6],
1 [T-5] record clerk,
2 [T-5] dental,
1 sanitary tech,
2 drivers)
1 2½-ton truck
1 jeep w/trailer

II [7]
32-0-884

II
4-0
2 carbines
2 pistols

HQ CO II
5-130
6(1) ¾-ton trucks[4]
0(1) amphib jeep[4]
15(19) jeeps[4]
0(5) ¼-ton trailers[4]
4 37mm AT guns
7 BARs, 9 M1903
w/gren.lnchr
41 rifles, 78 carbines

(rifle)
6-192
1(0) ¾-ton truck[4]
1(2) jeeps[4]
0(2) ¼-ton trailers[4]
3 60mm mortars
2 .30-cal LMGs
11 BARs, 9 M1903
w/gren.lnchr
133 rifles
35 carbines, 10 pistols

WPNS
5-178
16(2) ¾-ton trucks
(1 C&R)[4]
4(18) jeeps[4]
0(14) ¼-ton trailers[4]
6 81mm M1 mortars
8 .30-cal M1917A1 HMGs
7 BARs, 14 M1903
w/gren.lnchr
29 rifles, 105 carbines
28 pistols

Bn (Medical)
2-36
1 CPT, 1 1LT
(medical)
1 SSgt, 1 Cpl
(medical)
34 Pvts (15 surgical
techs [aidmen][6],
2 medical techs[6],
12 litter bearers,
2 drivers, 3 basic)
2 jeeps w/trailers

Notes:
Source: TO 7-11, April 1, 1942 with Change 1 of October 4, 1942.
1. Strengths in brackets apply only when the regiment has a band.
2. Normally, only one regiment per division had a band.
3. Selected jeeps without trailers replaced one for one by amphibious jeeps October 4, 1942.
4. ¾-ton weapons carriers replaced one for one by jeeps with trailers October 4, 1942.
5. Regiment has a pool of ten .50-cal machine guns, for issue at the rate of one per four 2½-ton trucks for anti-aircraft defense.
6. Of 54 surgical techs (aidmen) in the medical detachment, 9 are T-4 and 14 are T-5. Two of the seven medical techs are rated T-5.
   One aidman attached to each machine gun, rifle, mortar and antitank platoon.
7. All ¾-ton trucks are in the weapons carrier configuration except as noted.

This identification photo shows a 75mm gun motor carriage M3 (or T-12) at the Desert Training Center, Indio CA (June 8, 1942). In the infantry division this was the most commonly used equipment of the 75mm platoons of the regimental cannon companies. This example also carries an M1919A4 LMG.

US Army infantry regiment HQ company, April 1, 1942[1]

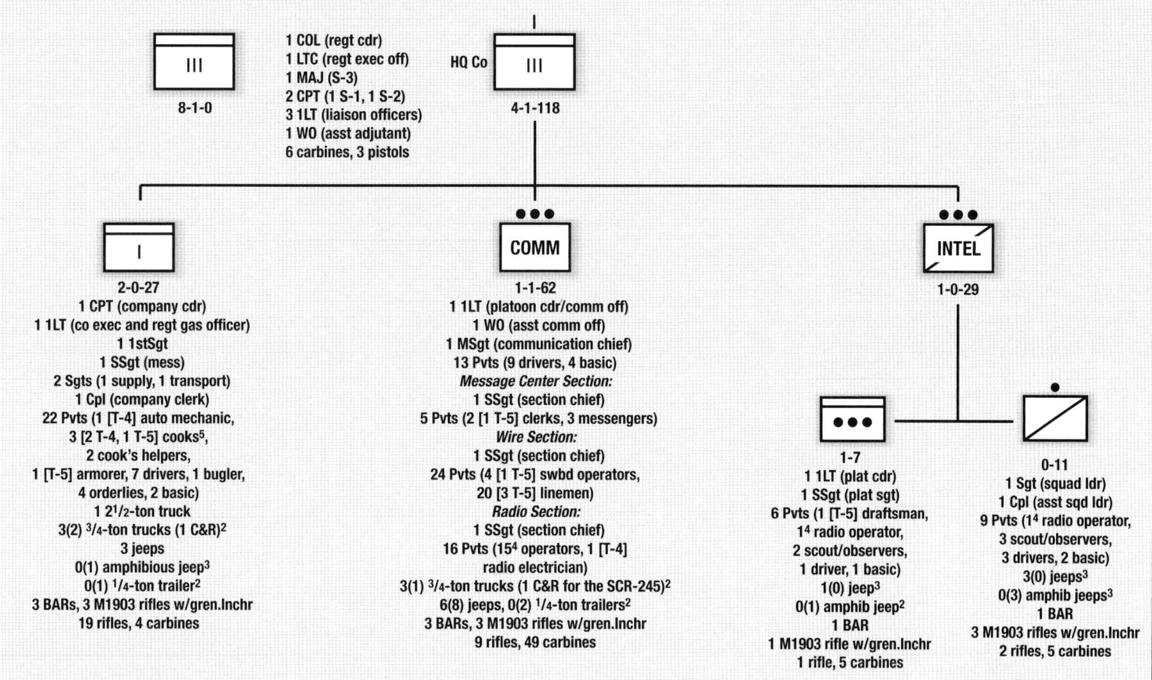

[III] 8-1-0

1 COL (regt cdr)
1 LTC (regt exec off)
1 MAJ (S-3)
2 CPT (1 S-1, 1 S-2)
3 1LT (liaison officers)
1 WO (asst adjutant)
6 carbines, 3 pistols

HQ Co **[III]** 4-1-118

[I] 2-0-27

1 CPT (company cdr)
1 1LT (co exec and regt gas officer)
1 1stSgt
1 SSgt (mess)
2 Sgts (1 supply, 1 transport)
1 Cpl (company clerk)
22 Pvts (1 [T-4] auto mechanic,
3 [2 T-4, 1 T-5] cooks[5],
2 cook's helpers,
1 [T-5] armorer, 7 drivers, 1 bugler,
4 orderlies, 2 basic)
1 2¹/₂-ton truck
3(2) ³/₄-ton trucks (1 C&R)[2]
3 jeeps
0(1) amphibious jeep[3]
0(1) ¹/₄-ton trailer[2]
3 BARs, 3 M1903 rifles w/gren.lnchr
19 rifles, 4 carbines

[COMM] 1-1-62

1 1LT (platoon cdr/comm off)
1 WO (asst comm off)
1 MSgt (communication chief)
13 Pvts (9 drivers, 4 basic)
Message Center Section:
1 SSgt (section chief)
5 Pvts (2 [1 T-5] clerks, 3 messengers)
Wire Section:
1 SSgt (section chief)
24 Pvts (4 [1 T-5] swbd operators,
20 [3 T-5] linemen)
Radio Section:
1 SSgt (section chief)
16 Pvts (15[4] operators, 1 [T-4]
radio electrician)
3(1) ³/₄-ton trucks (1 C&R for the SCR-245)[2]
6(8) jeeps, 0(2) ¹/₄-ton trailers[2]
3 BARs, 3 M1903 rifles w/gren.lnchr
9 rifles, 49 carbines

[INTEL] 1-0-29

1-7

1 1LT (plat cdr)
1 SSgt (plat sgt)
6 Pvts (1 [T-5] draftsman,
1[4] radio operator,
2 scout/observers,
1 driver, 1 basic)
1(0) jeep[3]
0(1) amphib jeep[2]
1 BAR
1 M1903 rifle w/gren.lnchr
1 rifle, 5 carbines

0-11

1 Sgt (squad ldr)
1 Cpl (asst sqd ldr)
9 Pvts (1[4] radio operator,
3 scout/observers,
3 drivers, 2 basic)
3(0) jeeps[3]
0(3) amphib jeeps[3]
1 BAR
3 M1903 rifles w/gren.lnchr
2 rifles, 5 carbines

Notes:
Source: TO 7-12, April 1, 1942 with Change 1 of October 4, 1942.
1. Signal equipment comprised:
*   1 SCR-245, 5 SCR-171, 284 or 288*
*   12 SCR-195 or 511 (I&R platoon has four)*
*   2 BD-72 switchboards, 12 EE-8 telephones*
*   4 TG-5 telegraph sets, 4 RL-31 reel units*
*   8 CE-11 reel equipment, 27 miles of wire (25 on DR-4 reels).*
*   Small-arms distribution was as follows:*
*   Pistols: majors, lieutenant colonels and colonels only.*
*   Carbines: all personnel not otherwised armed.*
*   M1 rifles: all enlisted members of company headquarters except the first sergeant, bugler, message center clerks, all basic privates and one driver*
*   from company HQ and three from the communication platoon.*
*   M1903 rifles with grenade launcher: I&R squad leaders, two drivers per I&R squad, the draftsman (I&R), and three drivers each in the company*
*   HQ and communication platoon.*
*   BAR: three drivers each per company HQ, communication platoon, and I&R platoon.*
2. As of October 4, 1942, one ³/₄-ton truck (weapons carrier) in Company HQ and two ³/₄-ton weapons carriers and a ³/₄-ton radio van in the
*   Communication Platoon were replaced by a ³/₄-ton command and reconnaissance truck and three jeeps with trailers.*
3. Standard jeeps replaced by amphibious jeeps as of October 4, 1942.
4. Six of the 18 radio operators in the company are T-4 technicians and six others are T-5.
5. One cook in company HQ is for the regimental officers' mess.

A T-19 self-propelled 105mm howitzer with .50-cal machine gun at a July 4th parade in Memphis Tennessee, 1942. In an infantry division this vehicle equipped the 105mm howitzer platoons of the infantry regimental cannon companies.

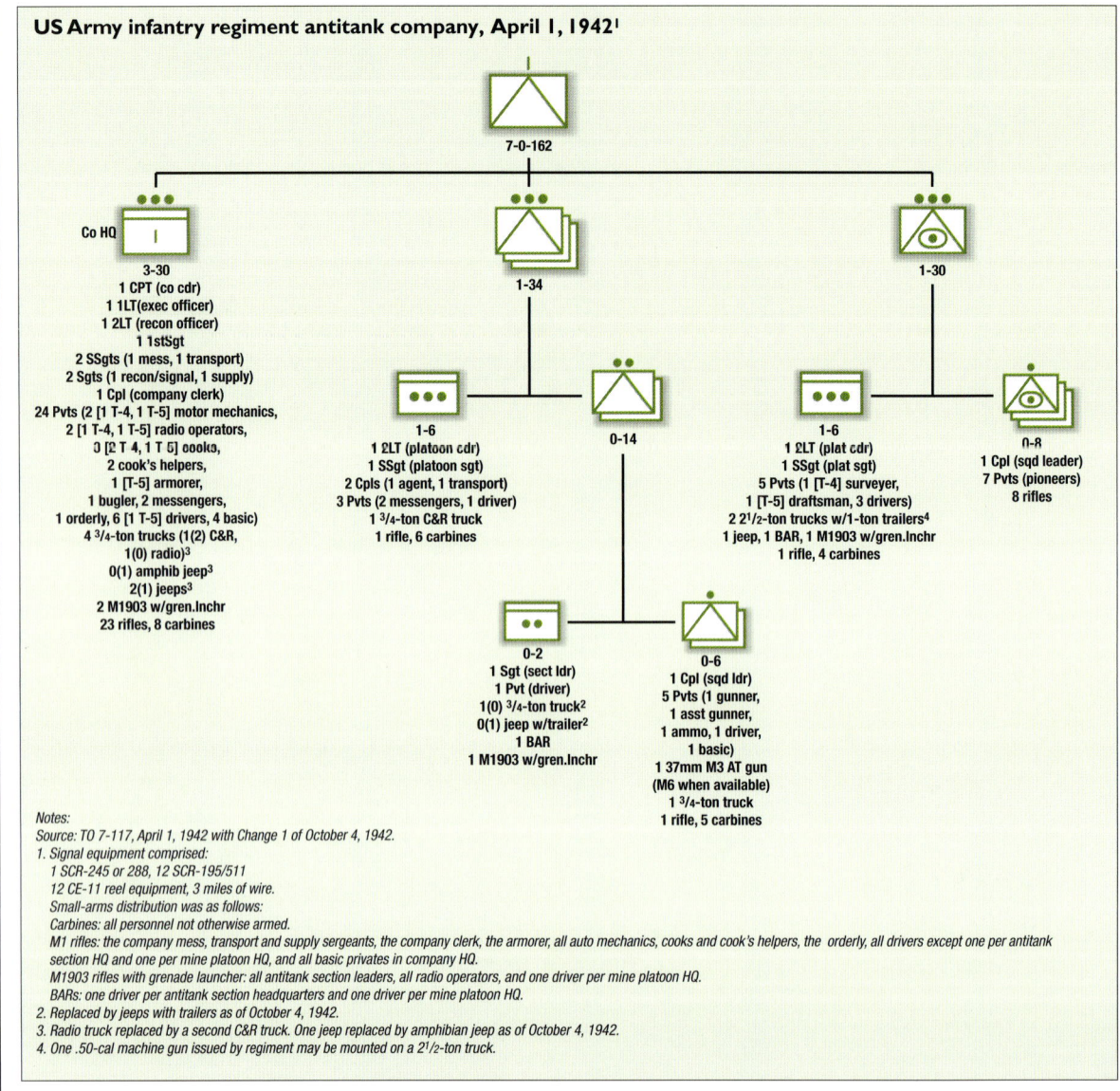

US Army infantry regiment antitank company, April 1, 1942[1]

7-0-162

Co HQ

3-30
1 CPT (co cdr)
1 1LT (exec officer)
1 2LT (recon officer)
1 1stSgt
2 SSgts (1 mess, 1 transport)
2 Sgts (1 recon/signal, 1 supply)
1 Cpl (company clerk)
24 Pvts (2 [1 T-4, 1 T-5] motor mechanics,
2 [1 T-4, 1 T-5] radio operators,
3 [2 T-4, 1 T-5] cooks,
2 cook's helpers,
1 [T-5] armorer,
1 bugler, 2 messengers,
1 orderly, 6 [1 T-5] drivers, 4 basic)
4 ³/₄-ton trucks (1(2) C&R,
1(0) radio)[3]
0(1) amphib jeep[3]
2(1) jeeps[3]
2 M1903 w/gren.lnchr
23 rifles, 8 carbines

1-34

1-6
1 2LT (platoon cdr)
1 SSgt (platoon sgt)
2 Cpls (1 agent, 1 transport)
3 Pvts (2 messengers, 1 driver)
1 ³/₄-ton C&R truck
1 rifle, 6 carbines

0-14

0-2
1 Sgt (sect ldr)
1 Pvt (driver)
1(0) ³/₄-ton truck[2]
0(1) jeep w/trailer[2]
1 BAR
1 M1903 w/gren.lnchr

0-6
1 Cpl (sqd ldr)
5 Pvts (1 gunner,
1 asst gunner,
1 ammo, 1 driver,
1 basic)
1 37mm M3 AT gun
(M6 when available)
1 ³/₄-ton truck
1 rifle, 5 carbines

1-30

1-6
1 2LT (plat cdr)
1 SSgt (plat sgt)
5 Pvts (1 [T-4] surveyer,
1 [T-5] draftsman, 3 drivers)
2 2¹/₂-ton trucks w/1-ton trailers[4]
1 jeep, 1 BAR, 1 M1903 w/gren.lnchr
1 rifle, 4 carbines

0-8
1 Cpl (sqd leader)
7 Pvts (pioneers)
8 rifles

Notes:
Source: TO 7-117, April 1, 1942 with Change 1 of October 4, 1942.
1. Signal equipment comprised:
   1 SCR-245 or 288, 12 SCR-195/511
   12 CE-11 reel equipment, 3 miles of wire.
   Small-arms distribution was as follows:
   Carbines: all personnel not otherwise armed.
   M1 rifles: the company mess, transport and supply sergeants, the company clerk, the armorer, all auto mechanics, cooks and cook's helpers, the orderly, all drivers except one per antitank
   section HQ and one per mine platoon HQ, and all basic privates in company HQ.
   M1903 rifles with grenade launcher: all antitank section leaders, all radio operators, and one driver per mine platoon HQ.
   BARs: one driver per antitank section headquarters and one driver per mine platoon HQ.
2. Replaced by jeeps with trailers as of October 4, 1942.
3. Radio truck replaced by a second C&R truck. One jeep replaced by amphibian jeep as of October 4, 1942.
4. One .50-cal machine gun issued by regiment may be mounted on a 2¹/₂-ton truck.

their fire accordingly. The War Department saw the new 60mm and 81mm mortars as at least a partial cannon company substitute, but many officers believed that the infantry would need light cannon as well. They could not only outrange the mortars, but also use direct fire. Unfortunately, the US Army never developed any light artillery pieces suitable for a cannon company. Therefore the War Department substituted heavier weapons originally designed as division-level artillery. In order to give them sufficient mobility, it would mount them on M3-series armored half-tracks and thus make them self-propelled. Unfortunately, although tactically mobile these half-tracks were heavy, conspicuous, and poorly protected. They also needed a lot of fuel and maintenance and they consumed excessive amounts of shipping space.

The one remaining element of the regiment was its medical detachment. This was really a medical company, but its personnel belonged to the Medical Corps and as such they could only be "attached" to an infantry regiment, and were not an organic part of it. The detachment manned aid stations for the regimental headquarters and each battalion and supplied stretcher teams and medical aidmen ("medics"). A medic was attached to each combat platoon.

US Army infantry regiment cannon company, April 1, 1942[1]

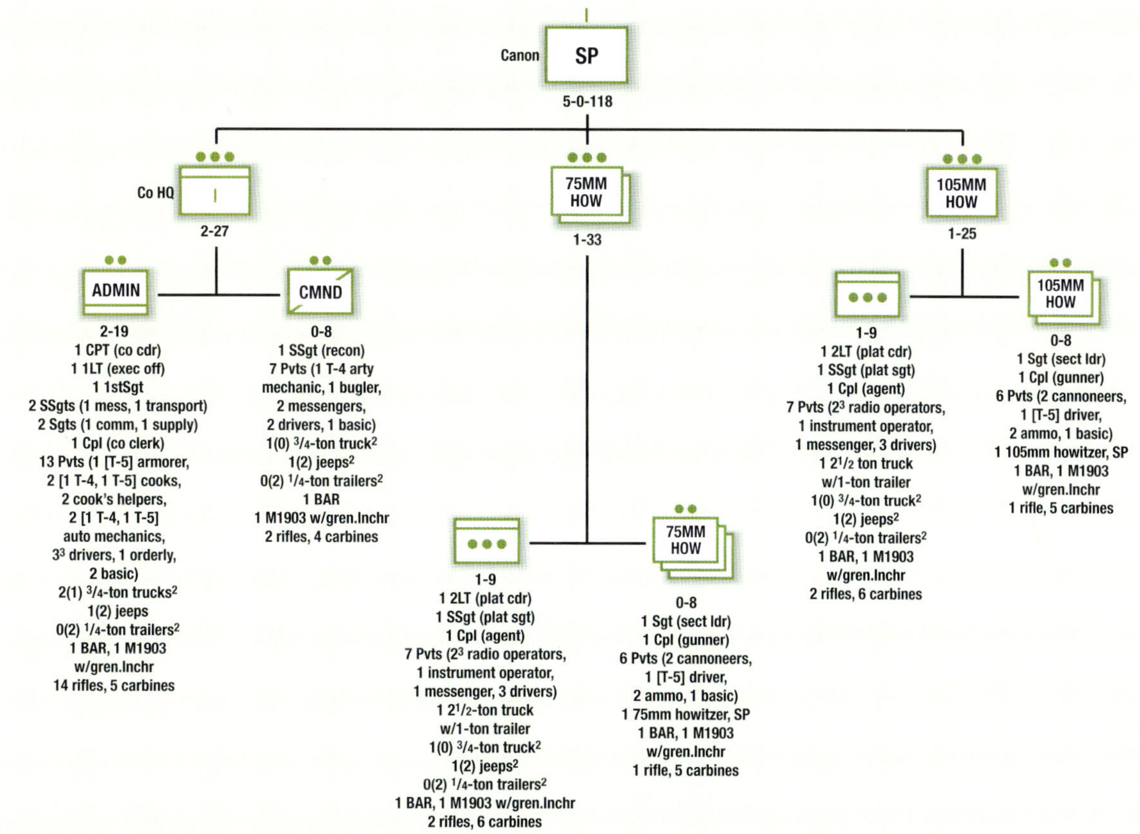

Canon SP
5-0-118

Co HQ I
2-27

75MM HOW
1-33

105MM HOW
1-25

ADMIN
2-19
1 CPT (co cdr)
1 1LT (exec off)
1 1stSgt
2 SSgts (1 mess, 1 transport)
2 Sgts (1 comm, 1 supply)
1 Cpl (co clerk)
13 Pvts (1 T-5 armorer,
2 [1 T-4, 1 T-5] cooks,
2 cook's helpers,
2 [1 T-4, 1 T-5]
auto mechanics,
3[3] drivers, 1 orderly,
2 basic)
2(1) 3/4-ton trucks[2]
1(2) jeeps
0(2) 1/4-ton trailers[2]
1 BAR, 1 M1903
w/gren.lnchr
14 rifles, 5 carbines

CMND
0-8
1 SSgt (recon)
7 Pvts (1 T-4 arty
mechanic, 1 bugler,
2 messengers,
2 drivers, 1 basic)
1(0) 3/4-ton truck[2]
1(2) jeeps[2]
0(2) 1/4-ton trailers[2]
1 BAR
1 M1903 w/gren.lnchr
2 rifles, 4 carbines

75MM HOW
1-9
1 2LT (plat cdr)
1 SSgt (plat sgt)
1 Cpl (agent)
7 Pvts (2[3] radio operators,
1 instrument operator,
1 messenger, 3 drivers)
1 2 1/2-ton truck
w/1-ton trailer
1(0) 3/4-ton truck[2]
1(2) jeeps[2]
0(2) 1/4-ton trailers[2]
1 BAR, 1 M1903 w/gren.lnchr
2 rifles, 6 carbines

75MM HOW
0-8
1 Sgt (sect ldr)
1 Cpl (gunner)
6 Pvts (2 cannoneers,
1 [T-5] driver,
2 ammo, 1 basic)
1 75mm howitzer, SP
1 BAR, 1 M1903
w/gren.lnchr
1 rifle, 5 carbines

105MM HOW
1-9
1 2LT (plat cdr)
1 SSgt (plat sgt)
1 Cpl (agent)
7 Pvts (2[3] radio operators,
1 instrument operator,
1 messenger, 3 drivers)
1 2 1/2 ton truck
w/1-ton trailer
1(0) 3/4-ton truck[2]
1(2) jeeps[2]
0(2) 1/4-ton trailers[2]
1 BAR, 1 M1903
w/gren.lnchr
2 rifles, 6 carbines

105MM HOW
0-8
1 Sgt (sect ldr)
1 Cpl (gunner)
6 Pvts (2 cannoneers,
1 [T-5] driver,
2 ammo, 1 basic)
1 105mm howitzer, SP
1 BAR, 1 M1903
w/gren.lnchr
1 rifle, 5 carbines

Notes:

Source: TO 7-14, April 1, 1942.

1. Precise signal equipment quantities are uncertain, as the records are incomplete, but included six SCR-195/511 (or VRC-1). Quantities and types of wire equipment are unknown.
   Small-arms distribution comprised:
   Carbines: all personnel not otherwise armed.
   M1 rifles: the company mess and supply sergeants, all corporals not serving as gunners, the armorer, the artillery mechanic, all auto mechanics, all cooks and cook's helpers,
   one driver in company HQ (admin/supply) and one in each gun platoon HQ, the orderly, and all basic privates.
   M1903 rifles with grenade launcher: each sergeant gun section leader, one driver each in the company admin/supply section, the command/recon section and in each gun platoon HQ.
   BAR: one driver each in the company admin/supply section, the command and recon section, and in each gun platoon HQ and each self-propelled gun driver.
2. All 3/4-ton weapons carriers, except one in the company HQ platoon, were replaced by jeeps with trailers as of October 4, 1942.
3. Two of the six radio operators in the company were T-4 technicians and two others were T-5. Radio operators also served as telephone operators when wire systems were in use.
   One truck driver was also a T-5 technician.

A rare shot taken near Velotte, France on September 15, 1944 of a T19 self-propelled howitzer serving with the 10th Field Artillery Battalion, 3d Infantry Division. The T19 had supposedly long been retired by this point. Apparently, the 10th Field Artillery, officially a towed 105mm howitzer battalion, had taken advantage of an opportunity to become self-propeled.

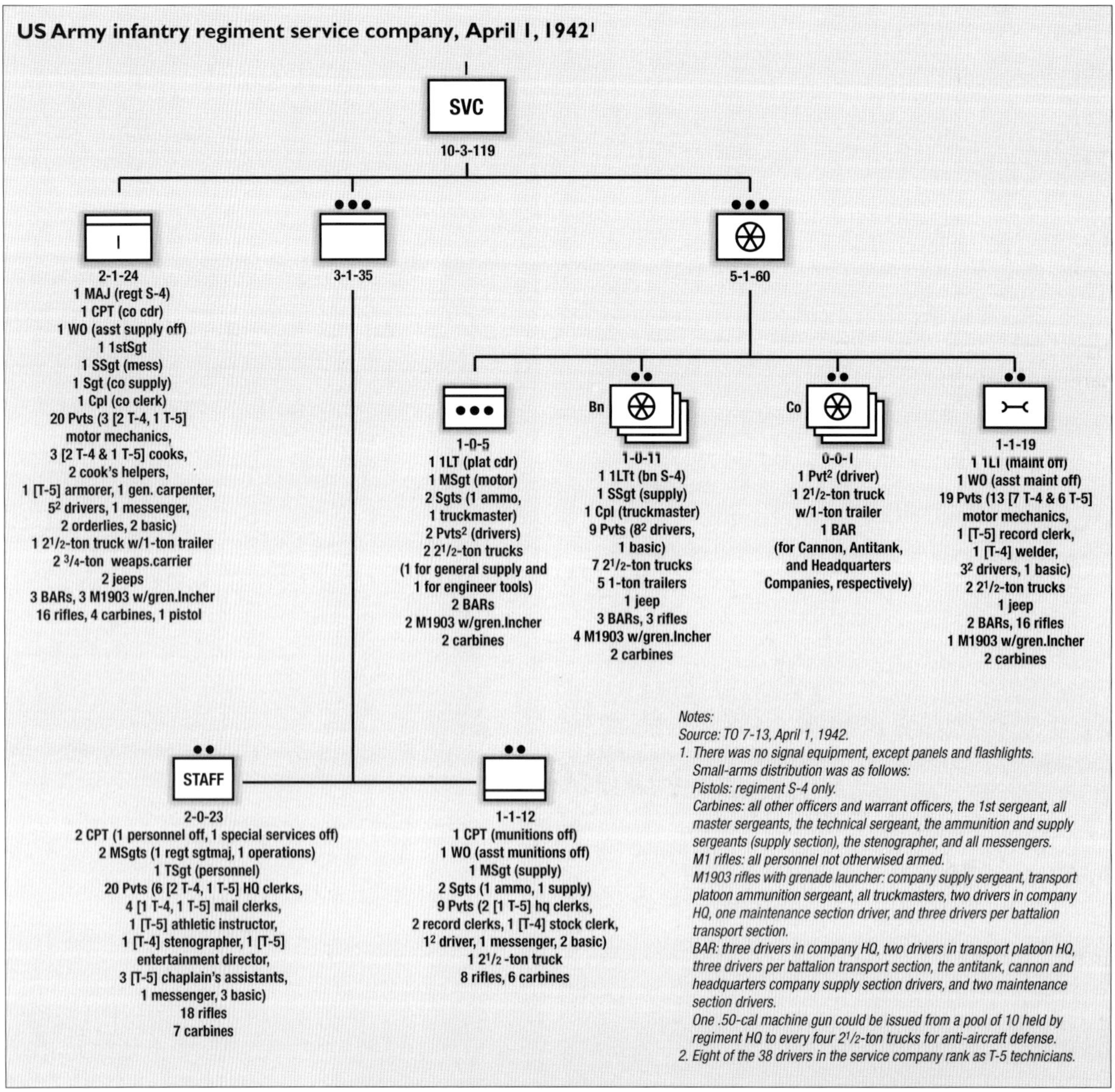

US Army infantry regiment service company, April 1, 1942[1]

SVC
10-3-119

I
2-1-24
1 MAJ (regt S-4)
1 CPT (co cdr)
1 WO (asst supply off)
1 1stSgt
1 SSgt (mess)
1 Sgt (co supply)
1 Cpl (co clerk)
20 Pvts (3 [2 T-4, 1 T-5]
motor mechanics,
3 [2 T-4 & 1 T-5] cooks,
2 cook's helpers,
1 [T-5] armorer, 1 gen. carpenter,
5[2] drivers, 1 messenger,
2 orderlies, 2 basic)
1 2¹/₂-ton truck w/1-ton trailer
2 ³/₄-ton weaps.carrier
2 jeeps
3 BARs, 3 M1903 w/gren.lncher
16 rifles, 4 carbines, 1 pistol

3-1-35

⚙ 5-1-60

1-0-5
1 1LT (plat cdr)
1 MSgt (motor)
2 Sgts (1 ammo,
1 truckmaster)
2 Pvts[2] (drivers)
2 2¹/₂-ton trucks
(1 for general supply and
1 for engineer tools)
2 BARs
2 M1903 w/gren.lncher
2 carbines

Bn ⚙
1-0-11
1 1LTt (bn S-4)
1 SSgt (supply)
1 Cpl (truckmaster)
9 Pvts (8[2] drivers,
1 basic)
7 2¹/₂-ton trucks
5 1-ton trailers
1 jeep
3 BARs, 3 rifles
4 M1903 w/gren.lncher
2 carbines

Co ⚙
0-0-1
1 Pvt[2] (driver)
1 2¹/₂-ton truck
w/1-ton trailer
1 BAR
(for Cannon, Antitank,
and Headquarters
Companies, respectively)

⊢⊣
1-1-19
1 1Ll (maint off)
1 WO (asst maint off)
19 Pvts (13 [7 T-4 & 6 T-5]
motor mechanics,
1 [T-5] record clerk,
1 [T-4] welder,
3[2] drivers, 1 basic)
2 2¹/₂-ton trucks
1 jeep
2 BARs, 16 rifles
1 M1903 w/gren.lncher
2 carbines

STAFF
2-0-23
2 CPT (1 personnel off, 1 special services off)
2 MSgts (1 regt sgtmaj, 1 operations)
1 TSgt (personnel)
20 Pvts (6 [2 T-4, 1 T-5] HQ clerks,
4 [1 T-4, 1 T-5] mail clerks,
1 [T-5] athletic instructor,
1 [T-4] stenographer, 1 [T-5]
entertainment director,
3 [T-5] chaplain's assistants,
1 messenger, 3 basic)
18 rifles
7 carbines

1-1-12
1 CPT (munitions off)
1 WO (asst munitions off)
1 MSgt (supply)
2 Sgts (1 ammo, 1 supply)
9 Pvts (2 [1 T-5] hq clerks,
2 record clerks, 1 [T-4] stock clerk,
1[2] driver, 1 messenger, 2 basic)
1 2¹/₂-ton truck
8 rifles, 6 carbines

Notes:
Source: TO 7-13, April 1, 1942.
1. There was no signal equipment, except panels and flashlights.
Small-arms distribution was as follows:
Pistols: regiment S-4 only.
Carbines: all other officers and warrant officers, the 1st sergeant, all master sergeants, the technical sergeant, the ammunition and supply sergeants (supply section), the stenographer, and all messengers.
M1 rifles: all personnel not otherwised armed.
M1903 rifles with grenade launcher: company supply sergeant, transport platoon ammunition sergeant, all truckmasters, two drivers in company HQ, one maintenance section driver, and three drivers per battalion transport section.
BAR: three drivers in company HQ, two drivers in transport platoon HQ, three drivers per battalion transport section, the antitank, cannon and headquarters company supply section drivers, and two maintenance section drivers.
One .50-cal machine gun could be issued from a pool of 10 held by regiment HQ to every four 2¹/₂-ton trucks for anti-aircraft defense.
2. Eight of the 38 drivers in the service company rank as T-5 technicians.

A shell is rammed into an M1918 155mm howitzer on Arundel Island, September 24, 1943. This weapon, probably from the 136th or 192d Field Artillery, is firing on Japanese positions near Vila, on Kolombangara Island following the capture of Munda airfield, New Georgia. Officially, US forces were only supposed to use their outdated M1918 howitzers for training, since the much more modern M1 155mm howitzer was intended to replace them. However, even combat photos of 155mm howitzer units taken prior to 1944 rarely show any M1 howitzers. The M1918 appears to have been the dominant weapon up until then.

The division artillery

The division artillery was organized as a brigade headquarters controlling four separate battalions. Three of the battalions used the excellent M2 105mm howitzer, one of the best weapons of its type used during the war. They were intended for the direct support of the three infantry regiments. The fourth battalion was supposed to be equipped with the very successful M1 155mm howitzer, but earlier in the war the older and shorter-ranged M1918 howitzers were frequently substituted.

In June 1942, the AGF ordered a reduction in the number of $2\frac{1}{2}$-ton trucks assigned to the artillery in order to save shipping space, fuel, rubber, and maintenance man-hours. In October 1942, the AGF gave each headquarters battery in the division artillery a pair of light observation aircraft to identify targets and direct fire on them.

Table 3: Infantry division towed artillery (1942–43)

Model no.	Type	Description
M2A1	105mm howitzer	This was the standard division-level light howitzer. It used a sliding breech and fired a semi-fixed 33-pound HE shell (a complete round weighed about 40 pounds) out to 12,200 yards (11,000 meters). The rate of fire was relatively fast (up to 10 rounds per minute). WP, smoke, AT, and canister ammunition became available for it later in the war. At 4,980 pounds the weapon was fairly heavy and had to be towed by a $2\frac{1}{2}$-ton truck.
M1918	155mm howitzer	This World War I medium howitzer needed replacement because its carriage's very limited traverse (three degrees) made it difficult for it to shift its fire to new targets. However, photographic evidence indicates that this weapon saw much combat use through late 1943. It weighed nearly 8,200 pounds and could fire a 95-pound HE shell (a complete round weighed about 108 pounds) to 12,400 yards (11,330 meters). Smoke and chemical ammunition was also available.
M1	155mm howitzer	This was a much more modern but heavier weapon than the M1918. It fired nearly (but not quite) identical ammunition out to 16,350 yards (14,950 meters). It could traverse 30 degrees but its 12,000-pound weight was a heavy load for its 4-ton prime mover. It was not until 1943 that there were enough M1 howitzers to relegate the M1918 howitzer to training duties and the lend-lease equipping of lesser allies. Like the M1918 it used an interrupted screw breech and separate loading ammunition, allowing a maximum rate of fire of three rounds per minute.

US Army infantry division artillery, April 1, 1942[1]

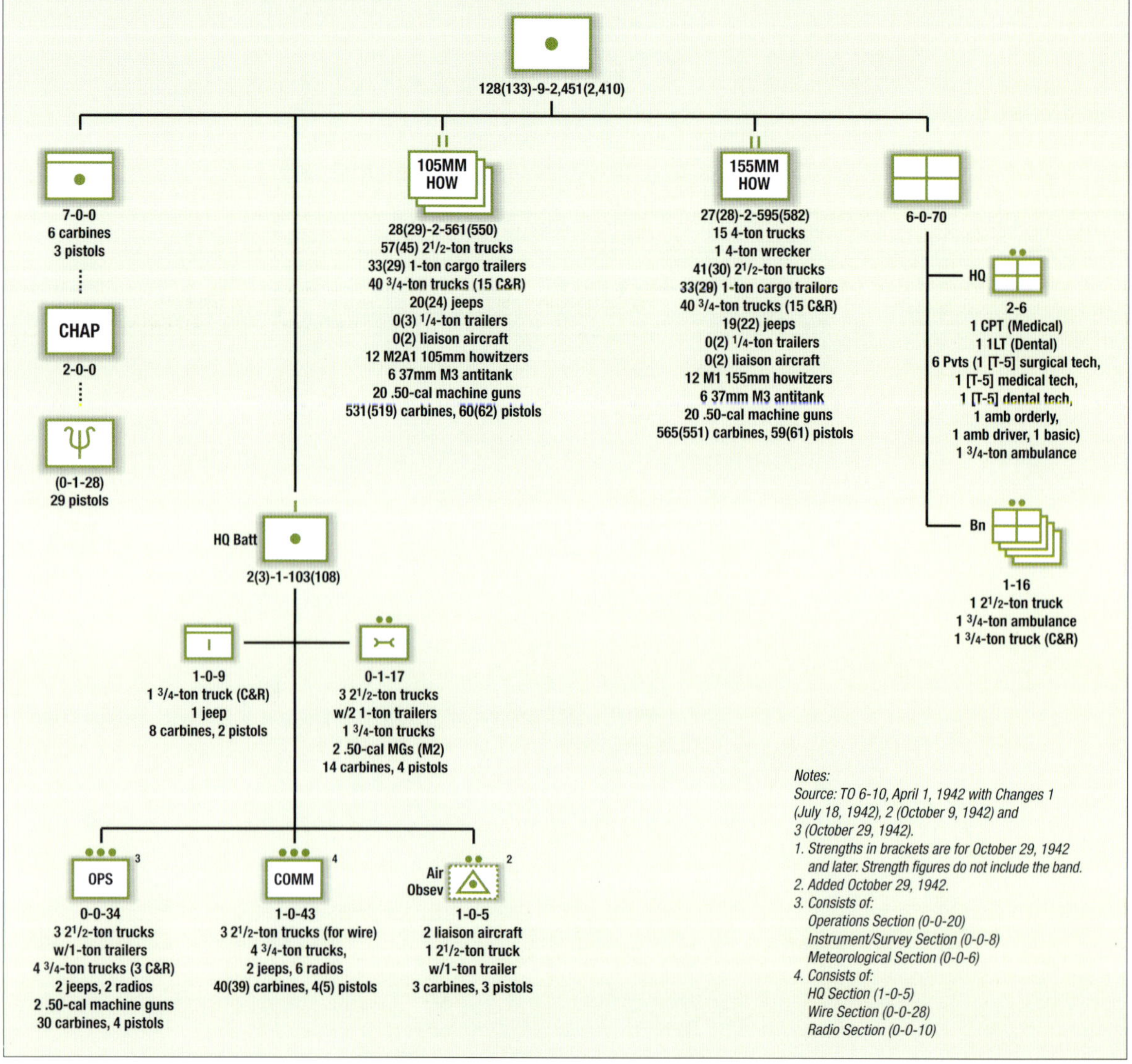

128(133)-9-2,451(2,410)

[Chaplain/HQ]
7-0-0
6 carbines
3 pistols

CHAP
2-0-0

(0-1-28)
29 pistols

105MM HOW
28(29)-2-561(550)
57(45) 2½-ton trucks
33(29) 1-ton cargo trailers
40 ¾-ton trucks (15 C&R)
20(24) jeeps
0(3) ¼-ton trailers
0(2) liaison aircraft
12 M2A1 105mm howitzers
6 37mm M3 antitank
20 .50-cal machine guns
531(519) carbines, 60(62) pistols

155MM HOW
27(28)-2-595(582)
15 4-ton trucks
1 4-ton wrecker
41(30) 2½-ton trucks
33(29) 1-ton cargo trailers
40 ¾-ton trucks (15 C&R)
19(22) jeeps
0(2) ¼-ton trailers
0(2) liaison aircraft
12 M1 155mm howitzers
6 37mm M3 antitank
20 .50-cal machine guns
565(551) carbines, 59(61) pistols

[Medical]
6-0-70

HQ
2-6
1 CPT (Medical)
1 1LT (Dental)
6 Pvts (1 [T-5] surgical tech,
1 [T-5] medical tech,
1 [T-5] dental tech,
1 amb orderly,
1 amb driver, 1 basic)
1 ¾-ton ambulance

Bn
1-16
1 2½-ton truck
1 ¾-ton ambulance
1 ¾-ton truck (C&R)

HQ Batt
2(3)-1-103(108)

[HQ section]
1-0-9
1 ¾-ton truck (C&R)
1 jeep
8 carbines, 2 pistols

[Maintenance]
0-1-17
3 2½-ton trucks
w/2 1-ton trailers
1 ¾-ton trucks
2 .50-cal MGs (M2)
14 carbines, 4 pistols

OPS [3]
0-0-34
3 2½-ton trucks
w/1-ton trailers
4 ¾-ton trucks (3 C&R)
2 jeeps, 2 radios
2 .50-cal machine guns
30 carbines, 4 pistols

COMM [4]
1-0-43
3 2½-ton trucks (for wire)
4 ¾-ton trucks,
2 jeeps, 6 radios
40(39) carbines, 4(5) pistols

Air Obsev [2]
1-0-5
2 liaison aircraft
1 2½-ton truck
w/1-ton trailer
3 carbines, 3 pistols

Notes:
Source: TO 6-10, April 1, 1942 with Changes 1
(July 18, 1942), 2 (October 9, 1942) and
3 (October 29, 1942).
1. Strengths in brackets are for October 29, 1942
and later. Strength figures do not include the band.
2. Added October 29, 1942.
3. Consists of:
Operations Section (0-0-20)
Instrument/Survey Section (0-0-8)
Meteorological Section (0-0-6)
4. Consists of:
HQ Section (1-0-5)
Wire Section (0-0-28)
Radio Section (0-0-10)

Two gun crews with M2 105mm howitzers prepare for firing positions against the "enemy" during artillery maneuvers in Australia, May 20, 1943. The M2 was probably the best World War II howitzer in its class. It was available in quantity at an early stage, and a slightly updated version, the M101, is still in limited use by US forces today.

US Army 105mm howitzer battalion, April 1, 1942[1]

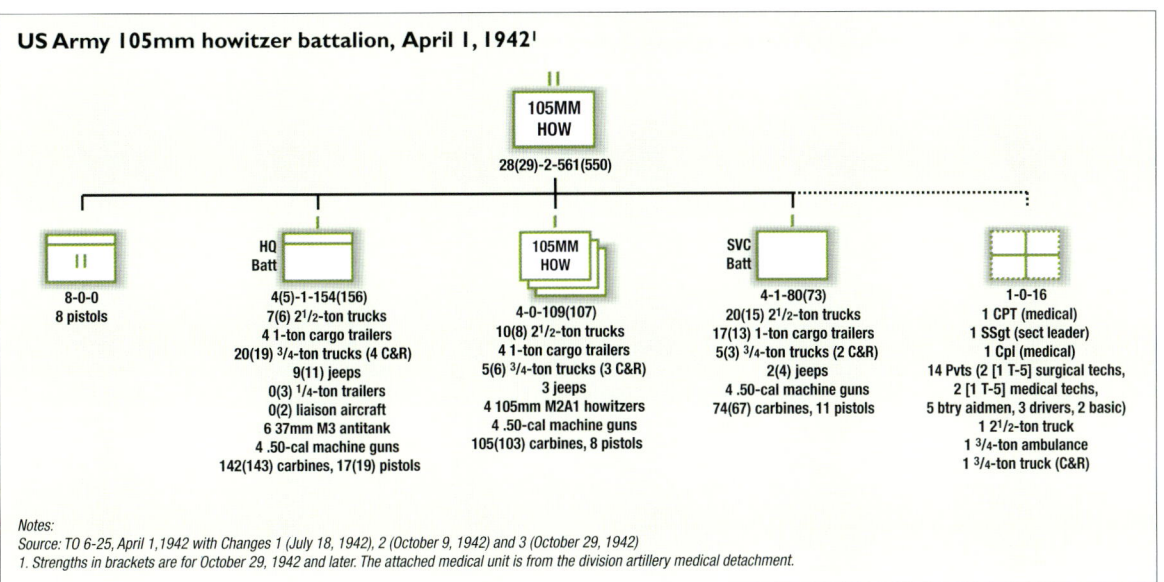

105MM HOW

28(29)-2-561(550)

8-0-0 8 pistols	**HQ Batt** 4(5)-1-154(156) 7(6) 2½-ton trucks 4 1-ton cargo trailers 20(19) ¾-ton trucks (4 C&R) 9(11) jeeps 0(3) ¼-ton trailers 0(2) liaison aircraft 6 37mm M3 antitank 4 .50-cal machine guns 142(143) carbines, 17(19) pistols	**105MM HOW** 4-0-109(107) 10(8) 2½-ton trucks 4 1-ton cargo trailers 5(6) ¾-ton trucks (3 C&R) 3 jeeps 4 105mm M2A1 howitzers 4 .50-cal machine guns 105(103) carbines, 8 pistols	**SVC Batt** 4-1-80(73) 20(15) 2½-ton trucks 17(13) 1-ton cargo trailers 5(3) ¾-ton trucks (2 C&R) 2(4) jeeps 4 .50-cal machine guns 74(67) carbines, 11 pistols	**1-0-16** 1 CPT (medical) 1 SSgt (sect leader) 1 Cpl (medical) 14 Pvts (2 [1 T-5] surgical techs, 2 [1 T-5] medical techs, 5 btry aidmen, 3 drivers, 2 basic) 1 2½-ton truck 1 ¾-ton ambulance 1 ¾-ton truck (C&R)

Notes:
Source: TO 6-25, April 1,1942 with Changes 1 (July 18, 1942), 2 (October 9, 1942) and 3 (October 29, 1942)
1. Strengths in brackets are for October 29, 1942 and later. The attached medical unit is from the division artillery medical detachment.

US Army 155mm howitzer battalion, April 1, 1942[1]

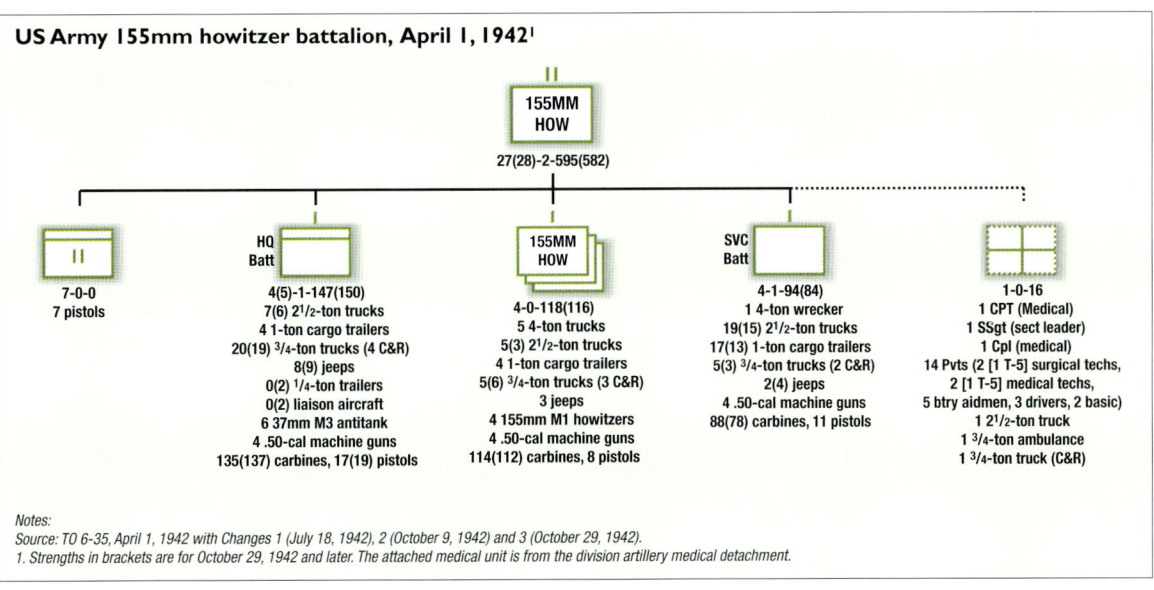

155MM HOW

27(28)-2-595(582)

7-0-0 7 pistols	**HQ Batt** 4(5)-1-147(150) 7(6) 2½-ton trucks 4 1-ton cargo trailers 20(19) ¾-ton trucks (4 C&R) 8(9) jeeps 0(2) ¼-ton trailers 0(2) liaison aircraft 6 37mm M3 antitank 4 .50-cal machine guns 135(137) carbines, 17(19) pistols	**155MM HOW** 4-0-118(116) 5 4-ton trucks 5(3) 2½-ton trucks 4 1-ton cargo trailers 5(6) ¾-ton trucks (3 C&R) 3 jeeps 4 155mm M1 howitzers 4 .50-cal machine guns 114(112) carbines, 8 pistols	**SVC Batt** 4-1-94(84) 1 4-ton wrecker 19(15) 2½-ton trucks 17(13) 1-ton cargo trailers 5(3) ¾-ton trucks (2 C&R) 2(4) jeeps 4 .50-cal machine guns 88(78) carbines, 11 pistols	**1-0-16** 1 CPT (Medical) 1 SSgt (sect leader) 1 Cpl (medical) 14 Pvts (2 [1 T-5] surgical techs, 2 [1 T-5] medical techs, 5 btry aidmen, 3 drivers, 2 basic) 1 2½-ton truck 1 ¾-ton ambulance 1 ¾-ton truck (C&R)

Notes:
Source: TO 6-35, April 1, 1942 with Changes 1 (July 18, 1942), 2 (October 9, 1942) and 3 (October 29, 1942).
1. Strengths in brackets are for October 29, 1942 and later. The attached medical unit is from the division artillery medical detachment.

This uncaptioned photo shows one of the rare T30 self-propelled 75mm howitzers, with which infantry regimental cannon companies using the April 1942 tables were supposed to have been equipped. It is probably in combat in Italy, 1943.

US Army artillery battalion HQ battery, April 1, 1942[1]

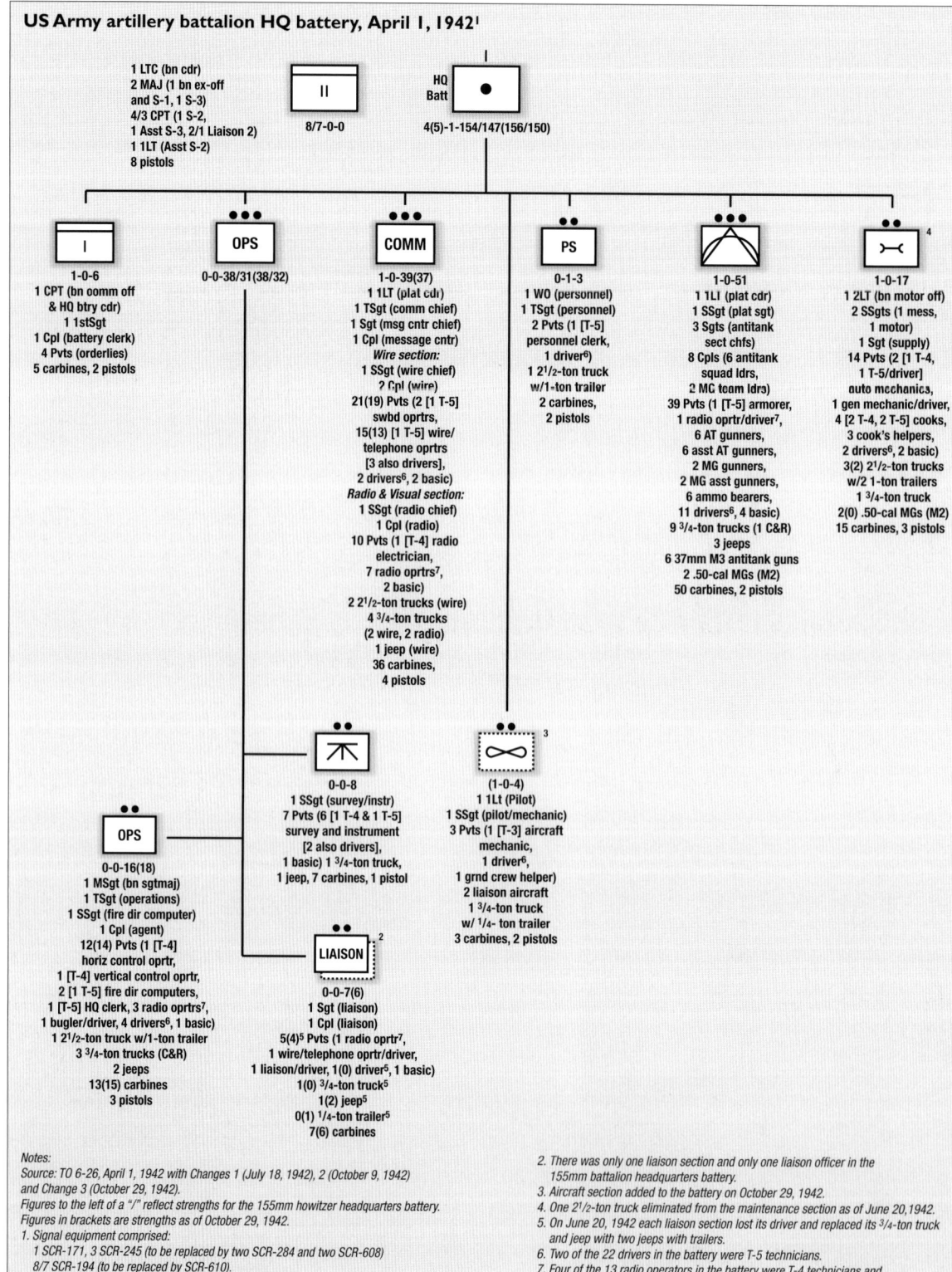

1 LTC (bn cdr)
2 MAJ (1 bn ex-off
and S-1, 1 S-3)
4/3 CPT (1 S-2,
1 Asst S-3, 2/1 Liaison 2)
1 1LT (Asst S-2)
8 pistols

II
8/7-0-0

HQ Batt
4(5)-1-154/147(156/150)

I
1-0-6
1 CPT (bn comm off
& HQ btry cdr)
1 1stSgt
1 Cpl (battery clerk)
4 Pvts (orderlies)
5 carbines, 2 pistols

OPS
0-0-38/31(38/32)

COMM
1-0-39(37)
1 1LT (plat cdr)
1 TSgt (comm chief)
1 Sgt (msg cntr chief)
1 Cpl (message cntr)
Wire section:
1 SSgt (wire chief)
2 Cpl (wire)
21(19) Pvts (2 [1 T-5]
swbd oprtrs,
15(13) [1 T-5] wire/
telephone oprtrs
[3 also drivers],
2 drivers[6], 2 basic)
Radio & Visual section:
1 SSgt (radio chief)
1 Cpl (radio)
10 Pvts (1 [T-4] radio
electrician,
7 radio oprtrs[7],
2 basic)
2 2¹/₂-ton trucks (wire)
4 ³/₄-ton trucks
(2 wire, 2 radio)
1 jeep (wire)
36 carbines,
4 pistols

PS
0-1-3
1 WO (personnel)
1 TSgt (personnel)
2 Pvts (1 [T-5]
personnel clerk,
1 driver[6])
1 2¹/₂-ton truck
w/1-ton trailer
2 carbines,
2 pistols

1-0-51
1 1Lt (plat cdr)
1 SSgt (plat sgt)
3 Sgts (antitank
sect chfs)
8 Cpls (6 antitank
squad ldrs,
2 MG team ldrs)
39 Pvts (1 [T-5] armorer,
1 radio oprtr/driver[7],
6 AT gunners,
6 asst AT gunners,
2 MG gunners,
2 MG asst gunners,
6 ammo bearers,
11 drivers[6], 4 basic)
9 ³/₄-ton trucks (1 C&R)
3 jeeps
6 37mm M3 antitank guns
2 .50-cal MGs (M2)
50 carbines, 2 pistols

[4]
1-0-17
1 2LT (bn motor off)
2 SSgts (1 mess,
1 motor)
1 Sgt (supply)
14 Pvts (2 [1 T-4,
1 T-5/driver]
auto mechanics,
1 gen mechanic/driver,
4 [2 T-4, 2 T-5] cooks,
3 cook's helpers,
2 drivers[6], 2 basic)
3(2) 2¹/₂-ton trucks
w/2 1-ton trailers
1 ³/₄-ton truck
2(0) .50-cal MGs (M2)
15 carbines, 3 pistols

0-0-8
1 SSgt (survey/instr)
7 Pvts (6 [1 T-4 & 1 T-5]
survey and instrument
[2 also drivers],
1 basic) 1 ³/₄-ton truck,
1 jeep, 7 carbines, 1 pistol

[3]
(1-0-4)
1 1Lt (Pilot)
1 SSgt (pilot/mechanic)
3 Pvts (1 [T-3] aircraft
mechanic,
1 driver[6],
1 grnd crew helper)
2 liaison aircraft
1 ³/₄-ton truck
w/ ¹/₄- ton trailer
3 carbines, 2 pistols

OPS
0-0-16(18)
1 MSgt (bn sgtmaj)
1 TSgt (operations)
1 SSgt (fire dir computer)
1 Cpl (agent)
12(14) Pvts (1 [T-4
horiz control oprtr,
1 [T-4] vertical control oprtr,
2 [1 T-5] fire dir computers,
1 [T-5] HQ clerk, 3 radio oprtrs[7],
1 bugler/driver, 4 drivers[6], 1 basic)
1 2¹/₂-ton truck w/1-ton trailer
3 ³/₄-ton trucks (C&R)
2 jeeps
13(15) carbines
3 pistols

LIAISON[2]
0-0-7(6)
1 Sgt (liaison)
1 Cpl (liaison)
5(4)⁵ Pvts (1 radio oprtr[7],
1 wire/telephone oprtr/driver,
1 liaison/driver, 1(0) driver[5], 1 basic)
1(0) ³/₄-ton truck[5]
1(2) jeep[5]
0(1) ¹/₄-ton trailer[5]
7(6) carbines

Notes:
*Source: TO 6-26, April 1, 1942 with Changes 1 (July 18, 1942), 2 (October 9, 1942)
and Change 3 (October 29, 1942).*
Figures to the left of a "/" reflect strengths for the 155mm howitzer headquarters battery.
Figures in brackets are strengths as of October 29, 1942.
1. Signal equipment comprised:
  1 SCR-171, 3 SCR-245 (to be replaced by two SCR-284 and two SCR-608)
  8/7 SCR-194 (to be replaced by SCR-610).
  2 BD-72 and 1 BD-71 switchboards, 19 EE-8 telephones
  30/25 miles of wire (18/13 on DR-4 reels, 12 on DR-8)
  1 RL-31, 1 RL-39 reel units, 1 TG-5 telegraph set
  Small-arms distribution was as follows:
  Pistols: staff sergeants and higher.
  Carbines: sergeants and below.

2. There was only one liaison section and only one liaison officer in the
  155mm battalion headquarters battery.
3. Aircraft section added to the battery on October 29, 1942.
4. One 2¹/₂-ton truck eliminated from the maintenance section as of June 20, 1942.
5. On June 20, 1942 each liaison section lost its driver and replaced its ³/₄-ton truck
  and jeep with two jeeps with trailers.
6. Two of the 22 drivers in the battery were T-5 technicians.
7. Four of the 13 radio operators in the battery were T-4 technicians and
  four others were T-5.

US Army 105mm howitzer battery, April 1, 1942[1]

```
                              105MM
                              HOW
                           4-0-109(107)
```

| (Battery HQ)
1-3
1 CPT (battery cdr)
1 1stSgt
1 Cpl (battery clerk)
1 Pvt (orderly)
2 carbines, 2 pistols

DETAIL
1-28(27)[2]
1 1LT (recon off)
1 SSgt (chief of detail)
1 Sgt (signal)
5 Cpls (1 agent/driver,
1 instrument,
2 scout, 1 wire)
21(20) Pvts (4 [1 T-4 & 1 T-5]
radio operators,
1 [T-5] switchboard operator,
9 wiremen/telephone operators
[1 is also a driver],
4(3) drivers[4], 1 bugler/driver 2 basic)[2]
1(0) 2½-ton truck[2]
4(5) ¾-ton trucks
(3 C&R)[2]
2 jeeps
27(26) carbines, 2 pistols

FIRING
1-63

FIRING
1-2
1 1LT (btry exec off)
2 Pvts (1 [T-4] artillery
mechanic,
1 instrument
operator and driver)
1 jeep
2 carbines
1 pistol

||| (gun sections)
0-11
1 SSgt (section ldr—
1st Section only)
1 Sgt (section ldr—2d, 3d
and 4th sections only)
1 Cpl (gunner)
9 Pvts (7 cannoneers,
1 driver[4], 1 basic)
1 2½-ton truck
1 M2A1 105mm howitzer
11 carbines (10 in 1st Section only)
1 pistol (in 1st Section only)

5TH SECT
0-17
1 Sgt (section ldr)
3 Cpls (2 MG team ldrs,
1 ammunition)
13 Pvts (6 cannoneers,
2 drivers[4], 2 MG gunners,
2 MG asst gunners, 1 basic)
2 2½-ton trucks
2 1-ton trailers
2 .50-cal HMGs (M2)
17 carbines

>—< (trains / combat train)
1-15(14)[3]
1 2LT (asst exec off)
1 SSgt (mess)
2 Sgts (1 motor, 1 supply)
12(11) Pvts (2(1) [1 T-4, 1(0) T-5]
auto mechanics/drivers[3],
2 [1 T-4, 1 T-5] cooks,
2 cook's helpers,
2 drivers[4],
1 general mechanic, 3 basic)
3(2) 2½-ton trucks
2 1-ton trailers
1 ¾-ton truck
14(13) carbines, 2 pistols

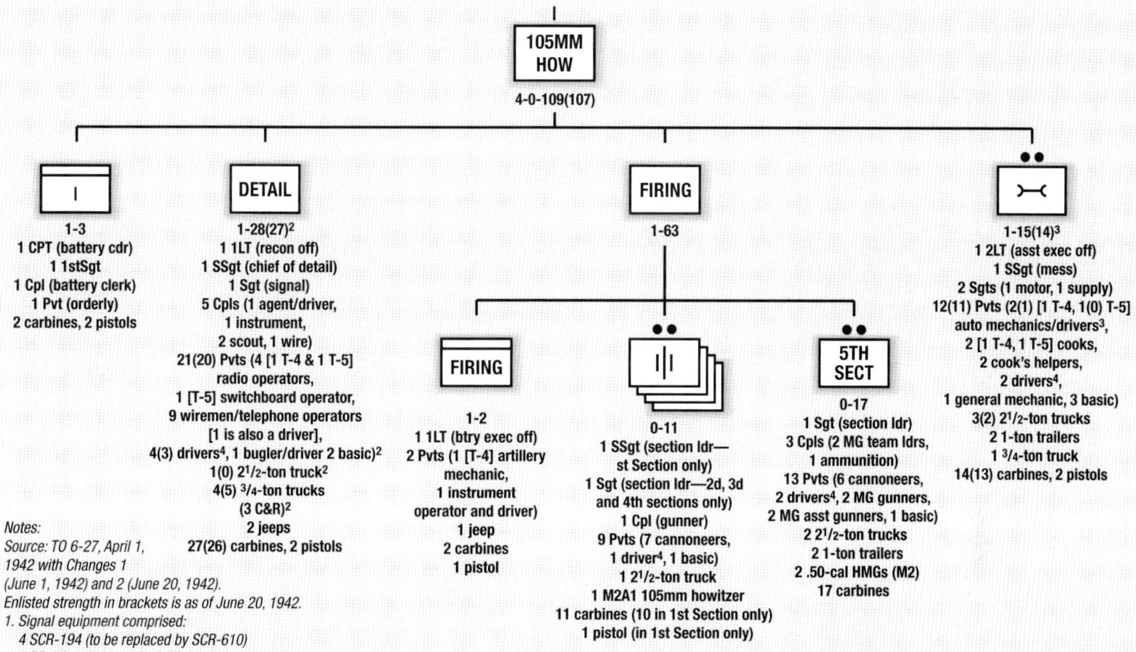

Notes:
Source: TO 6-27, April 1,
1942 with Changes 1
(June 1, 1942) and 2 (June 20, 1942).
Enlisted strength in brackets is as of June 20, 1942.
1. Signal equipment comprised:
  4 SCR-194 (to be replaced by SCR-610)
  2 BD-71 switchboards, 9 EE-8 telephones
  1 RL-31, 1 RL-39, 10 miles of wire (8 on DR-4 reels, 2 on DR-8).
  Small-arms distribution was as follows:
  Pistols: staff sergeants and higher.
  Carbines: sergeants and below.
2. In June 1942, a 2½-ton truck and its driver was replaced by a ¾-ton weapons carrier with no designated driver.
3. One T-5 auto mechanic and one 2½-ton truck was eliminated in June 1942.
4. Four drivers in the battery are rated as T-5 technicians.

US Army 155mm howitzer battery, April 1, 1942[1]

```
                              155MM
                              HOW
                           4-0-118(116)
```

| (Battery HQ)
1-3
1 CPT (battery cdr)
1 1stSgt
1 Cpl (battery clerk)
1 Pvt (orderly)
2 carbines, 2 pistols

DETAIL
1-29(28)[2]
1 1LT (recon off)
1 SSgt (chief of detail)
1 Sgt (signal)
5 Cpls (1 agent/driver, 1 instrument,
2 scout, 1 wire)
22(21) Pvts (4 [1 T-4 & 1 T-5]
radio operators,
1 [T-5] switchboard operator,
9 wiremen/telephone operators
[1 is also a driver],
4(3) drivers[4],
1 bugler/driver, 3 basic)[2]
1(0) 2½-ton truck[2]
4(5) ¾-ton trucks (3 C&R)[2]
2 jeeps
28(27) carbines, 2 pistols

FIRING
1-71

FIRING
1-2
1 1LT (btry exec off)
2 Pvts (1 [T-4]
artillery mechanic,
1 instrument
operator and driver)
1 jeep
2 carbines
1 pistol

||| (gun sections)
0-13
1 SSgt (section ldr—
1st Section only)
1 Sgt (section ldr—2d, 3d
and 4th sections only)
2 Cpls (1 gunner,
1 ammunition)
10 Pvts (8 cannoneers,
1 driver[4], 1 basic)
1 4-ton truck
1 M1 155mm howitzer
13 carbines (12 in 1st Section only)
1 pistol (in 1st Section only)

5TH SECT
0-17
1 Sgt (section ldr)
3 Cpls (2 MG team ldrs,
1 ammunition)
13 Pvts (6 cannoneers,
2 drivers[4], 2 MG gunners,
2 MG asst gunners, 1 basic)
1 4-ton truck
1 2½-ton truck
2 1-ton trailers
2 .50-cal HMGs (M2)
17 carbines

>—< (trains / combat train)
1-15(14)[3]
1 2LT (asst exec off)
1 SSgt (mess)
2 Sgts (1 motor, 1 supply)
12(11) Pvts (2(1) [1 T-4, 1(0) T-5]
auto mechanics/drivers[3],
2 [1 T-4, 1 T-5] cooks,
2 cook's helpers, 2 drivers[4],
1 general mechanic, 3 basic)
3(2) 2½-ton trucks
2 1-ton trailers
1 ¾-ton truck
14(13) carbines, 2 pistols

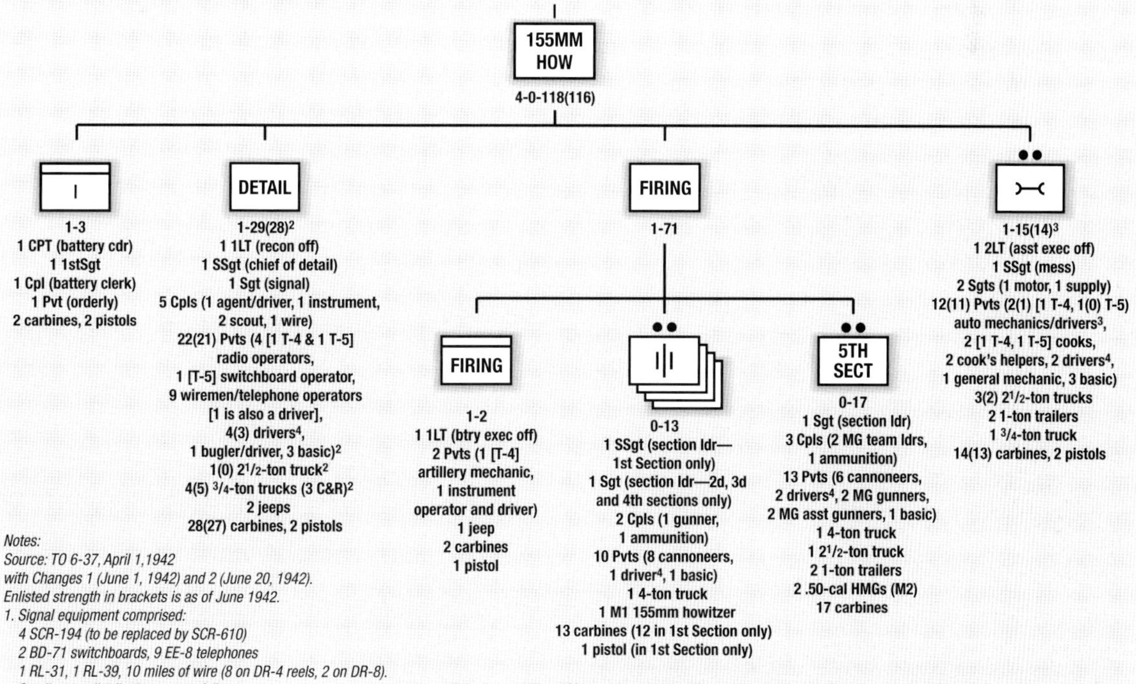

Notes:
Source: TO 6-37, April 1,1942
with Changes 1 (June 1, 1942) and 2 (June 20, 1942).
Enlisted strength in brackets is as of June 1942.
1. Signal equipment comprised:
  4 SCR-194 (to be replaced by SCR-610)
  2 BD-71 switchboards, 9 EE-8 telephones
  1 RL-31, 1 RL-39, 10 miles of wire (8 on DR-4 reels, 2 on DR-8).
  Small-arms distribution was as follows:
  Pistols: staff sergeants and higher.
  Carbines: sergeants and below.
2. In June 1942, a 2½-ton truck and its driver was replaced by a ¾-ton weapons carrier without a designated driver.
3. One T-5 auto mechanic and one 2½-ton truck eliminated in June 1942.
4. Four drivers in the battery were rated as T-5 technicians.

US Army light artillery battalion service battery, April 1, 1942[1]

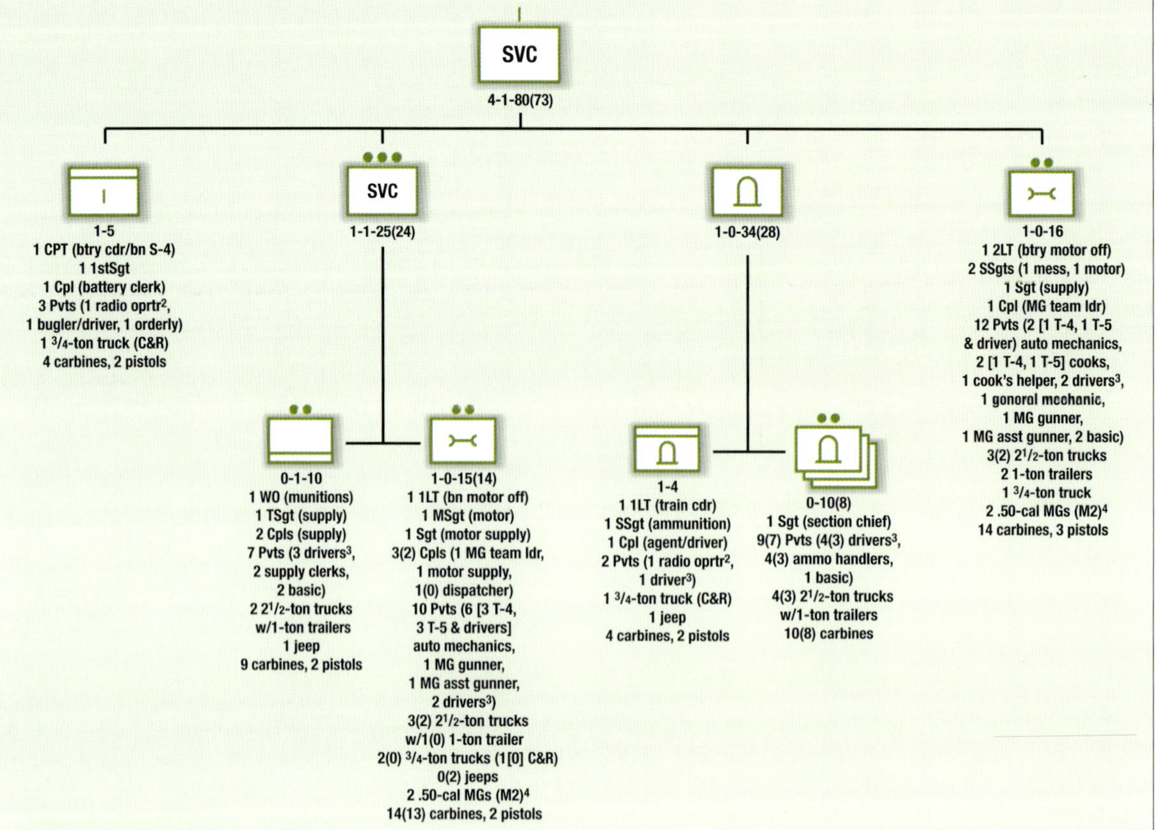

SVC
4-1-80(73)

I
1-5
1 CPT (btry cdr/bn S-4)
1 1stSgt
1 Cpl (battery clerk)
3 Pvts (1 radio oprtr[2],
1 bugler/driver, 1 orderly)
1 3/4-ton truck (C&R)
4 carbines, 2 pistols

SVC
1-1-25(24)

0-1-10
1 WO (munitions)
1 TSgt (supply)
2 Cpls (supply)
7 Pvts (3 drivers[3],
2 supply clerks,
2 basic)
2 2 1/2-ton trucks
w/1-ton trailers
1 jeep
9 carbines, 2 pistols

1-0-15(14)
1 1LT (bn motor off)
1 MSgt (motor)
1 Sgt (motor supply)
3(2) Cpls (1 MG team ldr,
1 motor supply,
1(0) dispatcher)
10 Pvts (6 [3 T-4,
3 T-5 & drivers]
auto mechanics,
1 MG gunner,
1 MG asst gunner,
2 drivers[3])
3(2) 2 1/2-ton trucks
w/1(0) 1-ton trailer
2(0) 3/4-ton trucks (1[0] C&R)
0(2) jeeps
2 .50-cal MGs (M2)[4]
14(13) carbines, 2 pistols

1-0-34(28)

1-4
1 1LT (train cdr)
1 SSgt (ammunition)
1 Cpl (agent/driver)
2 Pvts (1 radio oprtr[2],
1 driver[3])
1 3/4-ton truck (C&R)
1 jeep
4 carbines, 2 pistols

0-10(8)
1 Sgt (section chief)
9(7) Pvts (4(3) drivers[3],
4(3) ammo handlers,
1 basic)
4(3) 2 1/2-ton trucks
w/1-ton trailers
10(8) carbines

1-0-16
1 2LT (btry motor off)
2 SSgts (1 mess, 1 motor)
1 Sgt (supply)
1 Cpl (MG team ldr)
12 Pvts (2 [1 T-4, 1 T-5
& driver) auto mechanics,
2 [1 T-4, 1 T-5] cooks,
1 cook's helper, 2 drivers[3],
1 gonoral mcohanic,
1 MG gunner,
1 MG asst gunner, 2 basic)
3(2) 2 1/2-ton trucks
2 1-ton trailers
1 3/4-ton truck
2 .50-cal MGs (M2)[4]
14 carbines, 3 pistols

Notes:
Source: TO 6-29, April 1, 1942 with Change 1 (July 16, 1942).
Strengths shown in brackets are as of July 16, 1942.
1. Signal equipment comprised:
    2 SCR-194 (to be replaced by SCR-610).
    Small-arms distribution was as follows:
    Pistols: staff sergeants and higher.
    Carbines: sergeants and below.
    Five 2 1/2-ton trucks and four 1-ton cargo trailers were dropped from the battery, and jeeps replaced two 3/4-ton trucks in the battalion maintenance section, as of July 16, 1942.
2. One radio operator was rated as a T-5 technician.
3. Four drivers in the battery were rated as T-5 technicians.
4. Only half of the .50-cal machine guns in the battery had assigned gun teams.

Members of the 10th Engineers, 3d Division build a temporary bridge to cover a hole blown in the roadway near Point Calava on the north coast of Sicily by retreating Axis forces, August 14, 1943.

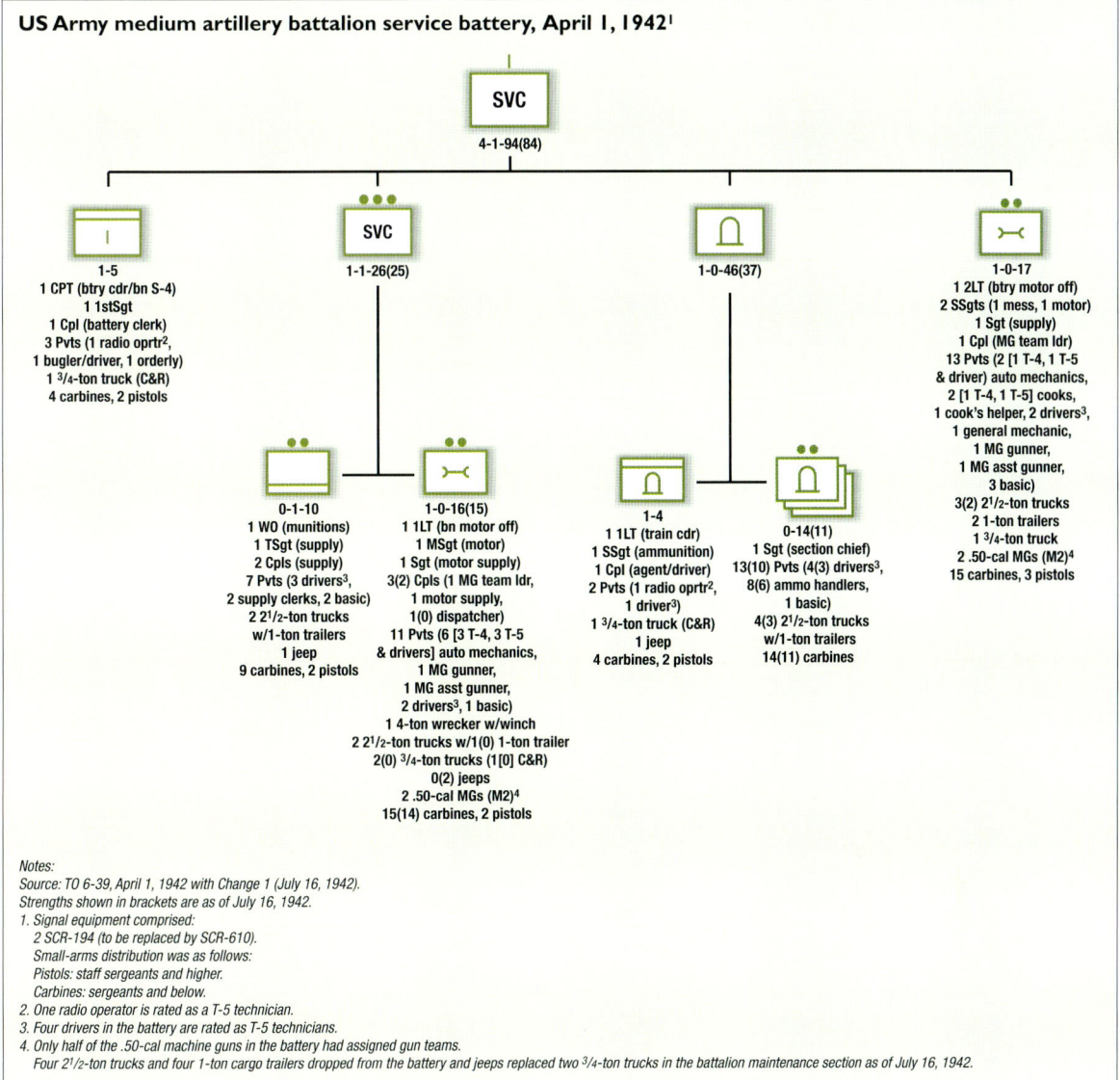

US Army medium artillery battalion service battery, April 1, 1942[1]

SVC
4-1-94(84)

|
1-5
1 CPT (btry cdr/bn S-4)
1 1stSgt
1 Cpl (battery clerk)
3 Pvts (1 radio oprtr[2],
1 bugler/driver, 1 orderly)
1 ³/₄-ton truck (C&R)
4 carbines, 2 pistols

SVC
1-1-26(25)

0-1-10
1 WO (munitions)
1 TSgt (supply)
2 Cpls (supply)
7 Pvts (3 drivers[3],
2 supply clerks, 2 basic)
2 2¹/₂-ton trucks
w/1-ton trailers
1 jeep
9 carbines, 2 pistols

1-0-16(15)
1 1LT (bn motor off)
1 MSgt (motor)
1 Sgt (motor supply)
3(2) Cpls (1 MG team ldr,
1 motor supply,
1(0) dispatcher)
11 Pvts (6 [3 T-4, 3 T-5
& drivers] auto mechanics,
1 MG gunner,
1 MG asst gunner,
2 drivers[3], 1 basic)
1 4-ton wrecker w/winch
2 2¹/₂-ton trucks w/1(0) 1-ton trailer
2(0) ³/₄-ton trucks (1[0] C&R)
0(2) jeeps
2 .50-cal MGs (M2)[4]
15(14) carbines, 2 pistols

∩
1-0-46(37)

1-4
1 1LT (train cdr)
1 SSgt (ammunition)
1 Cpl (agent/driver)
2 Pvts (1 radio oprtr[2],
1 driver[3])
1 ³/₄-ton truck (C&R)
1 jeep
4 carbines, 2 pistols

0-14(11)
1 Sgt (section chief)
13(10) Pvts (4(3) drivers[3],
8(6) ammo handlers,
1 basic)
4(3) 2¹/₂-ton trucks
w/1-ton trailers
14(11) carbines

✕
1-0-17
1 2LT (btry motor off)
2 SSgts (1 mess, 1 motor)
1 Sgt (supply)
1 Cpl (MG team ldr)
13 Pvts (2 [1 T-4, 1 T-5
& driver) auto mechanics,
2 [1 T-4, 1 T-5] cooks,
1 cook's helper, 2 drivers[3],
1 general mechanic,
1 MG gunner,
1 MG asst gunner,
3 basic)
3(2) 2¹/₂-ton trucks
2 1-ton trailers
1 ³/₄-ton truck
2 .50-cal MGs (M2)[4]
15 carbines, 3 pistols

Notes:
Source: TO 6-39, April 1, 1942 with Change 1 (July 16, 1942).
Strengths shown in brackets are as of July 16, 1942.
1. Signal equipment comprised:
   2 SCR-194 (to be replaced by SCR-610).
   Small-arms distribution was as follows:
   Pistols: staff sergeants and higher.
   Carbines: sergeants and below.
2. One radio operator is rated as a T-5 technician.
3. Four drivers in the battery are rated as T-5 technicians.
4. Only half of the .50-cal machine guns in the battery had assigned gun teams.
   Four 2¹/₂-ton trucks and four 1-ton cargo trailers dropped from the battery and jeeps replaced two ³/₄-ton trucks in the battalion maintenance section as of July 16, 1942.

The combat engineer battalion

This was a light engineering unit with limited construction, demolition, and river crossing capabilities. It was generally distributed in squad- or platoon-sized detachments throughout the division sector, but chiefly in forward areas. Engineer battalions attached to the division from corps and army would handle engineering tasks further to the rear.

Other divisional units

At first, a quartermaster battalion and a medical battalion handled division-level logistics (combat service support). The quartermaster battalion included a standard quartermaster truck company that functioned as the division transportation reserve. It also handled higher-level maintenance for all the trucks in the division. In August 1942, motor maintenance became a responsibility of the Ordnance Corps. The quartermaster battalion was reduced to a reinforced company (mainly by dropping its oversized

(continues on page 30)

US Army combat engineer battalion, April 1, 1942[1]

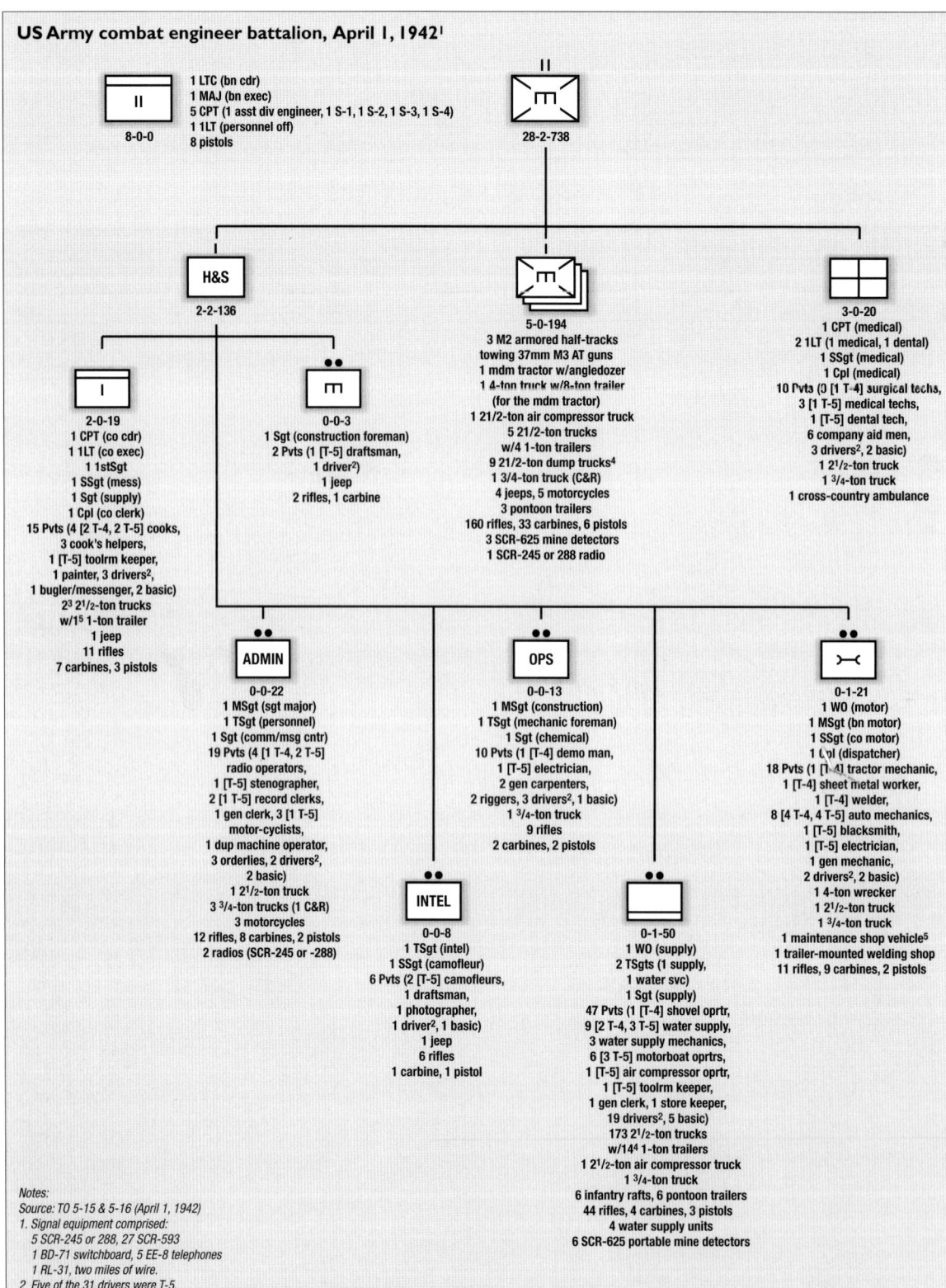

II — 8-0-0
1 LTC (bn cdr)
1 MAJ (bn exec)
5 CPT (1 asst div engineer, 1 S-1, 1 S-2, 1 S-3, 1 S-4)
1 1LT (personnel off)
8 pistols

II — 28-2-738

H&S — 2-2-136

I — 2-0-19
1 CPT (co cdr)
1 1LT (co exec)
1 1stSgt
1 SSgt (mess)
1 Sgt (supply)
1 Cpl (co clerk)
15 Pvts (4 [2 T-4, 2 T-5] cooks,
3 cook's helpers,
1 [T-5] toolrm keeper,
1 painter, 3 drivers[2],
1 bugler/messenger, 2 basic)
2[3] 2¹/₂-ton trucks
w/1[5] 1-ton trailer
1 jeep
11 rifles
7 carbines, 3 pistols

☰ — 0-0-3
1 Sgt (construction foreman)
2 Pvts (1 [T-5] draftsman,
1 driver[2])
1 jeep
2 rifles, 1 carbine

— 5-0-194
3 M2 armored half-tracks
towing 37mm M3 AT guns
1 mdm tractor w/angledozer
1 4-ton truck w/8-ton trailer
(for the mdm tractor)
1 2¹/₂-ton air compressor truck
5 2¹/₂-ton trucks
w/4 1-ton trailers
9 2¹/₂-ton dump trucks[4]
1 ³/₄-ton truck (C&R)
4 jeeps, 5 motorcycles
2 pontoon trailers
160 rifles, 33 carbines, 6 pistols
3 SCR-625 mine detectors
1 SCR-245 or 288 radio

— 3-0-20
1 CPT (medical)
2 1LT (1 medical, 1 dental)
1 SSgt (medical)
1 Cpl (medical)
10 Pvts (3 [1 T-4] surgical techs,
3 [1 T-5] medical techs,
1 [T-5] dental tech,
6 company aid men,
3 drivers[2], 2 basic)
1 2¹/₂-ton truck
1 ³/₄-ton truck
1 cross-country ambulance

ADMIN — 0-0-22
1 MSgt (sgt major)
1 TSgt (personnel)
1 Sgt (comm/msg cntr)
19 Pvts (4 [1 T-4, 2 T-5]
radio operators,
1 [T-5] stenographer,
2 [1 T-5] record clerks,
1 gen clerk, 3 [1 T-5]
motor-cyclists,
1 dup machine operator,
3 orderlies, 2 drivers[2],
2 basic)
1 2¹/₂-ton truck
3 ³/₄-ton trucks (1 C&R)
3 motorcycles
12 rifles, 8 carbines, 2 pistols
2 radios (SCR-245 or -288)

OPS — 0-0-13
1 MSgt (construction)
1 TSgt (mechanic foreman)
1 Sgt (chemical)
10 Pvts (1 [T-4] demo man,
1 [T-5] electrician,
2 gen carpenters,
2 riggers, 3 drivers[2], 1 basic)
1 ³/₄-ton truck
9 rifles
2 carbines, 2 pistols

⋈ — 0-1-21
1 WO (motor)
1 MSgt (bn motor)
1 SSgt (co motor)
1 Cpl (dispatcher)
18 Pvts (1 [T-4] tractor mechanic,
1 [T-4] sheet metal worker,
1 [T-4] welder,
8 [4 T-4, 4 T-5] auto mechanics,
1 [T-5] blacksmith,
1 [T-5] electrician,
1 gen mechanic,
2 drivers[2], 2 basic)
1 4-ton wrecker
1 2¹/₂-ton truck
1 ³/₄-ton truck
1 maintenance shop vehicle[5]
1 trailer-mounted welding shop
11 rifles, 9 carbines, 2 pistols

INTEL — 0-0-8
1 TSgt (intel)
1 SSgt (camofleur)
6 Pvts (2 [T-5] camofleurs,
1 draftsman,
1 photographer,
1 driver[2], 1 basic)
1 jeep
6 rifles
1 carbine, 1 pistol

— 0-1-50
1 WO (supply)
2 TSgts (1 supply,
1 water svc)
1 Sgt (supply)
47 Pvts (1 [T-4] shovel oprtr,
9 [2 T-4, 3 T-5] water supply,
3 water supply mechanics,
6 [3 T-5] motorboat oprtrs,
1 [T-5] air compressor oprtr,
1 [T-5] toolrm keeper,
1 gen clerk, 1 store keeper,
19 drivers[2], 5 basic)
173 2¹/₂-ton trucks
w/14[4] 1-ton trailers
1 2¹/₂-ton air compressor truck
1 ³/₄-ton truck
6 infantry rafts, 6 pontoon trailers
44 rifles, 4 carbines, 3 pistols
4 water supply units
6 SCR-625 portable mine detectors

Notes:
Source: TO 5-15 & 5-16 (April 1, 1942)
1. Signal equipment comprised:
   5 SCR-245 or 288, 27 SCR-593
   1 BD-71 switchboard, 5 EE-8 telephones
   1 RL-31, two miles of wire.
2. Five of the 31 drivers were T-5.
3. Six of these trucks carried bridging equipment, two carried personnel, four carried water-supply units, three carried antitank mines, and two carried supplementary equipment (including
   explosives). One of the two trucks in the Company HQ carried the field kitchen and water; the other had company supplies.
4. Trailers included one for kitchen and water (Company HQ), one for supplementary equipment, two for ammunition, one for maps, four for water-supply equipment, and six were for infantry
   entrenching sets. Although all but one of the trailers belonged to the supply section, three of them were hauled by trucks in the Company HQ, admin section and maintenance section.
5. Developmental type; not yet available.

A corduroy road built by the 114th Engineer Battalion, 32d Division to allow jeeps to carry supplies and ammunition over swampy areas, December 21, 1942. This road runs from Dobudura to Buna Village, New Guinea.

US Army combat engineer company, April 1, 1942[1]

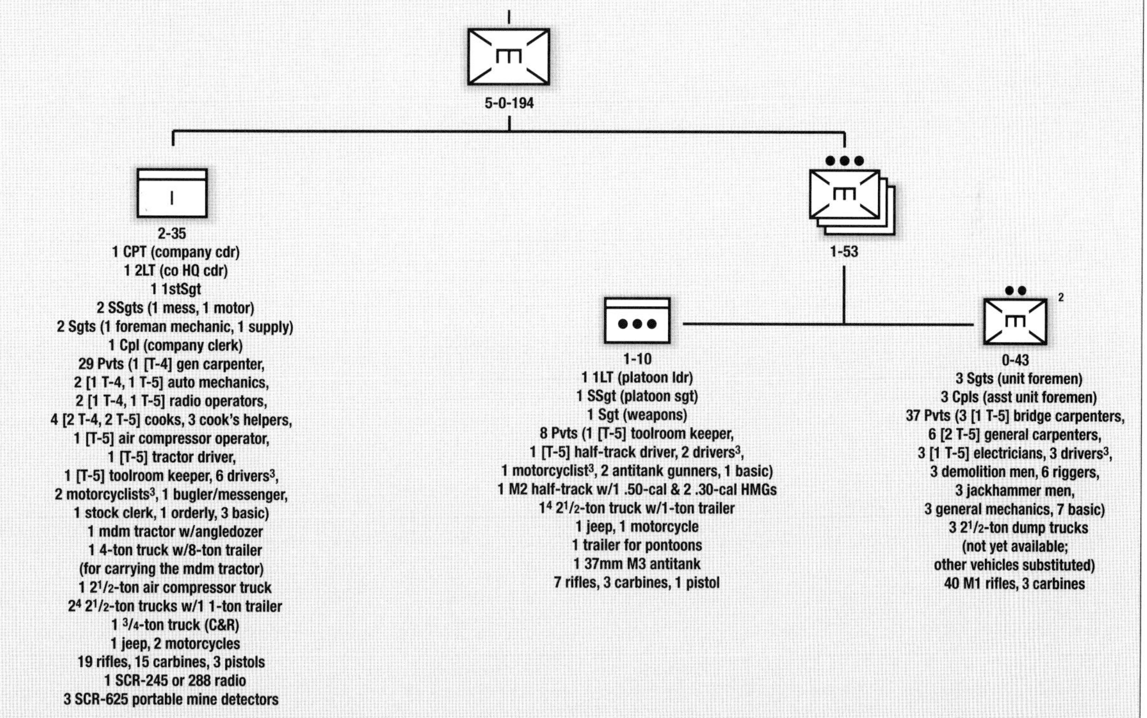

5-0-194

2-35
1 CPT (company cdr)
1 2LT (co HQ cdr)
1 1stSgt
2 SSgts (1 mess, 1 motor)
2 Sgts (1 foreman mechanic, 1 supply)
1 Cpl (company clerk)
29 Pvts (1 [T-4] gen carpenter,
2 [1 T-4, 1 T-5] auto mechanics,
2 [1 T-4, 1 T-5] radio operators,
4 [2 T-4, 2 T-5] cooks, 3 cook's helpers,
1 [T-5] air compressor operator,
1 [T-5] tractor driver,
1 [T-5] toolroom keeper, 6 drivers[3],
2 motorcyclists[3], 1 bugler/messenger,
1 stock clerk, 1 orderly, 3 basic)
1 mdm tractor w/angledozer
1 4-ton truck w/8-ton trailer
(for carrying the mdm tractor)
1 2¹/₂-ton air compressor truck
2[4] 2¹/₂-ton trucks w/1 1-ton trailer
1 ³/₄-ton truck (C&R)
1 jeep, 2 motorcycles
19 rifles, 15 carbines, 3 pistols
1 SCR-245 or 288 radio
3 SCR-625 portable mine detectors

1-53

1-10
1 1LT (platoon ldr)
1 SSgt (platoon sgt)
1 Sgt (weapons)
8 Pvts (1 [T-5] toolroom keeper,
1 [T-5] half-track driver, 2 drivers[3],
1 motorcyclist[3], 2 antitank gunners, 1 basic)
1 M2 half-track w/1 .50-cal & 2 .30-cal HMGs
1[4] 2¹/₂-ton truck w/1-ton trailer
1 jeep, 1 motorcycle
1 trailer for pontoons
1 37mm M3 antitank
7 rifles, 3 carbines, 1 pistol

0-43 [2]
3 Sgts (unit foremen)
3 Cpls (asst unit foremen)
37 Pvts (3 [1 T-5] bridge carpenters,
6 [2 T-5] general carpenters,
3 [1 T-5] electricians, 3 drivers[3],
3 demolition men, 6 riggers,
3 jackhammer men,
3 general mechanics, 7 basic)
3 2¹/₂-ton dump trucks
(not yet available;
other vehicles substituted)
40 M1 rifles, 3 carbines

Notes:
Source: TO 5-17 of April 1, 1942.
1. Note: nine SCR-593 normally issued to the company from the battalion communication platoon.
   Small-arms distribution was as follows:
   Pistols: officers and the 1st sergeant only.
   Carbines: all staff sergeants and sergeants, all radio operators, cooks and motorcyclists, the T-4 auto mechanic, the T-4 general carpenter, and the bugler.
   M1 rifles: all personnel not otherwise armed.
2. This formed three operating units.
3. Five of 21 drivers and two of five motorcyclists in the company were rated as T-5 techs.
4. At company HQ one 2¹/₂-ton truck and trailer was for the field kitchen and water. The other 2¹/₂-ton trucks carried platoon or company tools.

A WC-52 3/4-ton weapons carrier with its soft top erected. The WC-51 was the same but without the front-mounted power takeoff. (Recognition photo from about June 1942.)

maintenance platoon) and the division received a separate ordnance light maintenance company. This unit handled both motor and weapons maintenance. Previously, the only Ordnance Corps presence in the division was a small cell in division headquarters.

The medical battalion's three collecting companies collected wounded from the three infantry regiments and other divisional units as required. Then they forwarded them to the clearing company, which operated two small field hospitals (clearing platoons) for treatment and, if necessary, evacuation to higher-level (corps, army, or theater) hospitals.

For reconnaissance the division included a cavalry troop (company). The War Department refused to authorize a squadron (battalion) because the

US Army infantry division medical battalion, April 1, 1942[1]

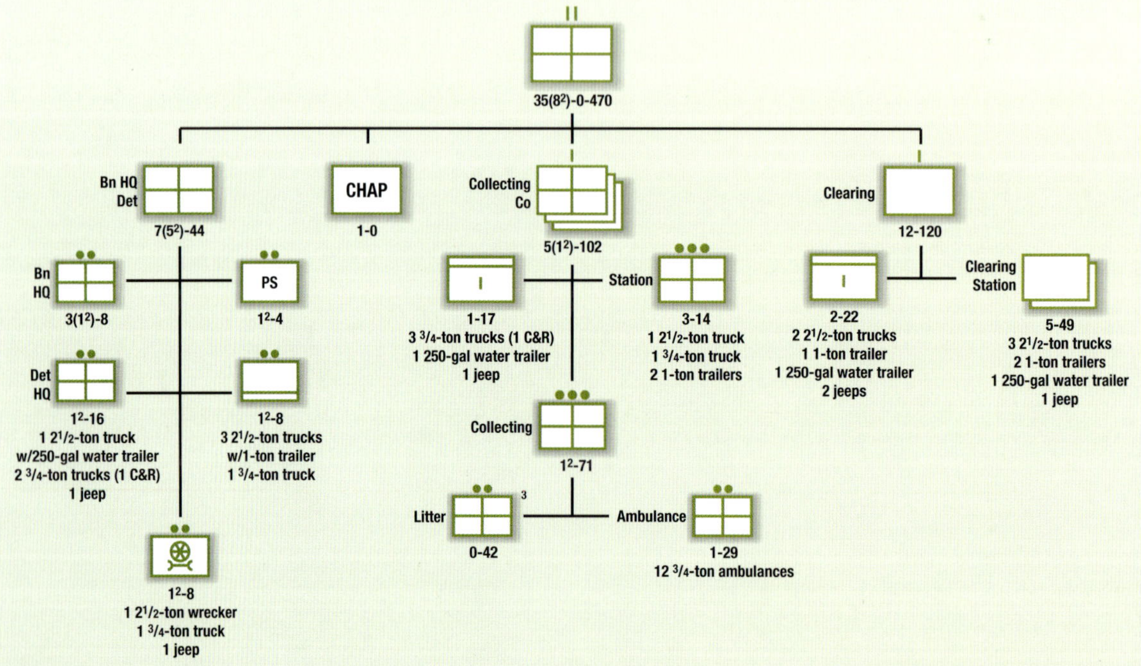

35(8[2])-0-470

Bn HQ Det — 7(5[2])-44

CHAP — 1-0

Collecting Co — 5(1[2])-102

Clearing — 12-120

Bn HQ — 3(1[2])-8

PS — 1[2]-4

Station — 1-17
3 3/4-ton trucks (1 C&R)
1 250-gal water trailer
1 jeep

Station — 3-14
1 2½-ton truck
1 3/4-ton truck
2 1-ton trailers

2-22
2 2½-ton trucks
1 1-ton trailer
1 250-gal water trailer
2 jeeps

Clearing Station — 5-49
3 2½-ton trucks
2 1-ton trailers
1 250-gal water trailer
1 jeep

Det HQ — 1[2]-16
1 2½-ton truck w/250-gal water trailer
2 3/4-ton trucks (1 C&R)
1 jeep

1[2]-8
3 2½-ton trucks w/1-ton trailer
1 3/4-ton truck

Collecting — 1[2]-71

Litter — 0-42

Ambulance — 1-29
12 3/4-ton ambulances

1[2]-8
1 2½-ton wrecker
1 3/4-ton truck
1 jeep

Notes:
1. Source: TO 8-15, 8-16, 8-17 & 8-18 (April 1, 1942).
2. Eight of the battalion's 35 officers were from the Medical Service Corps. These officers were not physicians or dentists. Instead, they supervised supply, administration, maintenance and other non-medical functions that were nevertheless vital to the medical battalion's success.
3. Consisted of nine four-man litter teams.

Members of Troop D, 102d Cavalry Regiment, in position and ready to fire from their M3A1 scout car during a practice reconnaissance exercise at Fort Jackson, SC. This car carries air-cooled M1919A4 light machine guns rather than the standard M1917A1 water-cooled guns. The radio operator operated one of the .30-cal machine guns; the other .30-cal and the .50-cal both had "full time" gunners. The M3A1 was the substitute armored fighting vehicle of the infantry division cavalry troop until the M8 armored car became available.

division was not expected to operate on a wide-enough frontage to justify one. For its fighting vehicles, the troop employed jeeps and armored cars. For its armored car, the War Department had chosen the T-22E2 prototype, but only in March 1943 did the first production vehicle leave the assembly line as the armored car M8. Until the M8 was available (in most units this was not before late 1943), M3A1 scout cars or M2 half-tracks served as substitutes. These vehicles frequently towed 37mm antitank guns in an attempt to replicate the superior firepower of the M8.

The signal company was the only Signal Corps element in the division. It formed the central communications node that tied all of the division elements together.

Finally, the division headquarters consisted of a series of staff sections. The general staff section performed most division-level planning and supervision of

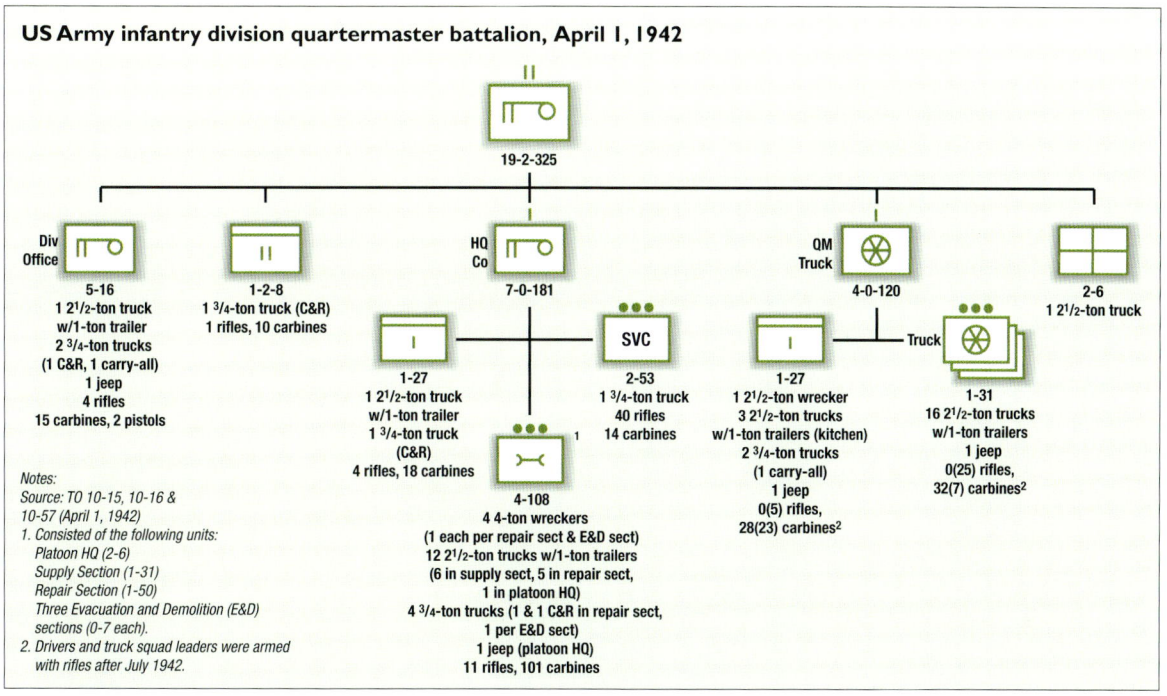

US Army infantry division quartermaster battalion, April 1, 1942

Notes:
Source: TO 10-15, 10-16 & 10-57 (April 1, 1942)
1. Consisted of the following units:
Platoon HQ (2-6)
Supply Section (1-31)
Repair Section (1-50)
Three Evacuation and Demolition (E&D) sections (0-7 each).
2. Drivers and truck squad leaders were armed with rifles after July 1942.

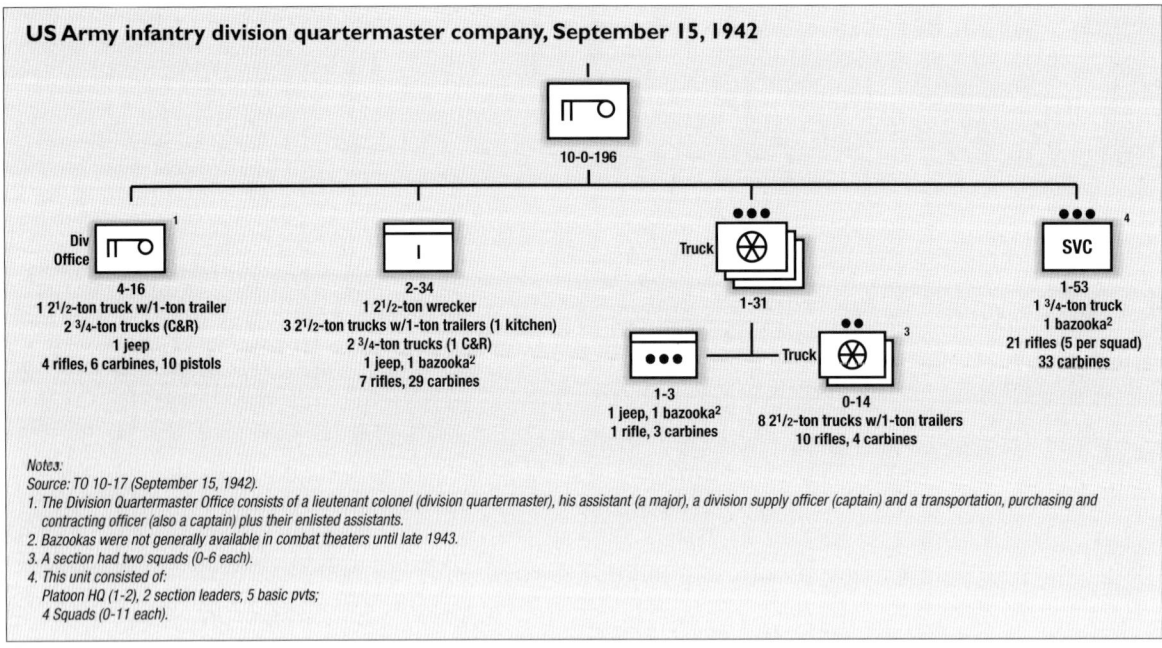

US Army infantry division quartermaster company, September 15, 1942

10-0-196

Div Office [1]
4-16
1 2½-ton truck w/1-ton trailer
2 ³⁄₄-ton trucks (C&R)
1 jeep
4 rifles, 6 carbines, 10 pistols

2-34
1 2½-ton wrecker
3 2½-ton trucks w/1-ton trailers (1 kitchen)
2 ³⁄₄-ton trucks (1 C&R)
1 jeep, 1 bazooka[2]
7 rifles, 29 carbines

Truck
1-31

1-3
1 jeep, 1 bazooka[2]
1 rifle, 3 carbines

Truck [3]
0-14
8 2½-ton trucks w/1-ton trailers
10 rifles, 4 carbines

SVC [4]
1-53
1 ³⁄₄-ton truck
1 bazooka[2]
21 rifles (5 per squad)
33 carbines

Notes:
Source: TO 10-17 (September 15, 1942).
1. The Division Quartermaster Office consists of a lieutenant colonel (division quartermaster), his assistant (a major), a division supply officer (captain) and a transportation, purchasing and
contracting officer (also a captain) plus their enlisted assistants.
2. Bazookas were not generally available in combat theaters until late 1943.
3. A section had two squads (0-6 each).
4. This unit consisted of:
Platoon HQ (1-2), 2 section leaders, 5 basic pvts;
4 Squads (0-11 each).

training and operations. The other sections were mainly advisory and liaison cells from other service branches or division components. Some were permanent parts of the division headquarters. Others were attached to the division headquarters from their parent organizations.

The division headquarters company provided administrative and logistical support for the division headquarters. It provided cooks, orderlies, drivers, and all the headquarters vehicles. It also supplied a defense platoon to provide some local security and division postal platoon. The headquarters company also supported the division military police platoon that worked directly for the division commander and G-1 and was not part of the headquarters company, although it was fed, supplied, and administered by it. The MP platoon provided both traffic-control and police services, but its size was inadequate and it needed reinforcement (usually from the infantry regiments) to carry out its duties.

Jeeps from the 102d Cavalry Regiment on maneuvers near Chistleton, England, January 23, 1943. Though they are not from an infantry division cavalry troop, the equipment is the same. The jeep on the left carries an air-cooled M1919A4 .30-cal LMG. The jeep on the right has the heavier M2 .50-cal machine gun. Combat experience soon revealed that the jeep was too light to serve as a stable gun platform for a .50-cal machine gun.

US Army infantry division ordnance light maintenance company, September 15, 1942

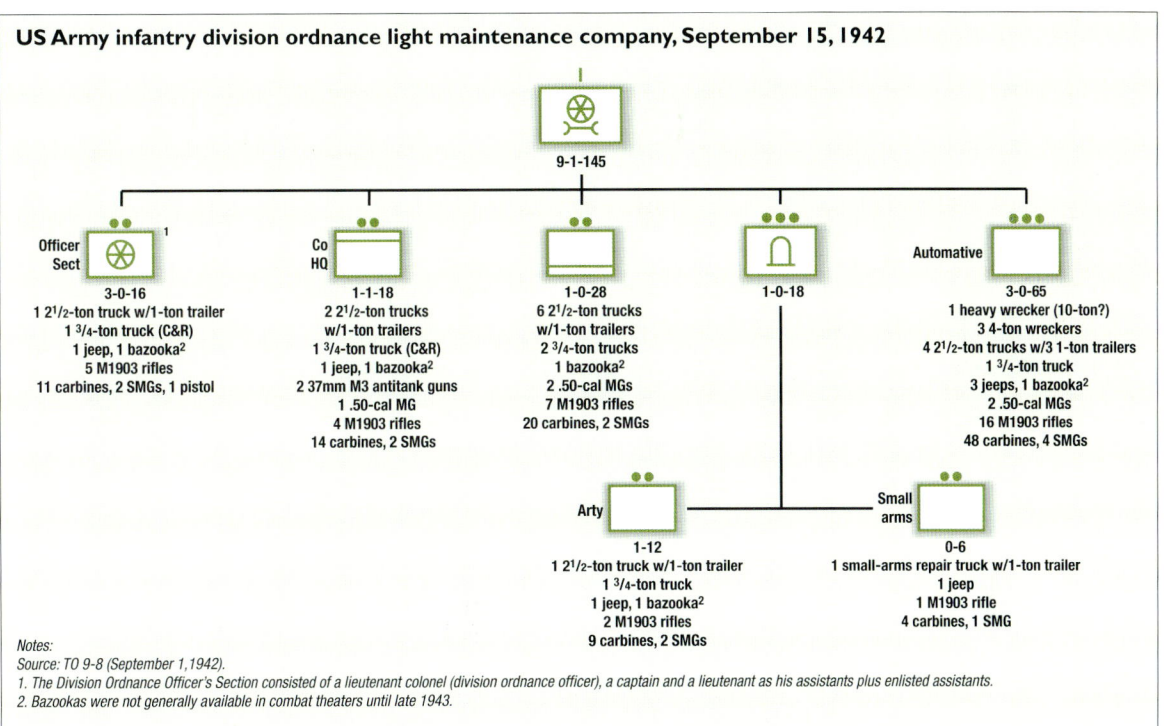

9-1-145

Officer Sect [1]
3-0-16
1 2½-ton truck w/1-ton trailer
1 ³/₄-ton truck (C&R)
1 jeep, 1 bazooka[2]
5 M1903 rifles
11 carbines, 2 SMGs, 1 pistol

Co HQ
1-1-18
2 2½-ton trucks
w/1-ton trailers
1 ³/₄-ton truck (C&R)
1 jeep, 1 bazooka[2]
2 37mm M3 antitank guns
1 .50-cal MG
4 M1903 rifles
14 carbines, 2 SMGs

1-0-28
6 2½-ton trucks
w/1-ton trailers
2 ³/₄-ton trucks
1 bazooka[2]
2 .50-cal MGs
7 M1903 rifles
20 carbines, 2 SMGs

1-0-18

Automative
3-0-65
1 heavy wrecker (10-ton?)
3 4-ton wreckers
4 2½-ton trucks w/3 1-ton trailers
1 ³/₄-ton truck
3 jeeps, 1 bazooka[2]
2 .50-cal MGs
16 M1903 rifles
48 carbines, 4 SMGs

Arty
1-12
1 2½-ton truck w/1-ton trailer
1 ³/₄-ton truck
1 jeep, 1 bazooka[2]
2 M1903 rifles
9 carbines, 2 SMGs

Small arms
0-6
1 small-arms repair truck w/1-ton trailer
1 jeep
1 M1903 rifle
4 carbines, 1 SMG

Notes:
Source: TO 9-8 (September 1, 1942).
1. The Division Ordnance Officer's Section consisted of a lieutenant colonel (division ordnance officer), a captain and a lieutenant as his assistants plus enlisted assistants.
2. Bazookas were not generally available in combat theaters until late 1943.

A high-angle shot shows the general layout of the auto repair shop of the 700th Ordnance Company, 45th Division at Vairano, Italy, November 28, 1943. A weapons carrier is in the center of the photo while an amphibious jeep sits just to the left of it.

US Army infantry division cavalry reconaissance troop, April 1, 1942[1]

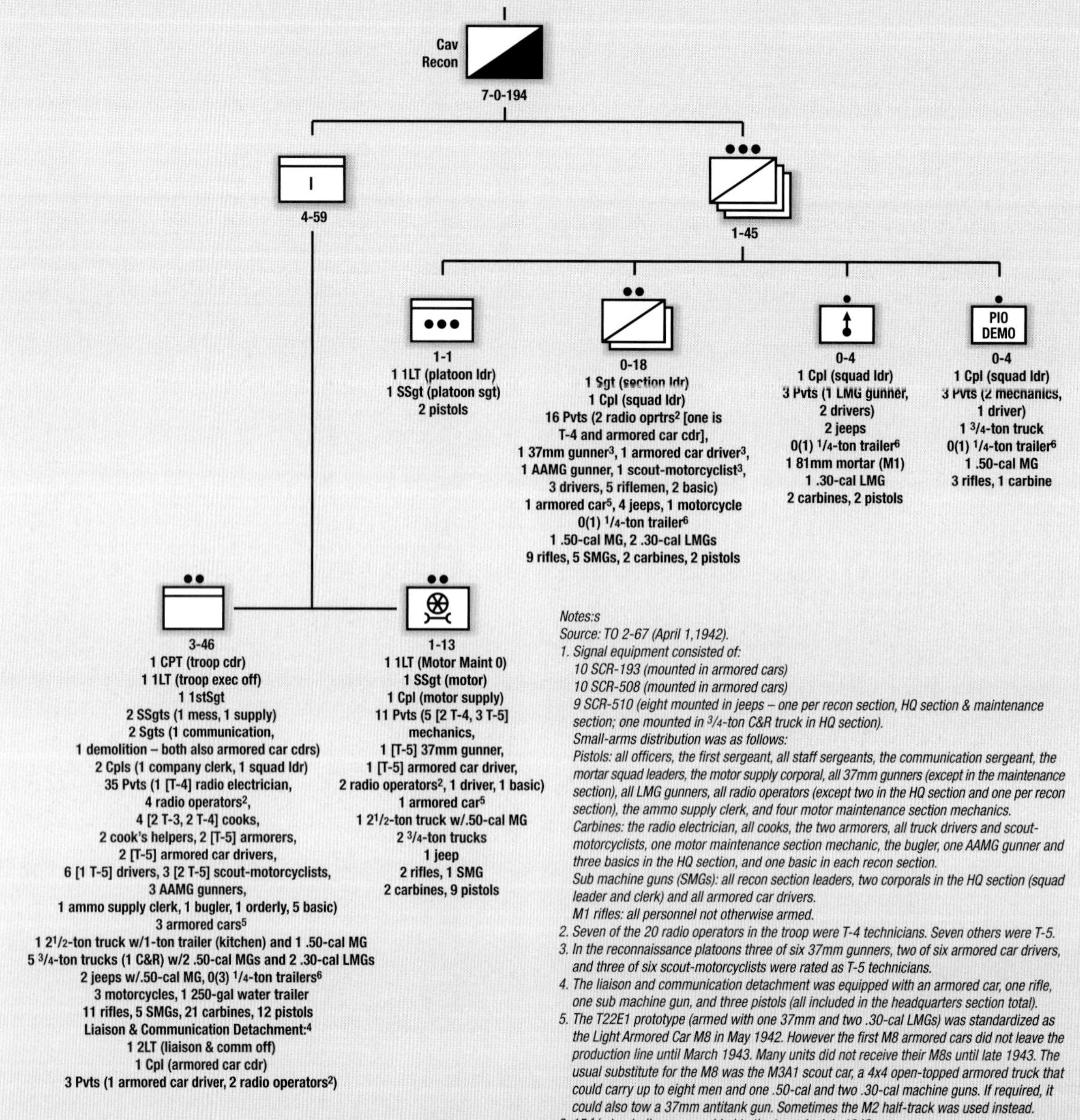

Cav Recon
7-0-194

4-59

1-45

1-1
1 1LT (platoon ldr)
1 SSgt (platoon sgt)
2 pistols

0-18
1 Sgt (section ldr)
1 Cpl (squad ldr)
16 Pvts (2 radio oprtrs[2] [one is
T-4 and armored car cdr],
1 37mm gunner[3], 1 armored car driver[3],
1 AAMG gunner, 1 scout-motorcyclist[3],
3 drivers, 5 riflemen, 2 basic)
1 armored car[5], 4 jeeps, 1 motorcycle
0(1) 1/4-ton trailer[6]
1 .50-cal MG, 2 .30-cal LMGs
9 rifles, 5 SMGs, 2 carbines, 2 pistols

0-4
1 Cpl (squad ldr)
3 Pvts (1 LMG gunner,
2 drivers)
2 jeeps
0(1) 1/4-ton trailer[6]
1 81mm mortar (M1)
1 .30-cal LMG
2 carbines, 2 pistols

PIO DEMO
0-4
1 Cpl (squad ldr)
3 Pvts (2 mechanics,
1 driver)
1 3/4-ton truck
0(1) 1/4-ton trailer[6]
1 .50-cal MG
3 rifles, 1 carbine

3-46
1 CPT (troop cdr)
1 1LT (troop exec off)
1 1stSgt
2 SSgts (1 mess, 1 supply)
2 Sgts (1 communication,
1 demolition – both also armored car cdrs)
2 Cpls (1 company clerk, 1 squad ldr)
35 Pvts (1 [T-4] radio electrician,
4 radio operators[2],
4 [2 T-3, 2 T-4] cooks,
2 cook's helpers, 2 [T-5] armorers,
2 [T-5] armored car drivers,
6 [1 T-5] drivers, 3 [2 T-5] scout-motorcyclists,
3 AAMG gunners,
1 ammo supply clerk, 1 bugler, 1 orderly, 5 basic)
3 armored cars[5]
1 21/2-ton truck w/1-ton trailer (kitchen) and 1 .50-cal MG
5 3/4-ton trucks (1 C&R) w/2 .50-cal MGs and 2 .30-cal LMGs
2 jeeps w/.50-cal MG, 0(3) 1/4-ton trailers[6]
3 motorcycles, 1 250-gal water trailer
11 rifles, 5 SMGs, 21 carbines, 12 pistols
Liaison & Communication Detachment:[4]
1 2LT (liaison & comm off)
1 Cpl (armored car cdr)
3 Pvts (1 armored car driver, 2 radio operators[2])

1-13
1 1LT (Motor Maint 0)
1 SSgt (motor)
1 Cpl (motor supply)
11 Pvts (5 [2 T-4, 3 T-5]
mechanics,
1 [T-5] 37mm gunner,
1 [T-5] armored car driver,
2 radio operators[2], 1 driver, 1 basic)
1 armored car[5]
1 21/2-ton truck w/.50-cal MG
2 3/4-ton trucks
1 jeep
2 rifles, 1 SMG
2 carbines, 9 pistols

Notes:s
Source: TO 2-67 (April 1,1942).
1. Signal equipment consisted of:
    10 SCR-193 (mounted in armored cars)
    10 SCR-508 (mounted in armored cars)
    9 SCR-510 (eight mounted in jeeps – one per recon section, HQ section & maintenance section; one mounted in 3/4-ton C&R truck in HQ section).
    Small-arms distribution was as follows:
    Pistols: all officers, the first sergeant, all staff sergeants, the communication sergeant, the mortar squad leaders, the motor supply corporal, all 37mm gunners (except in the maintenance section), all LMG gunners, all radio operators (except two in the HQ section and one per recon section), the ammo supply clerk, and four motor maintenance section mechanics.
    Carbines: the radio electrician, all cooks, the two armorers, all truck drivers and scout-motorcyclists, one motor maintenance section mechanic, the bugler, one AAMG gunner and three basics in the HQ section, and one basic in each recon section.
    Sub machine guns (SMGs): all recon section leaders, two corporals in the HQ section (squad leader and clerk) and all armored car drivers.
    M1 rifles: all personnel not otherwise armed.
2. Seven of the 20 radio operators in the troop were T-4 technicians. Seven others were T-5.
3. In the reconnaissance platoons three of six 37mm gunners, two of six armored car drivers, and three of six scout-motorcyclists were rated as T-5 technicians.
4. The liaison and communication detachment was equipped with an armored car, one rifle, one sub machine gun, and three pistols (all included in the headquarters section total).
5. The T22E1 prototype (armed with one 37mm and two .30-cal LMGs) was standardized as the Light Armored Car M8 in May 1942. However the first M8 armored cars did not leave the production line until March 1943. Many units did not receive their M8s until late 1943. The usual substitute for the M8 was the M3A1 scout car, a 4x4 open-topped armored truck that could carry up to eight men and one .50-cal and two .30-cal machine guns. If required, it could also tow a 37mm antitank gun. Sometimes the M2 half-track was used instead.
6. 15 1/4-ton trailers were added to the troop in July 1942.

A Chemical Warfare branch soldier demonstrates the M1A1 portable flamethrower for members of the Americal Division, October 5, 1943.

US Army infantry division signal company, April 1, 1942

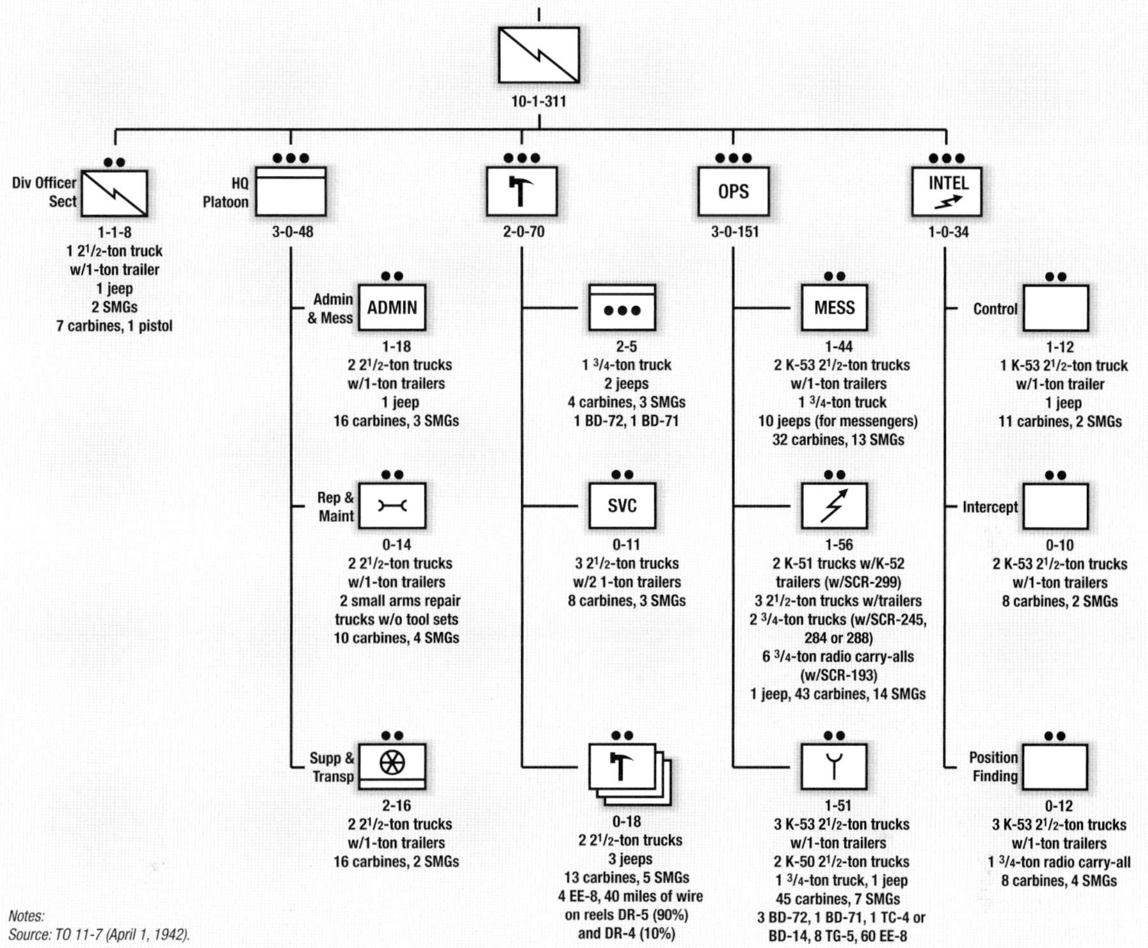

10-1-311

Div Officer Sect
1-1-8
1 2½-ton truck w/1-ton trailer
1 jeep
2 SMGs
7 carbines, 1 pistol

HQ Platoon
3-0-48

Admin & Mess — ADMIN
1-18
2 2½-ton trucks w/1-ton trailers
1 jeep
16 carbines, 3 SMGs

Rep & Maint
0-14
2 2½-ton trucks w/1-ton trailers
2 small arms repair trucks w/o tool sets
10 carbines, 4 SMGs

Supp & Transp
2-16
2 2½-ton trucks w/1-ton trailers
16 carbines, 2 SMGs

(Wire/Construction) T
2-0-70

2-5
1 ¾-ton truck
2 jeeps
4 carbines, 3 SMGs
1 BD-72, 1 BD-71

SVC
0-11
3 2½-ton trucks w/2 1-ton trailers
8 carbines, 3 SMGs

0-18
2 2½-ton trucks
3 jeeps
13 carbines, 5 SMGs
4 EE-8, 40 miles of wire on reels DR-5 (90%) and DR-4 (10%)

OPS
3-0-151

MESS
1-44
2 K-53 2½-ton trucks w/1-ton trailers
1 ¾-ton truck
10 jeeps (for messengers)
32 carbines, 13 SMGs

1-56
2 K-51 trucks w/K-52 trailers (w/SCR-299)
3 2½-ton trucks w/trailers
2 ¾-ton trucks (w/SCR-245, 284 or 288)
6 ¾-ton radio carry-alls (w/SCR-193)
1 jeep, 43 carbines, 14 SMGs

1-51
3 K-53 2½-ton trucks w/1-ton trailers
2 K-50 2½-ton trucks
1 ¾-ton truck, 1 jeep
45 carbines, 7 SMGs
3 BD-72, 1 BD-71, 1 TC-4 or BD-14, 8 TG-5, 60 EE-8

INTEL
1-0-34

Control
1-12
1 K-53 2½-ton truck w/1-ton trailer
1 jeep
11 carbines, 2 SMGs

Intercept
0-10
2 K-53 2½-ton trucks w/1-ton trailers
8 carbines, 2 SMGs

Position Finding
0-12
3 K-53 2½-ton trucks w/1-ton trailers
1 ¾-ton radio carry-all
8 carbines, 4 SMGs

Notes:
Source: TO 11-7 (April 1, 1942).

An SCR-284 radio mounted in a Jeep, September 13, 1943.

US Army infantry division HQ and HQ company, April 1, 1942[1]

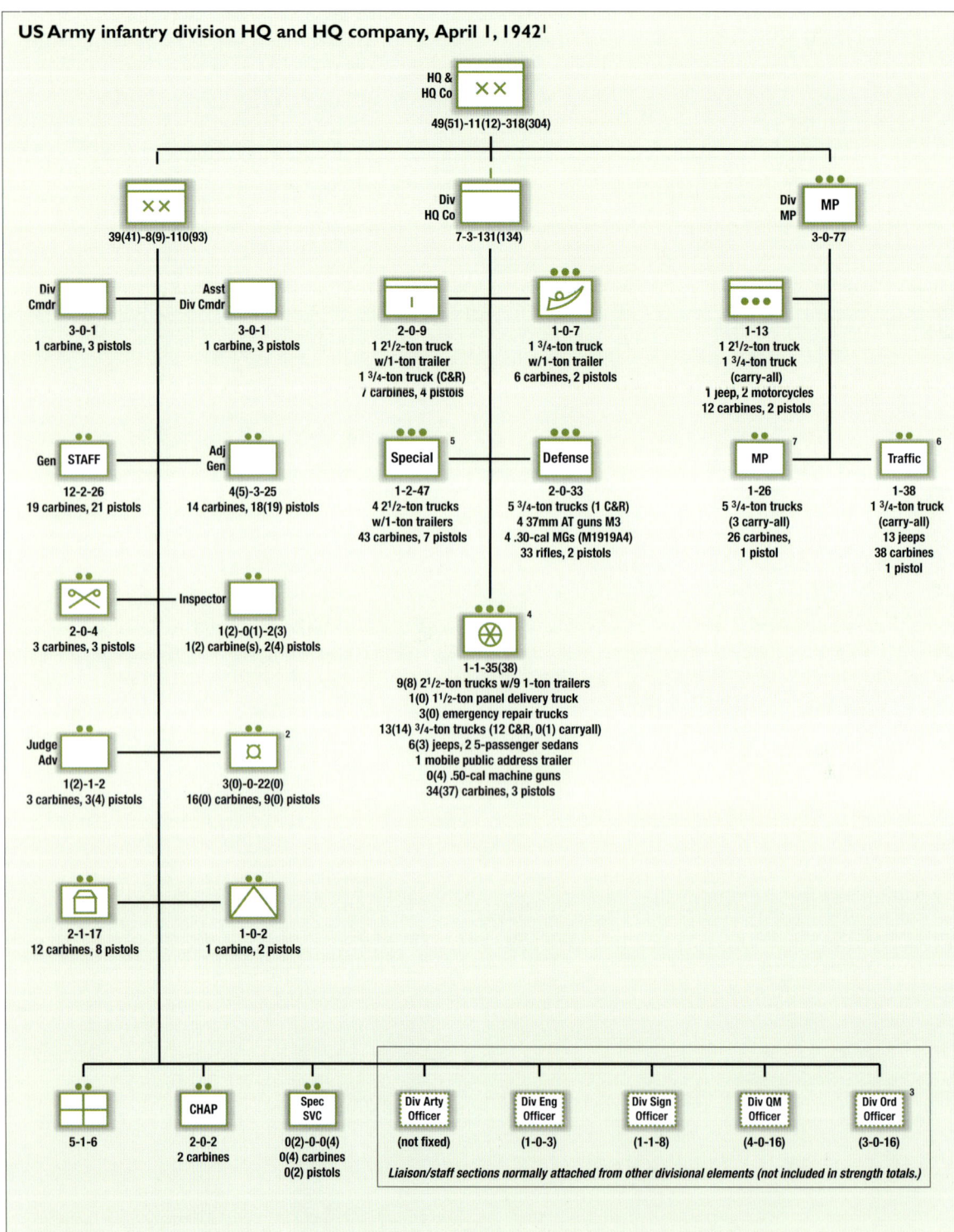

HQ & HQ Co ××
49(51)-11(12)-318(304)

Div HQ Co
7-3-131(134)

Div MP MP
3-0-77

××
39(41)-8(9)-110(93)

Div Cmdr
3-0-1
1 carbine, 3 pistols

Asst Div Cmdr
3-0-1
1 carbine, 3 pistols

I
2-0-9
1 2¹/₂-ton truck
w/1-ton trailer
1 ³/₄-ton truck (C&R)
7 carbines, 4 pistols

1-0-7
1 ³/₄-ton truck
w/1-ton trailer
6 carbines, 2 pistols

1-13
1 2¹/₂-ton truck
1 ³/₄-ton truck
(carry-all)
1 jeep, 2 motorcycles
12 carbines, 2 pistols

Gen STAFF
12-2-26
19 carbines, 21 pistols

Adj Gen
4(5)-3-25
14 carbines, 18(19) pistols

Special [5]
1-2-47
4 2¹/₂-ton trucks
w/1-ton trailers
43 carbines, 7 pistols

Defense
2-0-33
5 ³/₄-ton trucks (1 C&R)
4 37mm AT guns M3
4 .30-cal MGs (M1919A4)
33 rifles, 2 pistols

MP [7]
1-26
5 ³/₄-ton trucks
(3 carry-all)
26 carbines,
1 pistol

Traffic [6]
1-38
1 ³/₄-ton truck
(carry-all)
13 jeeps
38 carbines
1 pistol

✂
2-0-4
3 carbines, 3 pistols

Inspector
1(2)-0(1)-2(3)
1(2) carbine(s), 2(4) pistols

⊕ [4]
1-1-35(38)
9(8) 2¹/₂-ton trucks w/9 1-ton trailers
1(0) 1¹/₂-ton panel delivery truck
3(0) emergency repair trucks
13(14) ³/₄-ton trucks (12 C&R, 0(1) carryall)
6(3) jeeps, 2 5-passenger sedans
1 mobile public address trailer
0(4) .50-cal machine guns
34(37) carbines, 3 pistols

Judge Adv
1(2)-1-2
3 carbines, 3(4) pistols

♀ [2]
3(0)-0-22(0)
16(0) carbines, 9(0) pistols

⬡
2-1-17
12 carbines, 8 pistols

△
1-0-2
1 carbine, 2 pistols

⊞
5-1-6

CHAP
2-0-2
2 carbines

Spec SVC
0(2)-0-0(4)
0(4) carbines
0(2) pistols

Div Arty Officer
(not fixed)

Div Eng Officer
(1-0-3)

Div Sign Officer
(1-1-8)

Div QM Officer
(4-0-16)

Div Ord Officer [3]
(3-0-16)

Liaison/staff sections normally attached from other divisional elements (not included in strength totals.)

Notes:
Source: TO 7-1, 7-2 and 19-7 (April 1, 1942).
1. Strengths shown in brackets apply after September 15, 1942.
2. Division Ordnance Section replaced on September 15, 1942 by a division ordnance officer's section from the newly added Ordnance Light Maintenance Company.
3. After September 15, 1942.
4. Transportation platoon vehicles reserved for the use of the Ordnance Section, Division HQ were dropped as of September 15, 1942.
5. Includes division HQ mess and orderlies.
6. Consisted of Section HQ (1-2), and three squads (0-12 each). All traffic section vehicles were radio-equipped.
7. Consisted of Section HQ (1-2), and two squads (0-12 each).

Tactics

French soldiers firing .50-cal machine guns under American instruction, near Algiers, February 4, 1943.

Infantry tactical doctrine

In 1942 the US Army followed a tactical doctrine that was simple and conventional, as befitted a society that preferred direct and clear-cut solutions to problems. US Army doctrine continued to follow that of the French Army despite the catastrophic French defeat in 1940. Like the French Army, the US Army relied on massive firepower to overwhelm or wear down its opponents by attrition, reasoning that it was better by far to expend cannon shells than soldiers' lives. It saw maneuver as a means to seize geographical objectives and

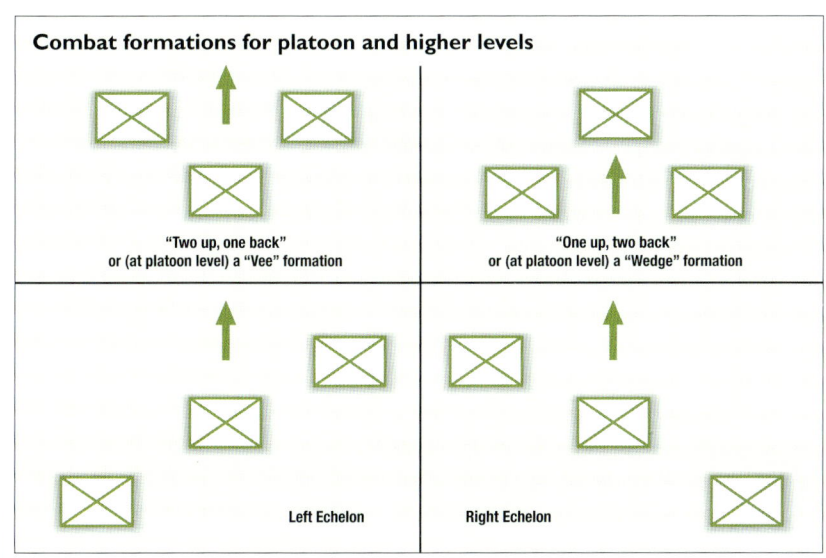

Combat formations for platoon and higher levels

"Two up, one back"
or (at platoon level) a "Vee" formation

"One up, two back"
or (at platoon level) a "Wedge" formation

Left Echelon

Right Echelon

Table 4: Infantry division small arms (1941–43)

Model no. and type	Caliber (muzzle velocity)	Effective range (yards)	Weight in pounds	Feed device
M1911A1 pistol	.45-cal ACP	50	2.43	7-round magazine
M1928, M1, M1A1 Thompson sub machine gun	.45-cal ACP (900 fps)	100	11.5	20- or 30-round magazine
M1 carbine semi-automatic	.30-cal Carbine (2,000 fps)	300	5.75	15- or 30-round magazine
M1903 bolt-action rifle	.30-06-cal (2,750 fps)	600	8.7	5-round clip
M1 semi-automatic rifle	.30-06-cal (2,750 fps)	500–600	10.3	8-round clip
M1918 and M1918A1 Browning Automatic Rifle	.30-06-cal (2,750 fps)	600	15.5	20-round magazine
M1918A2 Browning Automatic Rifle	.30-06-cal (2,750 fps)	600	21	20-round magazine
M26 hand grenade	n/a	15	1.31	n/a

Note: In combat the automatic rifleman, his assistant and one or more riflemen would carry a total of 320 rounds. Normally 200 rounds (10 magazines) were carried for each BAR that was not part of a rifle squad.

to reposition weapons to greater advantage. Its firepower had to be carefully orchestrated in order to avoid hitting friendly troops and to ensure that all targets were engaged with the weapons most effective against them. Although this doctrine made for a slower moving and more predictable battle, it was conceptually simple and logical and easy for newly minted officers to learn.

The dominant formation for both attack and defense was "two up, one back." This meant, to wit, that two maneuver elements deployed forward (for example, two rifle companies from an infantry battalion) while one stayed back in reserve. This concept required a triangular structure at every level from the three regiments in an infantry division down to the three rifle squads in a platoon. All rifle companies and larger units had their own base of fire element as well. All these echelons used similar tactics.

"One up, two back" was not the only combat formation, and it was not an option for the rifle squads. A squad had no sub-elements other than individual soldiers. The squad BAR was mainly a source of emergency firepower. The real firepower of the squad was supposed to come from its M1 rifles. Therefore a squad was usually unwise to deploy in depth because this would mask many of its rifles. Instead it usually adopted an irregular "skirmish line." However, a skirmish line was not easy for a squad leader to control because many of the men in it might be too far away to see or hear his commands. A skirmish line also exposed more men to enemy fire. A squad normally moved in a column, but might choose a "squad wedge" formation (like a skirmish line but

Sgt Tech Norman Brown of Grand Rapids, MI is shown loading a .50-cal machine gun in preparation for firing. This photo was taken in Australia, on November 15, 1942.

Notes

A Colt-Browning semi-automatic pistol. It was the Army's standard sidearm and was for personal defense only.

This weapon was issued mainly to armor and cavalry units. In 1943 the cheaper M3 "Grease Gun" began to replace it. The older M1928 version could use a 50-round drum magazine. Cyclic rate of fire was 700–800 rpm; the practical rate was 40–60 rpm. In the infantry division its issue was mainly to drivers in the signal company and the cavalry troop.

A personal defense weapon intended to replace most pistols. Well over six million were made but none reached the troops before 1942. It fired a special low-powered elongated pistol bullet that lacked stopping power.

The Army's standard rifle prior to 1936, this Mauser design had a relatively low rate of fire (10 rounds per minute at best) but it was very accurate, reliable, and popular. Used in 1942–43 mainly to employ the M1 rifle grenade launcher.

First adopted in 1936, this weapon had two to three times the rate of fire of the M1903. More than four million were made. After 1943, the M1 rifle with the new M7 launcher replaced most of the remaining M1903 rifles.

Declared obsolete in 1940, many of these BARs were converted to M1918A2, but unconverted weapons served throughout WWII. Cyclic rate of fire was 500 rpm but practical rate of fire was only 40 rpm due to rapid overheating. Also lacked stability in full automatic fire.

Converted from the M1918 and M1918A1, the M1918A2 featured a bipod at the muzzle, a butt monopod, hinged butt plate and better cooling. Also, the gunner could select low (350 rpm) or high (500 rpm) cyclic rates of fire. This plus greater weight gave it better stability in full automatic fire. Practical rate of fire was 40–60 rpm.

This pineapple-shaped fragmentation hand grenade had an effective casualty radius of 15 meters. It could not only be thrown but also fired from a rifle grenade launcher.

---

with the wings pulled back) if enemy contact was expected. For rifle platoons the manuals prescribed at least six different formations, but when approaching the enemy platoons tended to deploy one squad forward with the other two following it abreast. This later became known as a "wedge." In battle a platoon tended to deploy two squads forward and one back (just like larger units); this formation was later called a "V." Larger units rarely used "one up and two back" unless they were attacking on a narrow frontage or through difficult terrain. To guard an open flank, they might adopt an echelon formation.

Nevertheless, "two up, one back" was so prevalent that unit frontages were usually calculated on that basis. Thus, a squad in the offensive would deploy on a front of perhaps 50–100 yards, though this frontage could vary dramatically depending on the situation. The doctrinal frontage of a platoon comprised two squads. The frontage of a company was four squads or two platoons. The frontage of a battalion was eight squads or four platoons or two companies, and so forth.

Both offensive and defensive tactics centered on the terrain. Units were given specific geographic objectives, such as a hill or town, to capture or defend. The attack itself, usually supported by artillery and air strikes, would try to envelop an enemy flank. If this were not possible, the attack would go in frontally, trusting its supporting firepower to crush enemy resistance. Little subtlety was involved. The Germans noted with some surprise that, although they had no shortage of ammunition, the Americans rarely tried to mislead their enemies by firing at objectives other than those they intended to attack. While the Germans might not be strong enough to stop an American attack, they were seldom in doubt about where it was aimed at. Having seized an objective, the Americans tended to wait for orders, supplies or both and thus forfeit opportunities to exploit their success.

At the division level the emphasis in defensive combat was on firepower, although a corps could deploy a covering force of mechanized cavalry to screen and impede the enemy's advance. As the enemy approached the MLR (main

Table 5: Infantry crew-served weapons (1942–43)

Model no. and type	Caliber (muzzle velocity)	Effective range (yards)	Weight in pounds	Ammunition (weight in pounds)
M1919A4 Light Machine Gun (LMG), Air-Cooled	.30-06-cal (2,750 fps)	2,000	31 plus 14 for a tripod (two-man load)	Fires from a 250-round cloth belt. 3,000 rounds (12 belts) per gun normally kept in company weapons carriers.
M1917A1 Heavy Machine Gun (HMG), Water-Cooled	.30-06-cal (2,750 fps)	3,000	41 plus 53 for the tripod and 7 for a load of water	Fires from a 250-round cloth belt. 6,750 rounds (27 belts) weighing 554 plus four 23 water chests kept in the weapons carrier.
M2 .50-cal Machine Gun (MG), Air-Cooled, Heavy Barrel	.50-cal (2,935 fps)	2,000 (1,000 against aircraft)	83 plus 44 for a tripod or 84 for an antiaircraft mount	Fires from disintegrating metal link belts packed in 100-round metal boxes (about 29 each).
M2 60mm Mortar	60mm, could traverse 600 mils	1,985; minimum range was 200	42 (two-man load)	60 rounds per mortar (packed in five-round boxes) were carried on the rifle company weapons carriers.
M1 81mm Mortar	81mm; could traverse 700 mils w/o moving base-plate	3,300; minimum range was 200	143 (three-man load)	Light HE (9.1) 80 percent of the number of rounds carried; heavy HE (13.16) 20 percent of the ammunition carried. Chemical was 13.

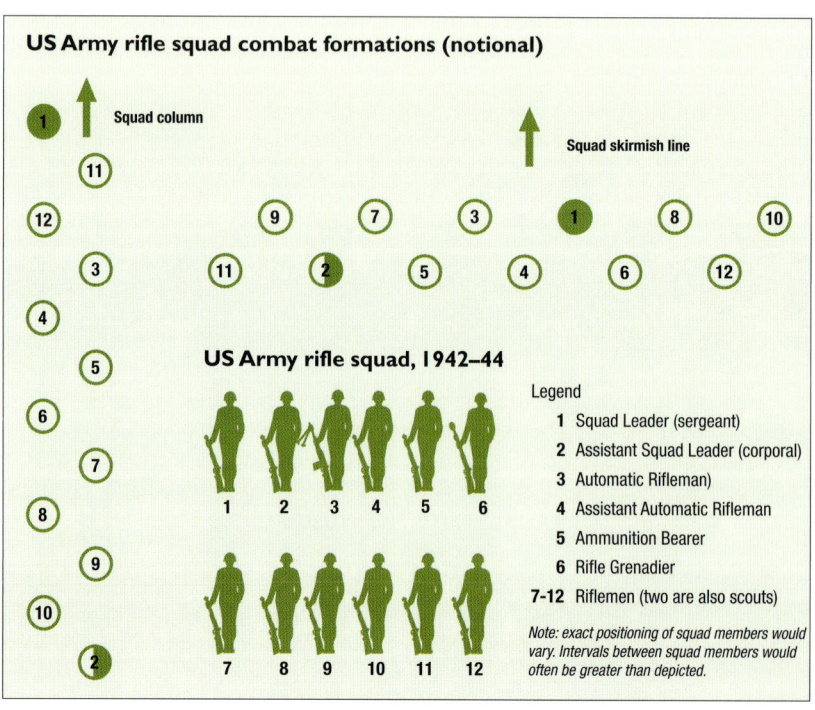

US Army rifle squad combat formations (notional)

Squad column

Squad skirmish line

US Army rifle squad, 1942–44

Legend
1 Squad Leader (sergeant)
2 Assistant Squad Leader (corporal)
3 Automatic Rifleman)
4 Assistant Automatic Rifleman
5 Ammunition Bearer
6 Rifle Grenadier
7-12 Riflemen (two are also scouts)

Note: exact positioning of squad members would vary. Intervals between squad members would often be greater than depicted.

Notes

Originally designed as a tank machine gun, it served as an intermediate weapon between the heavy M1917A1 machine gun and the BAR. The fact it could only be fired from its tripod limited it to defensive and supporting fire. Cyclic rate of fire was 400–550 rpm; practical rate was 60–120 rpm.

Designed for long-range shooting and high, sustained rates of fire, it was the standard battalion-level support weapon. Cyclic rate of fire was 450–600 rpm. Thanks to its water-cooling the gun had a practical rate of fire of 125 to 250 rpm. It could also serve as an antiaircraft weapon.

Originally an antitank weapon (AP ammo could defeat 28mm at 100 yards) but later used for air defense. Only certain guns had assigned crews. Effective and popular, its cyclic rate of fire was 400–600 rpm. Overheating held its practical rate of fire to 40–60 rpm.

This was a licenced produced version of the French Brandt M1935 60mm mortar. It fired mainly high explosive (HE) with an effective casualty radius of 15 meters. An illuminating round was also available.

Another Brandt design license produced in the USA. Its light high-explosive shell had a 25-meter effective casualty radius. The heavy HE shell, later discarded (max. range 1,300 yards), was for attacking hard targets. Chemical and illumination shells were also available but the former was rarely used.

line of resistance), he would be subjected to an increasing volume of fire as more weapons came within range. Upon signal, the artillery and mortars would fire "final protective fires" (FPF) to block specific enemy routes towards the MLR. Machine guns in flanking positions would fire "final protective lines" (FPL). An FPL was fired along a pre-selected azimuth at the maximum rate during the final stages of an enemy attack. The idea was to use interlocking FPLs to create a wall of bullets that the enemy would have to penetrate in order to reach the MLR. Mortar FPFs covered the "dead spaces" that machine guns or artillery could not reach.

Weapons platoons and companies

Fire-support units such as the rifle company weapons platoon or the infantry battalion weapons company operated differently (and usually separately) from the "maneuver" units. Unlike maneuver units, fire-support units were never held in reserve. The rifle company light machine gun (LMG) section, usually under the personal direction of the weapons platoon commander, delivered short to medium range automatic weapons fire, preferably from a flanking position that enabled it to fire across the company's entire front. The company commander usually controlled the 60mm mortar section, directing it to place itself in a defilade position (any fold in the ground would do) about 500 yards behind the company's forward positions. One or two section members would occupy an observation post within shouting or signaling distance of the guns and from which they could observe all or most of the company's frontline. The company commander or the mortar section leader chose the mortars' targets

Table 6: Infantry antitank weapons (1942–43)

Model and type	Weight (lb) and crew	Combat range	Ammunition (weights in lb)
M3 or M3A1 37mm Antitank Gun L/53.5	912. Crew of five	1,000+ yards. Can fire up to 20 rpm	Armor piercing (AP) projectile (1.9, 2,600 fps mv) pierces 36mm/0° at 500 yards. Armor Piercing Capped (APC) 92,900 fps mv) pierces 61mm/0° at 500 yards; HE projectile was 1.6.
M1 2.36in. (60mm) Bazooka	13.26. Crew of two	300 yards	Standard shaped charge antitank rocket weighed 3.4. Early versions could defeat 60–100mm of armor.
M9 and M9A1 rifle grenades	1.31 per grenade	100 (?) yards	The later M9A1 could defeat up to 100mm of homogeneous armor.

Table 7: Infantry division armored vehicles (1942–43)

Type and model	Weight and Gross Vehicle Weight	Total built
M3A1 Armored Scout Car 4x4	8,900, 11,750 (GVW)	20,918
T22E1 or M8 Light Armored Car 6x6	14,500, 17,200 (GVW)	8,523
M2 Armored Half-Track	14,160, 17,800 (GVW)	11,415
M2A1 Armored Half-Track	14,600, 18,600, (GVW)	1,643
T-30 Half-Track Self-Propelled Howitzer	19,600 (approx.)	500 (-108)
T-12 Half-Track Self-Propelled Gun (also known as the M3 or M3A1)	19,800	2,202 (-1,360)
T-19 Half-Track Self-Propelled Howitzer	21,000 (approx.)	324

based on his view of the situation. The mortars did not normally take calls for fire directly from the rifle platoons and they did not normally use radios or telephones. The Army believed that such equipment should be used to call in the fire of the division artillery. Using it to call for mortar fire would create dependency on communication equipment that the Army considered to be inherently unreliable. The whole point of having mortars was to give the infantry indirect fire weapons that it could use whether the radios or telephones worked or not. Though radios and telephones were sometimes used anyway, such use was the exception in 1942–43.

If the mortar section had to displace during combat, one gun could move while the other two continued to fire. Mortar squads were seldom attached to

This was an unlicenced copy of the Rheinmetall-Borsig Model 35/36, Germany's standard antitank gun in 1939–41. The US version differed mainly in the appearance of the carriage and shield. By 1942 the gun was becoming ineffective against German tanks but its ability to fire HE (and, later, canister) enabled it to serve as an infantry support weapon. Jeeps or 3/4-ton trucks served as prime movers. The Army built 18,700. In 1941–42 160 rounds (90 percent AP, 10 percent HE) were carried with each gun.

Designed in 1918 by Dr Robert Goddard, the development of a rocket with a shaped charge made it revolutionary. Used with some success in North Africa, but later upgrades were not enough to keep pace with increases in German armor.

Fired from the M1 grenade launcher on the M1903 rifle and later (1943) from the M7 (M1 rifle) or M8 (carbine) launchers. Later in the war it was often used against bunkers and pillboxes.

Remarks

Open-topped armored truck carrying a driver plus seven troops and armed with one .50-cal and two .30-cal HMGs on a rail running around the troop compartment. Could tow a 37mm antitank gun. Top speed was 55mph; cruising range was 550 miles (80-gal tank). Armor thickness was about 1/4 inch. It served as a substitute for the M8 armored car.

Had a crew of four and an open-topped turret mounting an M6 37mm gun (an armored vehicle variant of the M3 towed gun) and one .30-cal co-axial MG. A .50-cal could be carried on a ring mount above the turret. Armor thickness was 0.25–0.75in. Top speed 56mph; range 250 miles (54-gal). Not available in most divisions until late 1943.

Open-topped vehicle carrying a driver plus nine troops; armed with one .50-cal and two .30-cal HMGs on a rail running around the troop compartment. Could tow an M3 37mm antitank gun. Top speed 45mph; cruising range 175 miles (60-gal).

Same as the M2 but used a ring mount (over the cab for the .50-cal machine gun) and fixed sockets on pedestals for its .30-cal machine guns rather than a skate rail. Armor thickness was mostly 0.25in. (6.35mm).

M3 half-track mounting a 75mm pack howitzer M1 facing forward. The howitzer fired a 14-pound HE shell to 9,600 yards (8,800 meters). White phosphorus (WP) and chemical projectiles were also available. Later there was also antitank round (HEAT able to penetrate 90mm). Armor thickness for M3 series was mostly 0.25in. (6.35mm); 108 were converted to personnel carriers before production of this type was complete.

M3 half-track mounting a French-designed 75mm M1897 field gun facing forward. Intended as an interim tank destroyer, it also served with infantry cannon companies. The gun's 15-pound armor-piercing shell could defeat 70mm of armor at 500 yards. HE and WP were also available. Maximum traverse was 19° to the left or 21° to the right. The maximum elevation of only 29° would have restricted the gun's range to about 11,000 yards. The vehicle carried a crew of five and 59 rounds of 75mm ammunition; 1,360 T-12 (later standardized as the M3 or M3A1) were rebuilt as armored personnel carriers, at least 518 before initial issue and the rest later in the war.

Similar to the T-12, this M3 half-track variant mounted an M2A1 105mm howitzer. Of the 324 built some served with the cannon companies and others temporarily with the armored divisions as M7 self-propelled howitzer substitutes. The howitzer was too heavy a load for its half-track carrier. Armor thickness was mostly 0.25in. (6.35mm).

rifle platoons except for tactical movements, where little or no enemy resistance was expected, or in defensive situations where maximum local control was needed. The LMG section operated together under company control, though on rare occasions it might be attached to a rifle platoon.

The infantry battalion heavy weapons company operated in much the same way as the rifle company weapons platoon, but on a larger scale. Like the weapons platoon, the weapons company was the battalion commander's base of fire, and the mortar platoon operated under his personal control. The weapons company commander was responsible for his unit's training, supply, and administration. Assisted by his executive and reconnaissance officer, he reconnoitered firing positions for the company's weapons and march routes to

Two 32d Division soldiers fire a 60mm mortar on a range in Australia, October 14, 1942.

those positions. He would recommend the best of these to the battalion commander.

In battle the weapons company commander normally took direct control of the two HMG platoons. Unlike his rifle company counterpart, he also had some control over his mortars since the battalion commander was often too busy to control them himself. An HMG platoon or section operated much like an LMG section, but it could deliver accurate fire at much longer ranges. Unlike the rifle company weapons platoon, in which all five weapon squads had to share two weapons carriers, each HMG squad had its own weapons carrier. This was a light truck that carried a crew-served weapon plus its ammunition. At first most weapons carriers were $3/4$-ton trucks, but jeeps with trailers replaced many of them. A weapons carrier was purely a transport vehicle, not a gun platform. For an HMG squad it had to carry over 700 pounds of gun, ammunition, and water. A jeep weapons carrier could not also carry more than two squad members, and this caused a weapons company to divide itself, for movement purposes, into separate foot and motor echelons. Sometimes both moved together, but in open terrain the carriers would let the foot echelon move ahead and then catch up to them by moving in bounds. If enemy contact was imminent, or if there was danger from air attack, one section per HMG platoon would stand ready to provide "over-watch" fire while other sections moved.

Just prior to engaging the enemy, the HMG platoon leaders would confer with the weapons company commander about the objectives to be taken or reached, the localities the platoons should occupy, and where the "off carrier" positions should be. Platoon and section leaders selected the primary firing positions for their guns as well as supplemental positions for use if their primary positions became unusable. Alternate positions could be chosen for secondary missions such as guarding a flank. The "off carrier" position was where the gun crew offloaded their weapon and an initial supply of ammunition. From there they would carry the gun and ammunition to a firing position. The off carrier position had to be both accessible to a light truck and screened from enemy direct fire and observation. Observers from platoon headquarters would be posted within visual signaling distance of the guns. They would monitor the platoon sector, determine ranges, select reference points, identify targets, and adjust fire. Ideally the HMG platoon leader would personally control the fire of all his guns. If this were impossible, he would direct one gun section and leave the other to his platoon sergeant. It was considered unsafe to fire over the heads of friendly troops at targets that were less than 400 meters ahead. Overhead fire was most often used in attacks led by friendly tanks. HMG fire tended to concentrate on direct-fire heavy weapons placed behind the enemy's frontline, but they could also attack targets on reverse slopes. In the defense, HMG would be positioned by section to deliver flanking fire or a "final protective line" along the main line of resistance. HMG platoon leaders also supervised the positioning of the rifle company LMG sections and ensured they fitted into the overall battalion fire plan. Alternatively HMGs might be positioned in depth to deliver overhead fire or to block enemy penetrations. They could also occupy open positions forward of the MLR to deliver long-range harassing fire. As the main enemy attack began, the HMGs would withdraw to their primary positions on or behind the MLR, using covered routes.

The 81mm mortar platoon operated much like the HMG platoons. Its weapons carriers were more heavily loaded, each with over 1,000 pounds of mortar, ammunition, and accessories. This seemingly generous supply of ammunition could be expended in as little as 10 minutes, so keeping the mortars supplied was always a headache. During combat, if the mortars needed to displace they would do so by sections to ensure continuous coverage. Like the rifle companies' 60mm mortars, the 81mm mortars covered gaps and "dead space" left by the artillery. However, the mortar platoon commander kept in touch with the artillery observers and coordinated his fire with theirs. In offensive operations, the mortars attacked targets chosen by the battalion and weapons company commanders and the mortar platoon leader. The mortars would position themselves within 800 yards of the battalion frontline. Though they could range to 3,300 yards, they were not

A sergeant demonstrates the low recoil of the Thompson sub machine gun by firing it against his chin, Camp Hood, TX, 1943.

to engage targets beyond 2,000 yards because this distance was regarded as the limit of effective observation. In the defense, 81mm fire generally engaged one primary and one or more secondary preplanned targets. The platoon leader placed his mortars in defilade while setting up an observation post within shouting distance of the guns from which most of the battalion frontline could be seen. If the observation post had to be further away, there was enough wire equipment to link the observers to the guns by telephone. Ideally, all of the mortars should stay close enough together for the platoon commander to control them. If this was not possible, the mortars could deploy by sections or even individual guns. In poor visibility, or if the battalion was very dispersed, mortar sections might be attached to the rifle companies. If this happened, these sections would operate like the 60mm mortars. The 81mm mortars could screen friendly movement with smoke as well as high explosives. Mortar fire was considered especially effective against entrenched crew-served weapons, in road cuts, behind railway embankments, or on reverse slopes. They were not, interestingly enough, expected to engage antitank guns since it was believed that such weapons were better dealt with by flat-trajectory automatic weapons fire.

Tank–infantry cooperation and antitank tactics

Until bazookas became available, an infantry division in 1942–43 had only its rifle grenades and 37mm antitank guns to protect it from enemy armor. The purpose of these weapons was only to defeat very minor tank threats and to prevent the troops from feeling completely helpless against enemy armor. The 37mm guns could fire effective high explosive and canister ammunition in addition to armor-piercing shot, and this enabled them to engage enemy infantry as well as armor. The infantry divisions had no tanks or tank destroyers of their own, because they were not likely to need them all the time, and it was War Department policy to concentrate tanks not assigned to armored divisions and all its heavier antitank guns into separate battalions. These battalions could operate in groups to counter the larger armor threats, but they were available for attachment to infantry divisions when needed.

The US Army had originally designed its tanks mainly for infantry support. A tank platoon might support a rifle company or infantry battalion. A tank company could support a battalion or a regiment. Tank battalions supported divisions. Tank destroyers were lightly armored and it was risky to expose them to enemy direct fire. However, they could deliver supporting fire, especially from hull defilade positions behind friendly troops.

Members of a tank destroyer battalion man an M6 self-propelled 37mm antitank gun at Camp Chaffee, Arkansas, December 11, 1942. About 5,380 M6 were eventually built. They were originally to have equipped the infantry regimental antitank companies, but towed M3 or M3A1 antitank guns were used instead.

The division's field artillery

US Army doctrine held that the mission of the field artillery was to destroy, suppress, or neutralize the enemy so that the "maneuver arms" (infantry and tanks) could defeat what was left. Whenever possible the infantry division artillery received reinforcement from the very large pool of non-divisional artillery (105mm and larger) that existed for this purpose. Although the exact amount of artillery support that a division might receive varied widely, on average it was four battalions in addition to the four already belonging to the division. These additional battalions would frequently belong to a separate artillery brigade. Though an artillery observation battalion might be available, it was generally left to the division artillery to find and choose the targets that these battalions would engage.

The division's three 105mm battalions may be described as "direct support" (DS) battalions. Each was closely associated with an infantry regiment and supported it whenever possible. If the regiment had to be temporarily detached from the division, its associated DS battalion would accompany it. In battle the DS battalion populated the regiment's sector with observation posts (OP) and forward observer (FO) teams. Each battery would deploy an OP under its reconnaissance officer. The battalion headquarters would also deploy an OP. Ideally, the battery OP could observe a battalion-sized sector of the frontline (just like an 81mm mortar OP). The OP would observe the sector, report targets that the battalion fire direction center (FDC) might engage, and report the effects of previous fire and any other activity of interest to the artillery.

A good OP position could be hard to find. Therefore a battery would frequently supplement its OP with an FO team, which could observe parts of the battery sector that the OP could not. An FO team could even attach itself to a rifle company. No battery FO team was officially authorized, but the battery reconnaissance officer or the assistant executive officer (AXO) could lead an improvised team. The AXO was by far the most likely FO team leader. He was the most junior (and expendable) officer in the battery. His duties at the battery maintenance section could easily be passed to the first sergeant. Other FO team members would include an enlisted observer (usually a scout corporal), a radio operator, and a wireman and telephone operator. Combat experience showed that it was best to have an FO team with each rifle company, but this arrangement did not become possible until mid 1944.

In addition to establishing OPs and sending out FO teams, the DS artillery battalion sent liaison teams to two of the supported infantry regiment's battalions. The artillery battalion commander was supposed to act as artillery liaison officer to the infantry regiment, but he usually delegated these duties to a subordinate.

The division's sole 155mm howitzer battalion was for the general support (GS) of the division. Its fire could reinforce that of the 105mm battalions, or it could fire on targets as directed by the division commander. However, its range was too short to cover the entire division sector and reinforcing artillery had to cover what remained.

In 1942, artillery fire was mainly preplanned, but as the war continued, and communication improved, the proportion of fire missions directed against unplanned targets of opportunity increased. The liaison teams planned and coordinated artillery fire in close cooperation with the infantry they supported. This helped to prevent fratricide and ensured that all targets were engaged with appropriate ordnance. The division artillery also coordinated the fire of whatever reinforcing artillery that might be available.

Although an infantry division seldom had more than two infantry regiments in its frontline, it never held any artillery in reserve. Any DS battalion whose regiment was not engaged would either reinforce the fire of another DS battalion or conduct GS fire missions instead.

Every battalion and higher-level headquarters battery in the division included an FDC that calculated firing data for the guns. Firing batteries, however, did not rate an FDC. Army doctrine prescribed the use of massed fire. A battalion was supposed to direct all its batteries onto one target at a time. In practice, however, an artillery battery did sometimes have to fire independently. In such cases, it would improvise its own FDC, usually run by the battery executive officer and staffed by the range-finding instrument operators.

In October 1942 the division artillery's target acquisition capabilities were considerably increased by the addition of a section of two light liaison aircraft to each battalion or division headquarters battery. The "aerial OP" concept behind these aircraft had been extensively tested in February 1942. Air observation was seen as supplemental to ground observation. Slow and unarmed but stable and reliable aircraft, mainly L-4 "Piper Cubs" or L-5 "Stinson Sentinels," were used. The 10 aircraft per division generally based themselves on the same level field or straight stretch of road (these planes needed very little takeoff and landing space) and operated as a de facto squadron. The "squadron" flew continuous daylight patrols (missions lasting 60–90 minutes) and battalion commanders, though no longer in control of their own aircraft, could easily request its services. To ensure their own survival the planes only operated at low altitude and from behind friendly lines and quickly made themselves scarce whenever enemy fighters were detected. Spotter aircraft were especially valuable for locating enemy artillery.

To keep up with the tactical situation and keep its guns within range of the enemy, the artillery had to make frequent displacements. When this was necessary, each battalion would move only one battery at a time (preceded by a reconnaissance party) while the other two continued to fire. The artillery also had to be able to defend itself from air or ground attack, but its ability to do so was limited. Batteries were very lightly armed and, besides the guns themselves, .50-cal machine guns were the only crew-served weapons. These were of value against low-flying aircraft but their practical rate of fire was too low to offer a lot of protection from an infantry attack. No antitank shells would be available for the 105mm howitzers until later in the war. Each battalion headquarters battery, however, included an antitank and antiaircraft (AA-AT) platoon with 37mm antitank guns.

Combat engineers

In offensive combat, the primary role of the combat engineer battalion was to increase the mobility of the division by building or repairing roads and bridges and removing obstacles. The battalion could also support a water crossing, but would need boats, rafts, and bridging material. In defensive combat the battalion would reduce the enemy mobility by erecting obstacles and destroying roads and bridges. The battalion could also do minor construction work, mostly of a temporary nature and it had certain logistical functions (see *Combat operations*).

The engineer battalion normally worked directly under division control and did not customarily attach an engineer company to each infantry regiment. An infantry regiment might, of course, request engineers for a particular task, but only received the engineers required to perform that task. Most of the engineers stayed under battalion control. However, if the division broke up into separate regimental combat teams (RCT), as often happened during amphibious operations, each RCT would have a combat engineer company attached to it.

The obstacles that the engineers most often had to remove or emplace were roadblocks and minefields. Obstacle clearing could be done with explosives, but the best tool for building or removing roadblocks (and with such things as

Near Algiers, American instructors train French soldiers to use the M3 37mm towed antitank gun, February 9, 1943. Upon completion of the training, this equipment was handed over to the French.

road building, debris removal and burying enemy pillboxes) was the "medium tractor crawler type with angle-dozer," or bulldozer. Each engineer company had only one, but it was probably the single most useful piece of equipment it had. Since the bulldozer could not move very far on its tracks, a 4-ton truck with an 8-ton trailer stood ready to carry it over longer distances. The bulldozer itself was usually a converted commercial model with a diesel engine and (later) an optional armored cab.

One task that a bulldozer could not help with was the laying and clearing of minefields. This was a labor-intensive job with everything being done by hand. The Division G-3 (see *Command, Control, Communications, and Intelligence*), the engineer battalion commander, and the commander of the infantry regiment in whose sector the mines were to be placed, planned and coordinated minefields. The antitank mine platoons in the infantry regimental antitank companies with assistance from the infantry battalion pioneer platoons would do the bulk of the mine laying. The division engineers would furnish some advice and assistance. For clearing mines, the engineers had to do much of the work themselves, using explosives and portable mine detectors. The infantry battalion pioneers could also assist with this if they were not more urgently needed elsewhere.

Although the engineer battalion was actually designated a "combat" engineer battalion, its real ability to engage in infantry combat was very limited. They lacked mortars, light automatic weapons (like the BAR), and appropriate communication systems. In the offensive, they frequently provided small parties to accompany the infantry, mainly for obstacle removal. Their heavy tripod (or half-track) mounted machine guns and 37mm guns gave them a combat capability that was mainly defensive. If the engineers were to fight as infantry the usual procedure was to attach each engineer company to an infantry battalion, which could supply the mortars and radios that the engineers lacked.

As was the case with the artillery, the one engineer battalion organic to an infantry division could not satisfy division requirements in moderate to heavy combat. Corps, and army-level engineer brigades and groups provided additional units to work in the division rear areas, or for special capabilities such as bridge construction or landing craft operation. A division in combat might easily have two or three battalions (often under an engineer brigade or group headquarters) attached to it or working in direct support of it.

Command, control, communications, and intelligence

Command and control

Command and control at the infantry squad and platoon level was very simple. The squad or platoon leader led his unit by personal example, using voice commands, arm and hand signals, and an operations order given before a battle began. He also had an assistant to extend his span of control by relaying orders or taking his place if he became a casualty. Assistant squad leaders and platoon guides also marched in the rear of their respective formations to watch for stragglers.

The company commander had a relatively large headquarters that he usually organized into forward and rear command posts (CP). The forward CP consisted of the company commander himself and the men he needed to enable him tactically to command the company (for a rifle company this was usually the communication sergeant and some messengers). The rear CP, under the company executive officer, was for the company administration, mess, and supply although many personnel involved with these functions were not physically with the company for very much of the time. The rear CP would also take command of the company if the forward CP ceased to function. In the case of a battalion weapons company, the company executive officer was also the reconnaissance officer. With his reconnaissance sergeant and usually a jeep or $3/4$-ton truck and driver, he would go forward to identify firing positions for the guns and the routes to reach them as well as "off carrier" positions for the weapons carriers.

The regimental antitank company, on the other hand, had a separate reconnaissance officer while the cannon company had its headquarters formally divided between an administrative and supply (A&S) section and a command and reconnaissance (C&R) section. In battle the C&R section would, of course, deploy forward under either the company commander or executive officer even though both of these officers officially belonged to the A&S section.

In the case of headquarters companies (and infantry regimental supply companies or artillery service batteries) there was no forward CP. These companies never fought as companies, so there was no need for tactical control. However, the headquarters company commander also served as the headquarters commandant of the battalion or higher headquarters that his company supported. As such he was in charge of local security, administration, and logistics.

The US Army organized its higher headquarters under a system originally devised by the French and passed on to the American Expeditionary Force (AEF) in World War I. It broke down a headquarters into several theoretically co-equal sections whose heads reported to a chief of staff. Initially, there were only three sections. The first dealt with discipline, morale, and personnel administration (including current unit strengths and prisoners of war). Its head was also the adjutant of the unit. The second section was for intelligence. The third was in charge of planning and supervising operations. Before the end of the war, there was a fourth section for logistics and a fifth section for training. After the war, the third and fifth sections were combined and, in practice at least, the third section took precedence over the other three. This staff system was first used only at army level but later extended to corps. By the time World War II had broken out, the French Army had applied the system down to the division level. The French regarded this type of headquarters as too large and complex for smaller units and had no plans to extend it any lower. In 1921, however, the US Army carried it all the way down to the battalion level.

A WC-56 3/4-ton command and reconnaissance (C&R) truck with its soft top stowed; this vehicle does not have a radio installed. The WC-56 differed from the WC-57 in not having a front-mounted power takeoff (PTO) winch. (Recognition photo from about June 1942.)

There were several reasons for this. In World War I, an AEF battalion headquarters had consisted of the battalion commander (a major) and a couple of lieutenants (one of whom acted as intelligence officer) to serve as his assistants. The regimental headquarters company furnished a sergeant major and some messengers, orderlies, and signalers. The battalion would also get a section from the regimental medical detachment, a section from the regimental supply company, and a telephone detail from the division signal battalion. Both the French and German armies used similar systems and these served them well. Most of their commanders could plan in their heads, issue verbal orders, and lead by personal example. They would detail one lieutenant to run the battalion command post (at which the battalion commander was seldom present) and use the other as a kind of "empowered messenger" with the authority to resolve situations that the battalion commander was too busy to deal with himself. However, inexperienced AEF battalion commanders, who often lacked even the experience of commanding a company, had never learned how to plan in their heads, make rapid but sound decisions, or use subordinates properly, often found their jobs overwhelming.

The US Army's solution to this problem was twofold. First, it made battalion commanders lieutenant colonels. The intent was to give battalion command to more mature and experienced officers, but of course it meant that the Army would need many more lieutenant colonels and would have to promote majors to that rank before they had acquired the requisite experience and maturity. The Army's decision therefore ended up defeating much of its own purpose.

Secondly, the Army adopted the French staff system as an "overkill" method to ensure that its future battalion and higher commanders had plenty of help. It believed that enough indifferently trained officers, using a simple, "paint by the numbers" system for assessing a situation and reaching a decision, could generate output that, if less than brilliant, ought to be at least good enough. In combat, this hope proved to be largely fulfilled, but the system was labor-intensive and time consuming. It caused US units to react more slowly to changing situations and to favor methodical and slow-moving "set piece" battles. Even so, the War Department rejected solutions based on improvements in officer training and selection. This would be elitist and after mobilization could easily leave the Army without enough officers. Instead, the War Department believed it was better to have more officers rather than better ones and to break down any job into pieces small enough for nearly anyone of normal intelligence and education to handle.

To implement its "French Solution" the Army gave each staff section a designating letter and a number. A section in a division headquarters or higher always had the letter "G" plus a number corresponding to which section it was. Thus the division G-1 was the first (or personnel) section of the division staff. The G-1 was also the section head himself. Below division level, staff sections used the letter "S." A battalion or regimental headquarters consisted only of officers. Their enlisted assistants belonged to their headquarters companies or (in an infantry regimental headquarters company) the staff section of the service company.

Despite these changes, an infantry battalion headquarters was still very small, consisting only of the battalion commander, executive officer, S-2 and S-3. The S-1 was also the headquarters company commander. His S-1 responsibilities were not very onerous because the regimental staff section and the company clerks did most of the work. The regimental service company provided an S-4. Enlisted assistants for the S-2 and S-3 came from the battalion headquarters section of the headquarters company. The battalion executive officer also functioned as chief of staff and S-3. The nominal S-3 actually served as the assistant S-3.

An infantry regimental headquarters was similar. It had all the officers that a battalion headquarters had but with higher ranks. The S-3 was really the S-3 and the executive officer was only the executive officer. The S-4 himself and the enlisted assistants for the S-1, S-3, and S-4 belonged to the service company. Unlike a battalion S-1, the regimental S-1 had to be a full-time S-1 and needed a warrant officer assistant because he really was responsible for personnel administration throughout the regiment. The company and regimental staff section personnel clerks worked under his supervision.

Finally, regimental headquarters also included three liaison officers. Their job was to keep the regimental commander informed of what was happening elsewhere in the division and to represent his interests. One would typically be placed with each of the other two regiments in the division and the third would go to division headquarters.

A division headquarters was a far larger and more complex organization than a regimental headquarters. At its core was the general staff section. Presided over by a chief of staff (a colonel) it included all four staff section heads (G-1, G-2, G-3 and G-4: all lieutenant colonels) plus officer assistants for the G-2, G-3, and G-4 (all majors), a G-4 motor officer (major), and warrant officer assistants for the G-1 and assistant G-4 (motor). The three remaining officers (captains) were the division liaison officers. Their duties were generally the same as those of regimental liaison officers except that two went to adjacent divisions and the third was stationed at the army corps headquarters that the division served under (divisions were not normally employed outside of a corps structure). Unlike battalion or regimental headquarters, the division general staff section included all the enlisted assistants for the G-2 and G-3.

The general staff section did most of the planning and supervised the execution of the division's operations. The remaining sections all performed special functions. They provided expertise within certain areas, or served as advisors and liaison for other service arms within the division. The finance, administration (adjutant general's section), legal services (judge advocate general), morale (special services), and chaplain operated under the purview of the G-1. The chemical and antitank sections provided special expertise to

This uncaptioned photo shows an EE-8 field telephone in use, probably during a training exercise in the United States c. 1942.

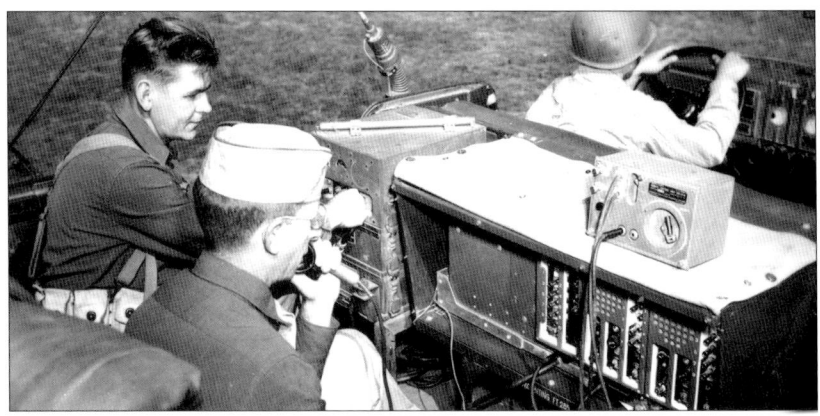

This uncaptioned photo, probably taken during a 1943 field exercise in either England or the United States, shows a 3/4-ton C&R truck serving as a communication vehicle. It mounts an SCR-508 FM radio on the left and a larger SCR-510 on the right. The longer-ranged SCR-193 system used in the infantry division signal company took up the same space as both of these smaller radios.

the G-3. The division artillery, engineer battalion, ordnance, quartermaster, and signals all maintained their own liaison sections with division headquarters.

Command and control within the division artillery was similar to what it was for the infantry, although it was easier to accomplish, since the artillery operated further away from the enemy. The division artillery headquarters and headquarters battery only provided command and control and certain fire-direction services to its battalions. The latter included a meteorological section that corrected firing data to conform to atmospheric conditions.

The division artillery commander kept in close touch with division headquarters. He participated in the division's planning and served as the division commander's artillery advisor. He chose the general locations where his battalions would operate and assigned them their missions, ordering necessary changes as the battle unfolded. His headquarters battery could direct the fire of two or more battalions onto the same targets.

Howitzer batteries normally fired under the control of their respective battalions although they could fire independently. Massed fire was preferred because to cause maximum damage it was desirable to hit a target with as many shells as possible, as quickly as possible, thus depriving the target of any opportunity to move away or take cover. Three batteries firing together were much more effective than the same three batteries firing separately.

The battalion headquarters controlled their batteries' movement as much as possible also. Ideally, batteries should occupy firing positions previously surveyed for them by the battalion survey and instrument section. A surveyed location was, of course, much more precise than one estimated from a map. When directing artillery fire it is at least as important to know the exact locations of one's own guns as it is to know the location of their targets; hence surveyed positions, when available, contributed significantly to artillery accuracy.

Communication equipment

In 1942 the US Army had four principal means of communication (other than speaking face-to-face). These were field telephone, radio, messenger, and visual. Field telephones were fairly clear, secure, and reliable, but they were not mobile and had to be connected by wire cables. Laying such cable over any distance could be arduous and time consuming and the cables, once laid, were frequently cut by artillery fire or the passage of motor vehicles. Burying the cables offered some (but not complete) protection but naturally it was much slower than just laying the cable on the surface. Telephone cables could also serve to transmit telegraph messages, which, of course, had to be in Morse

(continues on page 56)

Table 8: Selected non-radio infantry division signal equipment (1942–43)

System	Type	Description
EE-8	Field telephone	Standard field telephone with ringing equipment and leather case. Battery powered, its talking range was about five miles (using W-130 wire) or 14 miles (using W-110 wire).
TP-3	Field telephone	Shorter-ranged (up to five miles), lightweight, sound-powered field telephone.
BD-71	Switchboard	Relatively portable six-line battalion-level switchboard. It weighed 45 pounds.
BD-72	Switchboard	Relatively portable 12-line regimental-level switchboard. It weighed 75 pounds.
BD-14	Switchboard	40-line switchboard; three issued per division headquarters until replacement by the TC-4.
TG-5	Telegraph set	Portable field set for manual keying (Morse code) and receiving; weighed 6 pounds.
TC-4	Telephone exchange	Multi-line telephone exchange. A division headquarters had three (manned by signal company personnel). They were connected to BD-89 and BD-96 switchboards.
TL-122	Flashlight	A flashlight with a pushbutton that enabled it to serve as a signal lamp. It replaced most purpose-designed signal lamps and was issued in large quantities (nearly 800 per infantry regiment).
CE-11	Reel equipment	Combination of an RL-39 reel unit with $1/4$-mile of W-110 phone wire (usually on a DR-8 spool) and a sound-powered telephone (TP-3). Used to lay wire by hand.
RL-16	Reel unit	A two-wheeled handcart mounting two DR-4 drums. Few saw combat use prior to 1944.
RL-26	Reel unit	A heavy reel unit using a gas-engine drive, it was carried in a vehicle but being an older system its laying and recovery speeds were slow. Faster units began to replace it at the end of the war.
RL-31	Reel unit	Tubular A-frame, able to hold one DR-5 or two DR-4 spools. Brake and crank units to control speed of wire lay or recovery and to allow multiple reels to operate independently of each other. Could be used on the ground or (with an installation kit) from a vehicle (usually a jeep).
RL-39	Reel unit	Chest-type unit with carrying handles, straps, and a crank for rewinding. Used with the DR-8 drum to lay or recover wire by hand over short circuits in forward areas or difficult terrain.
DR-4	Spool	Metal spool container for laying or recovery of field wire, holding about a mile of W-130 wire. A full spool weighed 80 pounds and was a two-man load.
DR-5	Spool	Metal spool container for laying or recovery of field wire, holding about $2^{1}/_{2}$ miles of wire. It was usually mounted on a reel unit RL-31.
DR-8	Spool	Metal spool container for laying or recovery of field wire; used with the CE-11 and RL-39 holding about $1/4$-mile of W130 field telephone wire. It weighed about 20 pounds when full.
W-110	Telephone wire	The standard field telephone wire type. Weighing about 130 pounds per mile it had a talking range of 12–20 miles (buzzer communication range would be significantly greater). Due to its weight it was generally laid or recovered by a motor vehicle equipped with an RL-31 or RL-26.
W-130	Telephone wire	Lightweight field telephone wire weighing about 30 pounds per mile but with a talking range of only five miles. Its lighter weight enabled linemen to carry sufficient wire for hand laying.

Note: Updated versions of the CE-11, RL-31, RL-39, DR-5, and DR-8 were still in use in 2005.

Table 9: Infantry division radio equipment (1942–43)

System	Year	Type	Weight (lb)	Modulation	Freq. range	Tx range (miles)
SCR-171	1935	HF ground	179	AM	2–3 MHz	15 (CW only)
SCR-178	1941	HF ground	200?	AM	2.4–3.7 MHz	15 (CW only)
SCR-193	1941	HF air-ground vehicular	Over 100	AM	1.5–18 MHz	60 (CW), 40 (tone), 20 (voice)
SCR-194	1938	Man-pack	26.8	AM	28–52 MHz	2–3 (voice)
SCR-195	1938	Man-pack	26.8	AM	52–66 MHz	2–3 (voice)
SCR-245	1938	HF vehicular	186	AM	1.5–18 MHz	45 (CW), 35 (tone), 20 (voice)
SCR-284	1943	Ground or vehicular	250 (max)	AM	3.8–5.8 MHz	30 (CW), 20 (tone), 10 (voice)
SCR-288	1940	HF ground	60	AM	3.5–6.5 MHz	30 (CW), 15 (voice)
SCR-299	1941	Mobile HF station	Carried in a K-51 truck	AM	2–8 MHz	100 (voice) several hundred miles (CW)
SCR-508	1942	Vehicular	Heavy	FM	20–27.9 MHz	10 (voice only)
SCR-510	1943	Vehicular	No data	FM	20–27.9 MHz	5 (voice)
SCR-511	1941	Cavalry	20?	AM	2–6 MHz	3 (voice)
SCR-536	1942	Hand-held	6	AM	3.5–6 MHz	1 (voice)
SCR-593	1941	Man-pack receiver	22.5	AM	2–6 MHz	Receiver only
SCR-608	1942	Vehicular	Heavy	FM	27–38.9 MHz	10 (voice)
SCR-610	1943	Portable	No data	FM	27–38.9 MHz	5 (voice)

Notes: Only the more common types before 1944 are shown above. Transmission ranges apply when both transmitting and receiving station

Power	Notes
Battery or hand generator	Older CW-only system transported by vehicle but operated from the ground. It was in fairly common use early in the war but the SCR-284, SCR-288, and SCR-608 would soon replace it. Used at the battalion and regimental/brigade levels.
Battery or hand generator	Older HF field radio carried by vehicle and operated from the ground. Used in the artillery at brigade level.
Vehicle power	Heavy medium-range HF vehicular radio used at the division level and higher.
Battery Battery	The Army's first man-pack radio. The SCR-194 and SCR-195 were the artillery and infantry versions, respectively of this radio. Best used as a ground system. In "receive" mode the radio emitted a signal that jammed all radios on the same frequency and within about 1,500 yards except the radio that it was receiving from. The SCR-511 and then the SCR-300 in the infantry and the SCR-610 and later the SCR-619 in the artillery would replace it. Used mainly at the company/battery and battalion levels.
Vehicle power	Early vehicular radio originally used in the infantry regiment headquarters company and antitank company and in artillery battalion and brigade-level headquarters companies. The SCR-284 would replace it.
Battery, or hand generator, or vehicle power	Used at battalion level and higher, this set came in pack, ground and vehicular versions. In the infantry division it was typically mounted in a jeep. One man operated the set while another operated the generator. In combat the set proved to be too heavy and too fragile and late in the war the SCR-694 would replace it.
Battery, or hand generator	Used as a temporary replacement for the SCR-161, 171, 178, and 245 until the SCR-284 was available. Not a vehicular set.
Power unit PE-95 or batteries	Heavy division-level radio communication center mounted on a K-51 2½-ton truck towing a K-52 1-ton trailer (for the generator). Served successfully in North Africa and Sicily but the SCR-399 replaced it in 1944.
Vehicle power	The SCR-508 was first FM radio to see combat. SCR-608 was the artillery version. Though it could be used from the ground its weight normally dictated vehicular use. In the infantry division it served in the reconnaissance troop.
Vehicle power	Short-range vehicular radio, the artillery version (SCR-610) was also portable. SCR-510 served in the reconnaissance troop. SCR-610 served in the artillery at the battery and battalion levels. The battery-powered (artillery) version was the SCR-609.
Battery	Though designed as a cavalry radio for use by a man on horseback it was clearly superior to the SCR-194/195. Many served with the infantry in lieu of the SCR-195 but they were awkward to carry on foot. The SCR-300 replaced it in 1944.
Battery	Made its combat debut in Sicily in July 1943. Used in the rifle and heavy weapons companies of the infantry regiment. Only a technician could adjust the frequency and frequencies were assigned to specific companies. This usually prevented radios from one company from communicating with those from another.
Battery	This was the receiver portion of the SCR-543. A complete SCR-543 was too heavy to be man portable.
Vehicle power	The SCR-508 was first FM radio to see combat. SCR-608 was the artillery version. Though it could be used from the ground its weight normally dictated vehicular use. In the infantry division it served in the reconnaissance troop.
PE-97 power unit	Short-range vehicular radio, the artillery version (SCR-610) was also portable. SCR-510 served in the reconnaissance troop. SCR-610 served in the artillery at the battery and battalion levels. The battery-powered (artillery) version was the SCR-609.

y. Movement by either or both stations could reduce transmissions ranges by up to half.

code. Telegraph messages were typically only a sentence or two but a well-trained operator could transmit 30 per hour.

Radios did not require cable but were subject to the effects of unreliable batteries, variable atmospheric conditions, jamming, direction finding, and interception. Radios could transmit in voice, continuous wave (CW) or (in a few cases) tone mode. Only Morse messages could be sent via CW or tone, but Morse messages could be sent quickly (15–20 per hour) and reliably over long distances—but they required skilled operators. Voice radio transmissions, though not requiring trained operators, were much slower at 10–15 messages per hour. Encryption and decryption for Morse (but not voice) messages was slow but possible.

Early in the war all radio sets transmitted using amplitude modulation (AM). Sets using frequency modulation (FM) were first used in North Africa but did not become common until 1944. FM sets generated much less static, sending clearer messages that could be sent faster and with less chance of error. This was a revolutionary technology and only US forces had it.

Communication architecture

At the lowest level, platoons and squads (or sections) communicated within themselves by voice or hand and arm signals. Rifle and battalion weapons company commanders were allowed six hand-held SCR (Signal Corps Radio)-536 radios apiece. Normally, a company commander issued one to each of his platoon leaders and to the company command post (CP) while keeping one radio for himself to use when he was not in the CP. These sets constituted a company command net. In a weapons company the executive/ reconnaissance officer might also have a radio. Rifle companies had enough telephone equipment to operate an observation post (OP) during daylight or a listening post (LP) at night. The weapons company could connect its platoons by telephone with its own headquarters or its parent battalion headquarters.

Within a company or a battalion, messengers constituted a slower but more secure and reliable means of communication than radio. Messengers worked in pairs. A platoon leader, for example, stationed one of his messengers at the company CP while keeping the other one with him. If he needed to send a message one messenger would carry it to the company CP and send the other back with the reply. Messengers were usually selected from the better-quality soldiers because to reach their objectives they needed intelligence, initiative, and good land navigation skills (especially at night). Messengers working close to the frontline usually moved only on foot but those working further back might use jeeps or motorcycles.

Regimental and battalion communication platoons processed and sent most of the messages at their respective command echelons. They all used a similar structure and differed from one another mainly in size. The hub of any communication platoon was its message center. Outgoing messages had to be written in triplicate using a special message pad with carbon pages. The message center chief would then decide how to send it, be it by radio, telephone, messenger, or even a visual signal. He was expected to choose the fastest and most secure means. Message center clerks would write or process outgoing messages while receiving incoming messages, logging them, and then passing them on to whomsoever they were addressed.

The communication platoon's wire or telephone section was usually its largest and busiest. Whenever the parent unit halted, the section had to run cable (sometimes by vehicle but often by hand) to all subordinate headquarters and connect them through switchboards. This network needed constant repair and improvement. When it was time to move again the cables had to be recovered (even the rich Americans could not afford to abandon large amounts of cable), cleaned and rewound onto their spools. A battalion wire section had sufficient wire to hook all its companies, some Ops., and the antitank platoon into the battalion switchboard. The regimental communication platoon needed much more wire to reach its battalions and its cannon, antitank, and service companies. The antitank company could connect all its guns by wire.

Because of their low reliability and vulnerability to jamming and interception, radios were not considered a primary means of communication, but they were essential for any unit with no time to lay wire. In fact, battalion radio section personnel were also trained as visual signalers in case their radios became unnecessary or useless. The section maintained several heavier (30–40 pound) but longer-ranged man-pack radios both for its own use and for issue to its subordinate rifle and weapons company headquarters. The radios enabled these companies to join the battalion command net. The companies were not given operators for these sets but trained operators did man the ones used by the battalion headquarters and at higher echelons. Heavier (80 or more pound) sets operating from (or at least carried by) motor vehicles were used for regimental or higher-level communications. Each battalion also had one for use on the regimental tactical communication net. Only trained operators manned these sets. Sometimes they needed a second operator to man a generator.

Four of the 12 man-pack radios in the regimental headquarters company belonged to the intelligence and reconnaissance (I&R) platoon. The rest, plus six longer-ranged vehicle radios, were for the regimental commander to use as he saw fit. Although the antitank company was fully equipped with radios, the cannon company only had radios with its platoons, and neither the service company nor the medical detachment had any radio or telephone equipment at all. These, together with their operators, had to come from the regimental communication platoon. The radio section of this platoon also supplied one radio operator to the I&R platoon to operate the radio used to communicate with regimental headquarters.

Communication in the artillery was somewhat different. Each howitzer battery was allowed only four man-pack radios (no SCR-536). These were for communication between FDC (if one was set up), the gun line, the OP and an FO. However, wire was used whenever possible, especially for internal communication within the battery. The battalion communication platoon was also wire dependent. Its few radios were mainly for immediate communication with the liaison sections (assigned to infantry battalions) and for the fire-direction section (so it could always send fire commands to the batteries). A telephone network would displace the radios as quickly as it could be laid.

The division signal company, as the division headquarters' communications unit, was the hub of the division's communication network. The operations, construction, and radio intercept platoons were the company's key elements. The operations platoon was merely a collective designation for the company's message center, radio and telephone, and telegraph (or wire) sections. It functioned like a much-expanded version of a battalion or regimental communication platoon. The radio section could form as many as three watches to conduct 24-hour operations. It also included the SCR-299 communication center. The construction platoon laid and recovered the more than 120 miles of wire that the company owned. The wire section operated the wire network once it was in place. The radio intelligence platoon, which was not really a communication unit, located the source of hostile radio transmissions and intercepted and hopefully read enemy radio traffic.

Intelligence

The collection and reporting of information that could be processed into tactical intelligence was the responsibility of every soldier. However, in the infantry division very few soldiers did intelligence or reconnaissance work on anything like a full-time basis. An infantry battalion had only an S-2 (who was also the lowest-ranking member of the battalion staff) with a sergeant and six scout-observers. The S-2 could send a scout-observer to each rifle company to provide technical expertise and use the other three to man an observation post. Alternatively the S-2 could have his scouts accompany patrols provided by other units in order to collect whatever information the S-2 needed.

An infantry regimental commander, however, had an intelligence and reconnaissance (I&R) platoon as his personal reconnaissance unit. The I&R platoon spared him the need to improvise a substitute by weakening one of his battalions. Its functions included counterintelligence and assisting the S-2 in collecting, interpreting, and disseminating information either through office work, manning outposts, or accompanying patrols provided by other units. It could reconnoiter the terrain as well as the enemy. Neither its headquarters nor its two squads were meant for attachment to any battalion except for occasional missions of very limited duration. Though trained to carry out its mission on foot, the platoon operated primarily as a motorized unit. The armament of the platoon was deliberately defensive. It was not expected or encouraged to fight for its information. Generally, an I&R patrol would be of at least squad size, though the whole platoon (minus the S-2 office staff) might be used. Any patrol would include at least one radio since this was the fastest way to report whatever information it might obtain.

OP, reconnaissance, and FO parties, though hardly full-time intelligence personnel, were the "eyes and ears" of any artillery commander. They were expected to report not only targets but any other events or data that would keep the artillery commander abreast of the situation. Reconnaissance parties reported on terrain and potential firing positions for the guns. Liaison parties passed on information from the infantry.

The division cavalry troop was the division commander's personal reconnaissance unit. This unit was the product of years of experimentation but as of 1942 it had not yet evolved into anything satisfactory. Like the I&R platoon it was mainly for surveillance and did not normally fight for its information.

In an advance, the cavalry troop would precede the main body of the division by two to three hours. If a corps-level armored cavalry regiment was present the division troop could take the time to make a more detailed reconnaissance. The reconnaissance platoons were the basic tactical elements. They were not normally attached to the infantry regiments. Each platoon had a specified zone or route to reconnoiter but whenever practical the troop commander would hold a platoon in reserve. The troop frequently used dismounted scouts and patrols because it is hard to see or hear from a rapidly moving vehicle. Thanks to their low profile and noise signature the jeeps did most of the motorized scouting. A jeep with the .50-cal machine gun was supposed to provide air defense for each reconnaissance section but the vehicle proved to be too light to make a good gun platform for the .50-cal. The armored cars served as a base of fire for advancing or breaking contact. They could also relay reports with their long-range radios. Motorcyclists could serve as scouts or (should the radios fail) as messengers. If the enemy were near, each platoon would advance by bounds, one section covering the other's moves.

In the defense, the troop would delay the enemy, withdrawing from successive positions by bounds with sections and platoons covering each other. In battle, the troop had to be used with caution. Even after it had received its M8 armored cars it lacked the firepower to deal with tanks. Both its lightly armored and unarmored vehicles remained vulnerable to enemy fire and unable to traverse terrain that was boulder strewn, too hilly, too heavily forested, or had steep ditches or cliffs. They worked best on the roads (their "march" speed was 35 miles per hour in daylight or 15 after dark) but were at greater risk from mines or ambush. In the Pacific Theater, infantry division reconnaissance troops usually had to operate without their vehicles. In 1943 the cavalry troop was completely reorganized, though this reorganization did not begin to take effect in the combat theaters until the end the year.

Logistics

One key to the battlefield success of any 20th-century army has been the possession of a supply system that can resolve the often-competing demands of firepower and tactical mobility. This is because the quantity of supplies needed to maintain the fighting power of any combat unit for any length of time could easily ruin that unit's mobility if its transportation were not carefully managed. An efficient, high-demand, logistical system ensured mobility and flexibility by increasing the frequency, volume, and reliability of supply deliveries. If, for example, a combat unit could count on getting its food and water replenished each day, it need only carry one day of food and water. If it could count on getting ammunition within an hour of entering a battle, it would have to carry only one hour's worth of ammunition. These lighter loads would boost its tactical mobility. The US Army's new family of military trucks could rush supplies to the frontline unit in hours rather than days. Through the selective reinforcement of transportation assets it was possible to maintain delivery schedules despite difficult or extended routes or heavy demand. The heavily burdened fighting unit of World War I could become a thing of the past.

The new trucks made possible a complete reorganization of the Army's logistical system. They enabled regiments and separate battalions to go directly to army-level supply and ammunition points for everything they needed. Such points were typically 20 to 30 miles to the rear, or about one hour by truck one way. Army headquarters supplied laborers who sorted the supplies and loaded the trucks. Requesting units only had to send drivers to the supply points and did not have to reserve space in their vehicles for laborers. Under the new system division and corps-level headquarters were no longer part of the supply channel except in emergencies or in small theaters where they themselves were the highest-level headquarters.

However, the division was still closely involved with the collection, treatment, and evacuation of casualties. It still controlled small ordnance and quartermaster units that could maintain the division when it was not in

Like most civilian station wagons of this era, the WC-53 ¾-ton carry-all was of all-steel construction except for the roof, which was a wooden lattice framework covered by waterproof fabric. The driver's door could not be opened unless the spare tire was removed. Carry-alls frequently served as communication vehicles fitted with extensive electronic suites. In March 1943, the Army began to replace its carry-alls with additional C&R trucks. It found the carry-alls too conspicuous and top heavy for tactical use. (Recognition photo from about June 1942.)

Table 10: Classes of supply (1941)

Supply class	Description
Class I	Mostly rations and water, but the class covers all items consumed at generally uniform rates, in combat or out, that do not require special adaptation to meet individual requirements.
Class II	Non-consumable items appearing in a unit's table of equipment (TE) or table of basic allowances (TBA). It can include clothing, gas masks, weapons, trucks, radios, tools, and instruments.
Class III	All petroleum fuels and lubricants for both vehicles and aircraft. It can also include solid fuels such as coal.
Class IV	Items other than Class III or V that do not appear in a unit's TE or TBA but are required to support current or planned operations. It can include barbed wire, machinery, and construction materials.
Class V	Ammunition of all types, including pyrotechnics, mines, and chemical munitions.

Note: Since 1945 this system has been revised to include nine different supply classes.

Table 11: Types of field rations

A ration is an allowance of food and/or water for one person for one day.

Ration type	Description
Field Ration A	Similar to the garrison ration using cooked commercial-type food and including perishable items requiring refrigeration.
Field Ration B	Similar to Field Ration A except that canned or other non-perishable equivalents replace the perishable items.
Field Ration C	A cooked balanced ration consisting of three cans of meat and vegetables and three of crackers, sugar, coffee, etc. Although it could be heated, it was not considered a hot meal.
Field Ration D	An emergency ration, consisting of three four-ounce chocolate bars, issued in addition to or in lieu of C Rations. The bars had a slightly bitter flavor to discourage consumption if not needed.

A G7117 1½-ton cargo truck with hard top. (Recognition photo from about June 1942.)

A CCKW-352 2½-ton short wheel base (SWB) cargo truck with front winch; in an infantry division, SWB trucks mainly served as prime movers in the division artillery. Winch-equipped trucks often served as wreckers in 1942–43. Later production vehicles had soft-top cabs. (Recognition photo from about June 1942.)

combat and meet emergency requirements when it was. The division G-4 monitored the supply situation in order to know what support the division needed and to keep the division commander informed. The basic workings of this system are described below.

Infantry logistics

For an infantry regiment, the service company was the hub of the new supply system. This company was structured to release the greatest number of men for combat service while filling all routine supply requirements. The regimental supply officer (S-4) was a member of the company but his assistant S-4 actually commanded it. As company commander the assistant S-4 was responsible for discipline, administration, and training (except for the special training conducted by regimental staff officers). He also commanded the regimental motor echelon. This consisted of the service company transportation platoon (less detachments), plus any rifle or weapons company vehicles that might temporarily fall under regimental control.

Like most other company headquarters, that of the service company included a command group with the vehicles, messengers, and orderlies who worked for the company commander and S-4. An administrative group handled "housekeeping" for the service company itself.

The rest of the service company was split between a regimental headquarters platoon that did most of the paperwork and a transportation platoon that did much of the physical work.

The regimental headquarters platoon was simply a collective title covering the regimental staff and supply sections. The staff section contained all of the officer and enlisted assistants for the regimental S-1 (adjutant) and S-3 (operations and training officer). For the S-1 there was a personnel staff and a "special service" staff. A personnel officer with his own clerks plus the clerks from all 19 companies in the regiment constituted the personnel staff. Its sole function was centrally managed personnel administration. The "special service" staff handled anything connected to morale and welfare. It included chaplain's assistants, mail clerks, and even an athletic instructor and an entertainment director. The S-3 portion of the staff section consisted of the regimental sergeant major, an operations chief, a stenographer, and clerks.

Table 12: Infantry division motor vehicles (1942–43)

Type/model	Body type	Weight	GVW	No. built	Remarks
Harley-Davidson WLA	Solo motorcycle	583	763	60,486	Top speed 70mph; 124-mile range
¼-ton (jeep) 4x4	**Max speed for all jeeps = 45mph; cruising range = 285 miles (15 gal)**				
Ford GPW[1]	Personnel	2,450	3,650	350,349	Open topped; seats 3–4
Willys MB[1]	Personnel	2,450	3,650	281,578	Open topped; seats 3–4
Ford GPA[1,2]	Amphibious	unknown	4,460	12,778	Open topped; 5.5mph in water; seats 4
MBT ¼-ton trailer[1]	Cargo trailer	565	1,065	140,000+	Able to float when loaded
Dodge ¾-ton 4x4[1]	**Max speed for ¾-ton trucks (all variants) = 54mph; cruising range = 240 miles (30 gal)**				
Model WC-51[3]	Weapons carrier	5,645	7,445	123,541	Open topped, cargo bed aft
WC-52[3]	Weapons carrier	5,940	7,740	59,124	Same but with 5,000 PTO winch
WC-53[4]	Carry-all	5,750	7,550	8,400	Station wagon body; wood roof
WC-54	Ambulance	5,920	7,720	26,002	Carries 4 litter and 6 sitting patients
WC-56 (C&R)[3]	Command & Recon	5,375	7,175	21,156	Seats a driver plus 5 passengers
WC-57 (C&R)[3]	Command & Recon	5,675	7,475	6,010	Same but with 5,000 PTO winch
Chevrolet 1½-ton 4x4	**Max speed for 1½-ton trucks (all variants) = 45mph; cruising range = 144 miles (18 gal)**				
G7107[5]	Cargo truck	7,545	12,945	86,771	Hard-topped cab, commercial design
G7117[5]	Cargo truck	8,045	13,445	26,108	Same but with 10,000 PTO winch
G7106[5]	Dump truck	8,300	11,300	5,098	Hard-topped cab, commercial design
G7116[5]	Dump truck	8,700	11,800	9,297	Same but with 10,000 PTO winch
GMC 2½-ton 6x6[1]	**Max speed for 2½-ton trucks (all variants) = 45mph; cruising range = 300 miles (40 gal)**				
CCKW-352 (SWB)[6]	Cargo truck	11,000	16,000	412,385	352 had a 145in. and 353 a 164in. wheelbase; 10,000 PTO winch optional
CCKW-353 (LWB)[6]	Cargo truck	11,000	16,000		
CCKW Dump	Dump truck	11,850	16,850	48,345	10,000 PTO winch optional
CCKW Air Compressor	Air compressor	14,300	14,300	Unknown	Also carried set of air-powered tools
CCKW Wrecker[7]	Wrecker	Data unavailable – proved to be too light and soon withdrawn.			
CCKW Van	Van and mobile shop	11,930	16,930	15,205	Enclosed shop van
Diamond-T 4-ton 6x6	**Max speed for 4-ton trucks (all variants) = 40mph (governed); cruising range = 180 miles (60 gal)**				
968A	Cargo truck	18,400	26,400	9,794	Optional 15,000 PTO winch
969A	Wrecker	21,350	29,350	6,203	150,000 PTO winch
G518 1-ton trailer[1]	Cargo trailer	1,300	4,300	Large	Could actually carry 1.4–1.5 tons
G527 water trailer[1]	Water tank trailer	1,500	3,500	Large	Carried 250 gallons

(Notes appear on page 62)

The supply section functioned as an office group, a receiving and distributing group, and an ammunition group. The office group maintained records, consolidated requisitions and receipts, and compiled reports. The receiving and distributing group, working under the service company commander, received all classes of supply except Class V (ammunition) from higher supply echelons. The group designated distributing points for Class I, Class III, and Class IV supplies (see table 10) and then sorted and apportioned the supplies among the different elements of the regiment for collection by their intended recipients. Since the group consisted of only a staff sergeant and a few clerks, the units receiving the supplies had to furnish the necessary work details needed to load, unload, sort, and distribute them.

The ammunition group (for Class V supplies) consisted only of the regimental munitions officer, his munitions sergeant, and a 2 1/2-ton truck and driver. It supervised the regimental ammunition point and took charge of ammunition vehicles operating under regimental control. For labor, it could call on the battalion pioneer platoons. The truck served as an additional ammunition vehicle in emergencies or for other special purposes.

The transportation platoon commander was also regimental motor transport officer and service company executive officer. He supervised the establishment, control, defense, and operation of the regimental train bivouac. He was responsible for the maintenance of his vehicles and for the training of his drivers and mechanics and their operations except when they were detached from the regiment or had passed to the control of the regimental munitions officer. The motor sergeant acted as platoon sergeant and supervised vehicle maintenance and the preparation of records and reports. The truck-master helped to control the operation of the regimental train and usually accompanied the kitchen and baggage vehicles when they were under regimental control.

Apart from the headquarters and maintenance sections, the transportation platoon consisted of truck sections for every battalion and separate company in the regiment. The lieutenant in charge of each battalion section was also the S-4 of the battalion that he supported. He had a sergeant to assist him. In the field the lieutenant was in charge of his trucks only when they operated under battalion control. Two trucks per section carried supplementary ammunition for the rifle companies. They had no cargo trailers so that they were free to tow water trailers supplied by higher headquarters. The other five trucks (with trailers) carried field kitchens, rations, and bedrolls for each company in the battalion. The trucks in the company sections and service company headquarters carried similar loads for the other companies in the regiment.

The vehicles and drivers from the service company and the regimental medical detachment constituted the regimental train. The Army defined a "train" as those transport vehicles operating under the immediate orders of a unit commander that are used primarily for supply, evacuation, and maintenance. The train did not normally include the weapons carriers in the rifle and weapons companies. An infantry regiment actually had four trains. To which train a given vehicle happened to belong at any given time depended on what that vehicle was concurrently doing. The ammunition, or "combat," train included all vehicles carrying ammunition. The kitchen-and-baggage or "field" train included the vehicles carrying water, rations, kitchens, and other gear not required for actual combat. There was also a medical train, and the transportation platoon maintenance section was also a train. When not released to the battalions or otherwise employed, regimental train vehicles occupied a bivouac area. This was normally some miles to the rear (outside the range of enemy light artillery) and chosen for its cover, concealment, and accessibility to motor vehicles. The maintenance section could operate there and baggage and bedrolls were staged there. The receiving and distributing group of the regimental supply section would establish a regimental supply point in the bivouac area. Non-ammunition supplies arrived here from higher headquarters supply points in the trucks of the field train. These would pass through a division supply point en route. At the regimental supply point they would either drop their loads or be directed to go further to the battalions and/or companies.

The company field kitchens and mess teams normally stayed in the regimental bivouac area (or sometimes a battalion bivouac area) during the day where they rested and prepared food to carry up to their companies. The meals themselves were part of a new system of standardized rations that the War Department had developed to meet situational requirements (see table 11). Field rations A and B were hot meals prepared by company field kitchens. Field rations C and D were not hot meals but needed no preparation. The goal was that two of the three meals a soldier received per day would be hot. Hot meals would commonly be served (and filled water and gasoline cans delivered) after

A CCKW 2¹/₂-ton combination cargo and dump truck (body raised) with hard-top cab. (Recognition photo from about June 1942.)

Table 13: Echelons of maintenance	
Echelon	**Description**
First	Driver maintenance: simple tasks within the skill of the average driver, using tools and supplies available on the vehicle.
Second	Using unit maintenance: tasks, other than driver maintenance, performed by the using arm or service; specifically this includes company, battery, or troop-level mechanics plus battalion or regimental maintenance sections; the tasks themselves include minor repairs, unit replacements, and certain inspections.
Third	Ordnance or quartermaster field maintenance: tasks performed in the field by ordnance or quartermaster units (at division level or higher) that are beyond the capabilities of user maintenance.
Fourth	Depot maintenance: more extended work performed by ordnance or quartermaster personnel at major field depots or repair facilities.
Note: Until September 1942, responsibility for Third and Fourth Echelon vehicle maintenance was split between the Ordnance and Quartermaster Corps; after September it became the responsibility of the Ordnance Corps only.	

A Model 968A 4-ton cargo truck with hard-top cab and winch; in an infantry division 15 of these trucks served as prime movers for the division's twelve 155mm howitzers. Later production vehicles had soft-top cabs. (Recognition photo from about June 1942.)

A Model 969A 4-ton wrecker with hard-top cab; this eventually became the standard light wrecker because the 2¹/₂-ton wreckers were not powerful enough. (Recognition photo from about June 1942.)

dark and just before dawn. Kitchen trucks could get much closer to the troops during hours of darkness without being detected by the enemy.

Notwithstanding the importance of other supply classes, efficient ammunition supply was key to the success of the whole supply system. Trucks carried ammunition as far forward as possible before unloading and final distribution to users. During combat and after he had dumped his organic load, the driver of any transport vehicle not needed for some other purpose was usually given a requisition for ammunition. He was expected to go to the ammunition supply points (ASP) of progressively higher units (corps, army, etc.) until he could get his requisition filled. When not in combat, trucks used for ammunition maintained an initial load that was additional to what the men carried on their persons. This initial supply was calculated to last until a regular flow of ammunition from a higher headquarters supply source could be established. The actual functioning of the system varied with the type of unit involved.

In the weapons company each gun squad would unload its weapon and as much ammunition as it could carry from its weapons carrier, once this vehicle had reached its "off carrier" position. In offensive operations the weapons carriers stayed as close to their gun squads as possible, keeping their ammunition on board so they could easily move it to follow the course of the battle. Squad ammunition bearers (or pioneer platoon members) would return to the carriers for more ammunition as required. When directed by the transport sergeant or corporals, a few carriers at a time would return to the rear to pick up more ammunition. In the defense, the weapons carriers usually dumped their ammunition as close to the guns as possible and then moved well to the rear. They might also create small additional dumps near command posts.

In the antitank company (and the battalion antitank platoons) the procedure was similar except that prime movers almost always remained with their guns. Each antitank company section had a ³/₄-ton truck and each battalion antitank squad had a jeep that could stand by as a mobile ammunition dump or be sent to the rear for more ammunition. The ammunition vehicle in each platoon in the cannon company was a 2¹/₂-ton truck and trailer.

In a rifle company, one weapons carrier carried the 60mm mortars and their ammunition and the other carried the two LMGs and their ammunition. Just prior to combat each rifleman would receive 96 rounds in addition to the 40 he was supposed to be carrying. Each BAR would get 300 additional rounds (divided evenly between the BAR man, his assistant, and one rifleman) in addition to 240 already carried. Hand and rifle grenades would be issued as well. The two service company ammunition trucks in the battalion transportation section would "top off" the rifle company weapons carriers, replacing whatever they had issued to their respective companies. The trucks would then drop whatever they had left at the battalion ASP and head for an army ASP to pick up another load.

The infantry battalion ASP would be positioned close to the companies it served, but where trucks could load or unload under cover. It could shift as necessary to conform to the tactical situation. The battalion pioneer platoon would operate it under the supervision of the battalion supply officer. Weapons carriers arriving there in search of ammunition would be loaded and sent back as long as ammunition remained. Thereafter, the weapons carriers would be placed under regimental control and ordered to proceed to the regimental ASP. Designated by the regimental commander with the advice of his supply officer (S-4) and operated by the regimental munitions officer, the regimental ASP could be two or three miles to the rear (depending on the road net) and on, or near, the MSR (main supply route). The ASP could move according to the tactical situation. Empty vehicles could be loaded here with any available ammunition or directed to an army level ASP by way of the division supply point (usually just a control point). Service company trucks were supposed to conduct these runs, but company weapons carriers might do so if the need was great. There, they picked up a new load of ammunition and returned to the regimental ASP by the same route. Upon arrival, loaded vehicles could be held in reserve, sent to a battalion ASP, or unloaded and sent back for more ammunition.

This identification photo shows a CCKW-352 2¹/₂-ton cargo truck (short wheel base) in side view. It was taken at the Desert Training Center, Indio, CA on June 8, 1942.

This process would continue until the fighting had ceased and all ammunition vehicles had recovered their rated loads. It was a race against time. The next load of ammunition had to arrive before the troops consumed the current supply. Naturally, shorter distances and better roads would mean that the system could work with fewer or smaller trucks (or both). However, a regiment in serious combat would almost always need more than its organic trucks to maintain its ammunition supplies. A lack of trucks could reduce firepower even more than a lack of heavy weapons. Truck reinforcements could come from the divisional quartermaster truck company but would be mainly from truck units serving under corps or army command.

Artillery logistics

The artillery supply system differed from the infantry system in that the artillery was fully motorized, operated further to the rear, and had a far larger requirement for ammunition. Most activity occurred at the battalion and battery levels. The division artillery headquarters battery had no logistics assets other than what it needed to maintain itself. Even more than the division S-4, the artillery S-4 could do little more than monitor the artillery supply situation and ask for help, as it was needed. He had so little to do as S-4 that he also served as S-1.

Every headquarters, howitzer, or service battery included a maintenance section. Although this maintenance section did include a few mechanics and, until June 1942 an extra 2¹/₂-ton truck to serve as a wrecker, it was really the battery supply section. The cooks, the supply sergeant, a .50-cal machine-gun team, and the kitchen and supply trucks were all part of it. A field kitchen when mounted in a truck could prepare meals on the move. The battery operated far enough from the frontline that the field kitchens could accompany their parent batteries.

Each artillery battalion service battery operated a service platoon and an ammunition train. The battery commander doubled as battalion S-4. The service platoon included a battalion maintenance section that really did fix trucks. Its supply section functioned like the supply section in the infantry regimental service company but without the ammunition group. Its two cargo trucks carried fuel and rations beyond that carried in the battery maintenance sections.

A howitzer battery was centered on its four gun sections, each with a howitzer and its crew and prime mover. A gun crew and its equipment did not leave a lot of space in the truck for ammunition. Therefore, each battery had a "fifth section" with a pair of cargo trucks with trailers in lieu of a gun. The fifth section was really the battery ammunition section but it provided local antiaircraft defense as well. Also, the battalion ammunition train included a section of three or four additional ammunition trucks for each firing battery.

Artillery ammunition was normally allocated as credits. This meant that a given amount of ammunition was reserved for a given unit at a given ASP within a given period of time. For example, the 3d Infantry Division Artillery might be told that it had a credit of five units of fire for all ammunition classes available for pickup at the First Army ASP Number 3 between 1800 hours on January 10 and 1800 hours on January 12. Since this ammunition was intended to support a particular operation, any amounts left undrawn when the credit expired would revert to the headquarters that had originally allocated it.

An artillery battalion usually hauled their own ammunition using trucks from the ammunition train and "fifth sections" (which were sometimes pooled with the ammunition train) almost exclusively. However, it might also get space for its ammunition in a corps or army quartermaster train. Although the army supply points were supposed to provide labor to load ammunition trucks, these vehicles carried extra ammunition handlers (one per truck for 105mm howitzers, two for 155mm). These were for unloading ammunition at a firing point or loading it from a nearby cache where other laborers might not be available. A 2^1/$_2$-ton truck carried racks for 36 155mm shells and could tow 18 more in a 1-ton or M10 ammunition trailer. A 4-ton carried racks for 54 155mm shells and could also tow a 1 ton ammunition trailer (it only carried 36 shells if it was towing a howitzer instead). The 105mm ammunition came in two-round wooden boxes (weighing a little over 100 pounds each) that could be stacked up to a vehicle's weight limit. By artillery standards this was not a lot of ammunition. A truck would have to make many trips to the ASP to keep its guns supplied. Under these conditions the ammunition handlers could also serve as relief drivers to maintain delivery schedules.

Whenever an artillery unit moved, it was very desirable that it do so with its normal organic load, including its full load of ammunition. Ideally, ammunition to be used from any given firing position should be staged there in advance and then used in lieu of the ammunition that the guns carried with them. Unused ammunition would have to be abandoned, though the battery concerned was required to notify the next senior headquarters of its location.

The medical treatment and evacuation system

By 1942 nearly every Army regiment or separate battalion had its medical detachment. This detachment was organized according to a scheme first introduced by Army Medical Corps Major Jonathan Letterman. Letterman was a Civil War veteran who had been appalled at the plight of wounded men who often lay for days on the battlefield before being picked up. After that they were

A WC-54 ^{3}/$_4$-ton ambulance. (Recognition photo from about June 1942.)

either operated on by overworked field surgeons under barbaric conditions or sent on a long journey to a permanent hospital while receiving little or no treatment along the way. Men who survived this ordeal were often maimed for life. Letterman's reforms began with detailing enough stretcher-bearers to get the wounded off the battlefield early and into the hands of trained medical orderlies. These medics furnished essential treatment only, and then sent a casualty through successive stations in a systematic evacuation chain. Each station could give more treatment than the previous one. The end of the chain would be a general hospital, but only the most gravely wounded needed to go that far. Men with less serious injuries could get rapid and adequate treatment at the lower stations well before shock, gangrene, or other complications set in. They would not only survive but could even return to full duty. Letterman's ideas, though sometimes implemented locally, ran into a great deal of opposition and were not officially adopted until the Spanish-American War. In the 1942 infantry regiment, the medical detachment had sections serving the regimental headquarters and each battalion. The battalion sections provided aidmen ("medics") for every rifle, heavy machine gun, 81mm mortar and antitank platoon. Only the pioneers and rifle company weapons platoons received none. Medics located wounded men and rendered essential first aid, calling for a stretcher party if the patient could not walk or directing him to an aid station if he could (and still needed treatment). One or two surgeons and their enlisted assistants manned each battalion aid station. They could offer more care than a medic but they only did what was needed to stabilize the patient and save life or limb.

Medics of Company "C," 118th Medical Battalion, 43d Division administering plasma on New Georgia, July 19, 1943. Like other collecting companies, Company "C" was mainly an ambulance and stretcher-bearer unit but it did include a small station platoon that could establish a dressing station like this one. More frequently, it merely augmented the battalion clearing company.

The regimental section included the regimental surgeon with an aid station and medics (but no stretcher teams) for the regimental headquarters, antitank, cannon and service companies. It also supplied essential dental care for the entire regiment. The division medical battalion, using its three collecting companies (one per regiment), collected wounded from the aid stations and evacuated them to its clearing platoons (division field hospitals). From there they would go to corps or army hospitals. The preferred evacuation method was by ambulance. Stretcher teams were only for evacuating wounded from terrain where the ambulances could not go.

Supply functions of the engineers

Besides maps and potable water, the Corps of Engineers furnished certain Class II supply items such as compasses, surveying instruments, and slide rules. It also supplied Class IV items such as fortification material, paint (except ordnance paint), and nails. The division combat engineer battalion was not normally involved in the stocking and issue of any of these items except water. Class II and Class IV supplies were allocated through the applicable G-4 or S-4 of the using unit, who arranged for the users to pick up the material from engineer depots or distributing points. Distribution of maps was similarly the province of the G-2 or S-2. However, the engineer battalion was involved with the issue of captured or locally furnished Class IV items and the issue of captured maps. If significant quantities of captured or local Class IV material had to be issued, the battalion headquarters and service company would set up a distribution point for that purpose. Using units would pick up these supplies themselves.

Potable water was the province of the supply section of the engineer battalion headquarters and service company. This section included four water supply units, each carried in a separate 2^1/2-ton truck. Only three units had crews. These functioned as division-level water points (one per infantry regiment). They moved frequently to keep abreast of the combat situation. The fourth unit was a spare. The engineer battalion S-4 was also the division water officer.

Divisional ordnance and quartermaster units

Originally the division ordnance was only a small section in the division headquarters. The division quartermaster element was a small battalion with a headquarters company that included an oversized motor maintenance platoon for the Third-Echelon maintenance (see below) of the division's trucks. The battalion also had a standard quartermaster truck company. However, in September 1942 the Ordnance Corps received the responsibility for all motor maintenance.

This meant that the infantry division would only have a quartermaster company rather than a battalion, but it would also receive an ordnance light maintenance company to replace the earlier quartermaster battalion maintenance platoon and to perform weapons maintenance.

The Army classified maintenance into four "echelons" (see table 13). The drivers and mechanics in the user units, although not normally ordnance personnel, performed First and Second Echelon maintenance while Ordnance Corps units handled Third and Fourth. The ordnance company was far too small for a division. A large enough ordnance unit would need more men than the Army was willing to spare and would not be fully employed when the division was not in combat. The Army therefore authorized the battalion and regimental maintenance sections to perform not only Second-Echelon maintenance but also as much third echelon maintenance as they could. The ordnance company would limit itself to Third-Echelon jobs that required special tools or skills but not too much time. Lengthy repairs would go to a depot. The idea was to minimize the manpower devoted to maintenance, but in practice the ordnance company could only repair about one-third of the trucks that required its special expertise.

The new quartermaster company was the truck company that had previously been part of the old quartermaster battalion but was now reinforced with a division quartermaster section and a service platoon. The truck platoons were the division commander's transportation reserve. Each truck had an organic cargo load assigned to it, which made the truck platoons a reserve of supplies as well as transportation. If needed to carry special loads (or to transport infantry) they could do so after dropping their organic loads. However an infantry division needed six truck companies (18 platoons) in order to carry its nine infantry battalions (the rest of the division was already motorized). However, it would take much more than just the three truck platoons organic to the division to meet its supply requirements if it was engaged in serious combat. Therefore, the division almost always needed extra quartermaster truck companies (operating under the division quartermaster). Besides its truck platoons the quartermaster company had a service platoon. This was a labor unit meant to load and unload trucks and sort supplies into lots for user unit pickup. It was a holdover from when the division was a normal part of the supply chain. However, the Quartermaster Department insisted that it was still needed because it was the only source of division-level labor. Casual labor was indeed needed at the division level, although not always in support of quartermaster requirements.

Combat operations

The following section briefly describes campaigns that are examples of the early offensives, and the role of the infantry divisions in 1942–43.

Papua New Guinea

In March 1942 General Douglas MacArthur arrived in Australia from the Philippines to assume command of the Southwest Pacific Area (see map on page 70). The US 41st Infantry Division arrived in Australia during April to help defend it from the Japanese. Nearly all of Australia's combat-experienced soldiers were either fighting under British command in North Africa and the Middle East or had surrendered to the Japanese at Singapore and elsewhere. The Australian government immediately called its overseas forces home but the British government promised that if Australia left one infantry division in North Africa until the end of 1942, the United States would send another of its divisions to Australia. The 32d Infantry Division reached Australia later in May.

The Japanese threat to Australia did not take long to materialize. Since 1906, Papua, which is the southeastern quarter of New Guinea, had been an Australian possession. In 1920 Australia had received a League of Nations Mandate over the former German territories in northeastern New Guinea, New Britain, and the Admiralty and Solomon Islands. Australia regarded these territories as a buffer zone against an attack from Japan. The Japanese saw them as a buffer to protect their newly won empire from attack from the south. In January 1942, the Japanese seized New Britain and began to occupy the other islands as well. By May the Japanese decided that they needed to extend their buffer by seizing the Papua Territory, including the south coast port and airfield at Port Moresby. Japanese aircraft and submarines based at Port Moresby and in the southern Solomons could attack the sea communication between Australia and the United States. A Japanese seaborne attempt to capture Port Moresby was turned back in May 1942. In July the Japanese put a force ashore at Buna on the Papuan north coast to attack Port Moresby across the Papuan peninsula.

Two soldiers from the 128th Infantry, 32d Division on New Guinea examine a Japanese pillbox for possible booby traps and land mines, December 21, 1942. This pillbox was near Cape Endaiadere, about two miles east of Buna Mission.

USSR

CANADA

NORTH PACIFIC AREA

UNITED STATES

CENTRAL PACIFIC AREA

JAPAN

CHINA

$P \quad A \quad C \quad I \quad F \quad I \quad C \qquad O \quad C \quad E \quad A \quad N$

$A \quad R \quad E \quad A \quad S$

FORMOSA

Midway

HAWAIIAN IS.

PHILIPPINE IS.

MARSHALL IS.

.Palmyra
.Fanning
. Christmas

GILBERT IS.

NETHERLANDS INDIES

NEW
GUINEA

Canton

SOLOMON IS.

SAMOA

*SOUTHWEST
PACIFIC AREA*

FIJI

AUSTRALIA

NEW
CALEDONIA

SOUTH PACIFIC AREA

NEW
ZEALAND

——— Area boundaries

·········· Subdivision boundaries

0	1,000	2,000 mi
0	1,000	2,000	3,000km

The Pacific areas of operations,
August 1, 1942.

Members of the cannon company,
186th Infantry, 41st Division firing
an Australian 25-pounder (87.6mm)
field gun during beach practise at
Buna Mission Point, New Guinea
on May 20, 1943. The self-propelled
guns originally supplied for the
cannon companies of regiments
operating in the Pacific Theater
were clearly of little use in most
situations, so the cannon companies
frequently experimented with
alternative, lighter weapons.

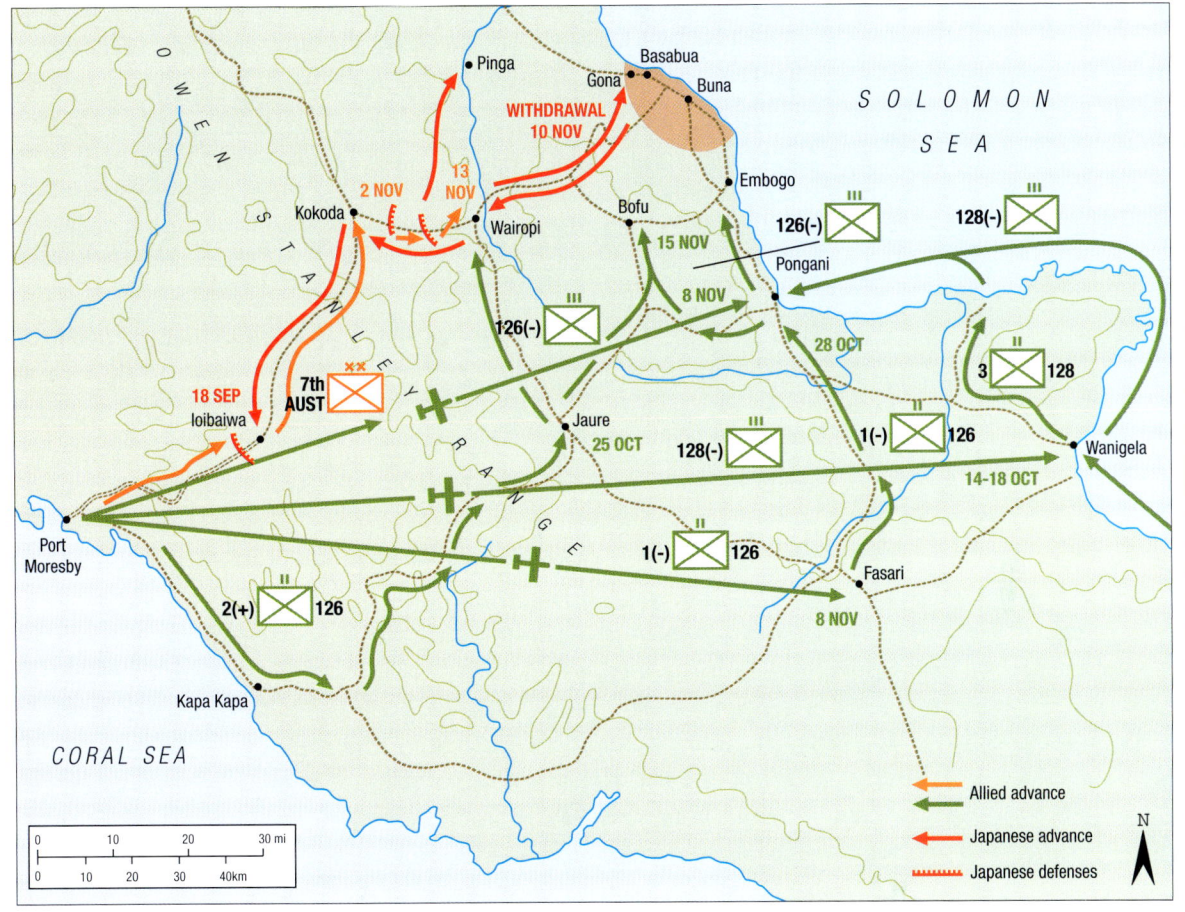

The fight for the Owen Stanley Range and the Kokoda Trail, New Guinea, September 18–November 15, 1942.

Australia took alarm at this development and heavily reinforced Port Moresby, but it was not until September that Australia was able to turn back the Japanese advance, and then only after the Japanese had covered three-quarters of the distance between Buna and Port Moresby. It had taken four Australian brigades (equivalent to infantry regiments) to defeat two Japanese regiments, which had no air cover and were suffering much more than the Australians from a lack of food, water, and ammunition, and from a hot, damp, mountainous, roadless, jungle wasteland. For the Australians it may not have been the most glorious victory ever won, but it was won and the Japanese retreat soon became a rout, with the Australians in hot pursuit.

To exploit this victory and to clear the Japanese out of their north-coast bases at Buna, Gona, and Sanamanda (which would eliminate any threat to Port Moresby) General MacArthur decided to send the 32d Division to New Guinea. This 32d was unprepared for the Pacific. Originally earmarked for Northern Ireland, its orders were changed at the last moment. Its men came mainly from northern states with cold winters and were not in the best physical shape. Attempts at instituting realistic combat training in Australia were interrupted by frequent moves. There were equipment deficiencies as well. The division had received no carbines and had to use pistols, supplemented with extra rifles and sub machine guns as substitutes. No jungle uniforms were available. Standard uniforms soon became unbearable in the extreme tropical heat. The division would fight in terrain that its planners never foresaw. Few radios would work in the heat and damp. The military trucks upon which the divisional logistics system depended would be largely useless. Supplies could only move by air, native bearer or in some cases by boat.

The division also had to make drastic changes in its organization. It had to leave all its artillery and nearly all of its antitank guns and trucks behind. Regimental cannon and antitank companies served as additional infantry without guns. Nearly all the stoves and field kitchens had to be left behind. The few that were brought along had to go to the medical units so they could sterilize their instruments. Units that had to march through the jungle could carry neither their 81mm mortars nor their heavy machine guns, but they were to be flown out to them later. In many cases the battalion weapons companies took over some or all of the rifle companies' 60mm mortars and M1919A4 air-cooled Brownings as lighter substitutes for their own weapons.

Initially General MacArthur sent two 32d Division regiments (the 126th and 128th) to New Guinea with the third regiment (the 127th) to follow on later. The plan was to assemble as much of the division as possible on the north coast to the south and east of Buna so that the Americans could launch a flanking attack to the northwest while the Australian 7th Division pressed northeastward from Kokoda and Wairopi. The bulk of the 128th Infantry would fly to Wanigela and then, together with the 18th Australian Brigade flown in from Milne Bay, would move (much of the way by boat) to Embogo. There it would prepare its attack on the Japanese at Buna, only seven miles away. The 126th Infantry would march through the jungle from Kapa Kapa (on the south coast) to Jaure and then, following a track parallel to but 30 miles to the south of the Australians, to Bofu. This march was a disaster. The first (and, as it turned out, only) unit to attempt it was the 2d Battalion, 126th Infantry (2d/126th). Though the distance was less than 80 miles and airdropped supplies were available, the march took 12 days. The heat, sharp kunai grass, leeches, fever-bearing insects, razor-backed mountain ridges that were so steep that one had to cling to vines to maintain one's footing, and five days of steady rain that flooded the rivers and made cooking impossible all took their toll. The battalion began straggling into Jaure on October 25, its men sickly, their clothes in tatters, and much of its equipment discarded or lost and in no state to meet the enemy. However, after a relatively easy march to Natunga the battalion rested for more than a week, replaced its equipment losses and reached Bofu by mid November. Its experience had made it clear that if troops were to reach a movement objective in a condition to fight, they would have to move by air or boat most of the way. The rest of the 126th Infantry therefore, using some newly discovered airfields, flew over the mountains and ended up at Pongani (1st/126th) and just south of Bofu at Natunga (3d/126th and regimental headquarters).

The 32d Division attack on Buna began on November 19. As of November 16 there were about 6,500 Japanese in the entire Buna-Gona area. Of these, about 1,300 were unarmed laborers; another 2,500 were sick or wounded; and 850 more were unarmed or lightly armed support troops. Combatants included a 900-man naval garrison for Buna plus a reduced strength antiaircraft battalion (250 men) also at Buna and the remains of the 15th Combat Engineer Regiment (450 men armed with rifles only). In addition, the remnants of the 41st and 144th Infantry Regiments, which had tried to capture Port Moresby, were outside the perimeter opposing the Australian advance. The Japanese situation was becoming desperate. Food and water were in critically short supply. Many men had to carry bamboo spears instead of rifles.

Although Allied intelligence erred in believing there were only about 2,000 to 2,500 Japanese in the Buna-Gona perimeter, Japanese intelligence fared worse. They paid so much attention to the Australian advance that they failed to detect the Americans on their left flank. When the 32d Division launched its attack, it caught the Japanese defenders of Buna completely by surprise. However, the Japanese had been fortifying Buna for months. Although they lacked proper materials and their trenches and underground bunkers filled with water whenever it rained, the fortifications presented a formidable obstacle.

For the attack on Buna, the 32d Division had only its 128th Infantry and a battalion of the 126th. The rest of the 126th was assisting the Australians. The biggest single problem was a lack of artillery. Only one American 105mm howitzer ever served in the campaign so the 32d Division artillery commander had to make use of lighter Australian weapons. Of these he managed to secure two 3.7in. mountain howitzers and four 25-pounder field guns (with more promised later). The deputy artillery commander also formed seventeen 81mm mortars into a massed battery that he himself directed. Inasmuch as there were no flamethrowers, troops had to rely on satchel charges and hand grenades to reduce Japanese pillboxes.

Adding to the Americans' difficulties Japanese destroyers in separate runs on the nights of November 17, 18, and 21 managed to deliver reinforcements. These were an infantry battalion (3d/229th Infantry), an attached mountain battery and 1,300 replacements for the 144th Infantry. The battalion and 500 replacements went to Buna. Together with the Navy garrison and the antiaircraft battalion they made a relatively formidable garrison.

As a result of all these limitations the 32d Division attack stalled. By December 2 the enemy fortifications were largely intact; the Americans had sustained 492 casualties and their morale was beginning to crack. Lieutenant General Robert Eichelberger, commanding the I Corps, which controlled the 32d and 41st Divisions, intervened at this point. He relieved the 32d Division commander and two of his principal subordinates. He improved the supply situation and ordered more bombing sorties from Fifth Air Force to defeat Japanese attempts to bring in supplies or reinforcements. The Australians also supplied five Bren gun carriers to give some much-needed armor support to "Warren" Task Force, which was the 32d Division designation for its forces attacking Buna to the northeast along the coast (mainly the 1st and 3d/128th Infantry). The attack soon ran into trouble as the Japanese quickly knocked out all five of the open-topped vehicles with hand grenades. However, to the west the "Urbana" Task Force (mainly 3d/128th and 1st/126th) did make some gains, one platoon penetrating all the way to the sea. Over the next few days, the missing 32d Division regiment, the 127th, was rushed by air to reinforce Urbana. Thus strengthened, Urbana took Buna village on December 14. Bolstered by four newly arrived Australian-manned M3 Stuart tanks and two battalions of Australian infantry, Warren Force renewed its attack on December 18. The tanks proved decisive and enabled Warren Force to penetrate the Japanese perimeter far enough to seize its two airfields. Although the Japanese had managed to bring in a few more reinforcements they were at this point completely out of food. Most of their leaders were dead and their defense began to collapse. Urbana Force overran their last stronghold at Buna Mission on January 2, bringing the battle for Buna to a close. The Australians reduced Gona and Sanamanda a few days later.

These battles had completely worn out the 32d Division. Out of 10,825 men in its three regiments it had suffered 9,609 casualties of whom 7,125 were sick, 804 had been killed or died of wounds and 1,680 were wounded. The 32d Division had received almost no replacements so it had all but ceased to function. Total Allied battle casualties were 3,095 killed and 5,451 wounded. The 163d Infantry of the 41st Division arrived in time to participate in the final battles (and sustain 97 killed, 524 wounded, and 83 missing). The rest of the 41st Division arrived in February to relieve the 32d Division and send its remnants home. Japanese losses to all causes (including many to disease or suicide but excluding wounded and sick who escaped or were evacuated) were about 12,000 of whom 350 were prisoners. Relative to the number of troops engaged these battles had been among the costliest of the Pacific War.

The Buna perimeter, New Guinea, November 16–21, 1942.

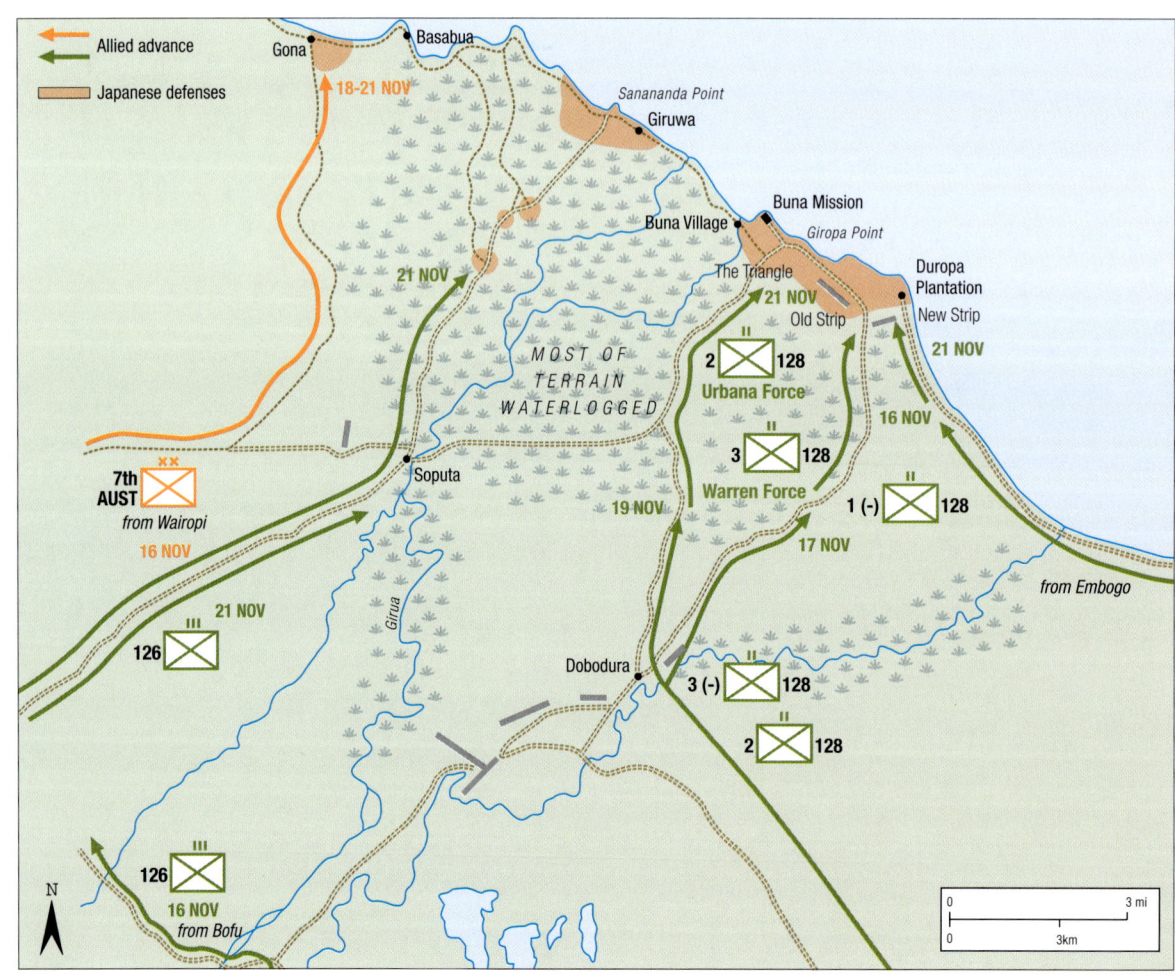

New Georgia

As early as July of 1942, General MacArthur was planning a series of offensives aimed at capturing Rabaul. Rabaul, the principal town on the island of New Britain, commanded an airfield and an excellent harbor. Its possession enabled the Japanese to continue to threaten the sea-lanes between the United States and Australia and to block Allied advances along northern New Guinea towards the Philippines. MacArthur's plan called for two mutually supporting advances that would culminate in a converging attack on Rabaul. One would be along the north coast of New Guinea. The other would be through the Solomon Islands. However none of this could occur until Guadalcanal and Papua were secure and even after that there were not enough Allied ground or air forces available for any offensives until mid 1943.

Forces from the South Pacific Area (adjacent to MacArthur's Southwest Pacific Area) would execute the advance through the Solomons. Their first objective was Munda Point on the island of New Georgia. The Japanese had completed an airfield there in December 1942 and another one at Vila on nearby Kolombangara (see map below). These airfields were intended to support the recapture of Henderson Field on Guadalcanal. Although this was no longer feasible the airfields were still a threat. In Allied hands they would greatly facilitate an advance on Rabaul.

A series of coral reefs effectively protected Munda from any seaborne assault. The Americans would have to attack it overland in an operation to be named *Toenails*.

Landings in New Georgia, June 21–July 5, 1943.

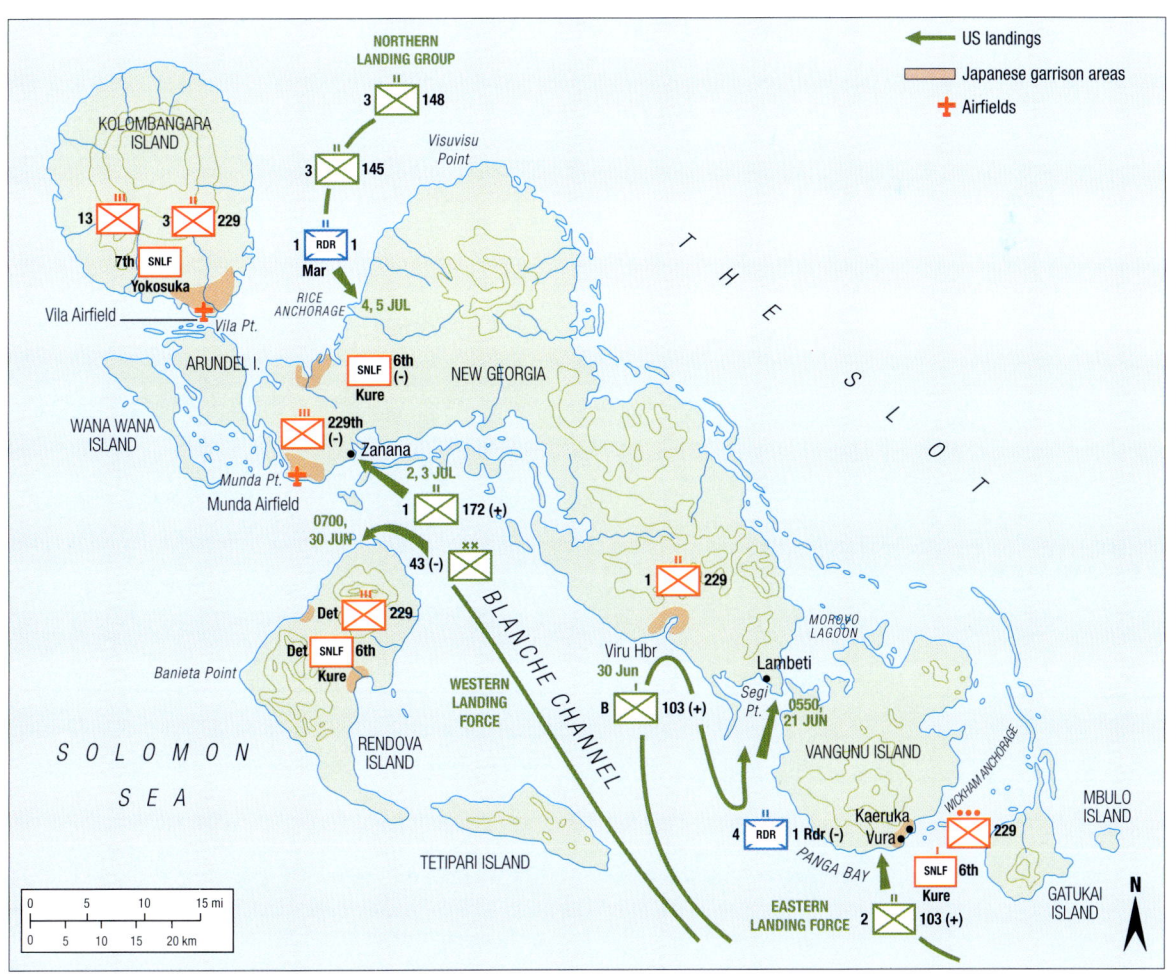

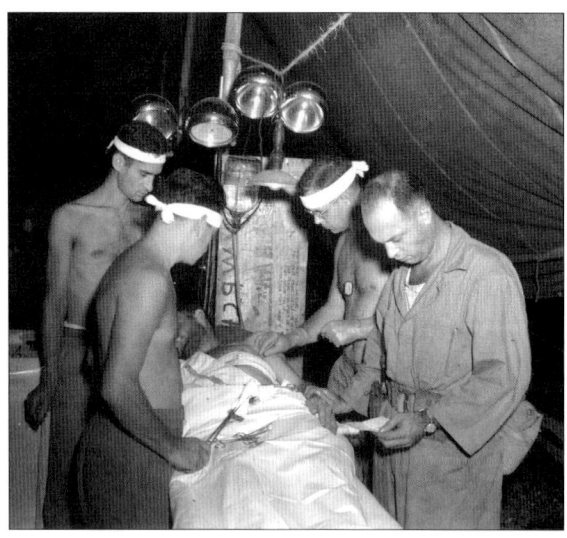

A view of surgical work being done in the field in New Georgia by members of the clearing company, 112th Medical Battalion, 37th Infantry Division. This photo shows the concluding procedure for treating sucking chest wounds. Air is being withdrawn from the patient's pleural spaces.

In terms of its climate, topography, and development, New Georgia was much like the rest of the Solomons and New Guinea. Their interiors were largely unexplored and they were hot, wet, swampy, mountainous, heavily vegetated, and unhealthy. However, compared to previous campaigns, American forces would be better prepared and the distances would be shorter. The ground force for *Toenails* would be built around the 37th and 43d Infantry divisions.

Operation *Toenails* opened with the seizure of Segi Point, Viru Harbor, and Wickham anchorage by about half of the 103d Infantry (reinforced) of the 43d Division plus the 4th US Marine Raider Battalion and Navy "Seabee" engineers to build an airfield at Segi Point. The Japanese forces in the vicinity were scattered in numerous detachments and could offer only sporadic resistance. At the same time (June 30) the main body of the 43d Division (6,000 men from the 169th and 172d Infantry, and other units) seized Rendova and adjacent islands and easily overwhelmed the small Japanese force stationed there. However a Japanese air strike on July 2 caused considerable damage to the mountains of supplies piled up on the beach. The plan was to use Rendova as a staging point for troops and supplies to be used in New Georgia and also as a firing position from which long-range artillery could keep Munda under pressure.

Rendova turned out to be too waterlogged to make a good supply base and it was not within easy artillery range of Munda. However, the "outer islands" off the New Georgia southwest coast provided much firmer ground. Field artillery positioned in these islands could not only hit Munda but also support a land campaign along the south coast.

Toenails had as its objective not only Munda but also Bairoko, about nine miles due north of Munda (see map on page 78). Bairoko harbor, on the Kula Gulf, was important because it was the only point on New Georgia where large ships could approach. For the Japanese it was the logical supply and retreat route. Beginning on July 3, a southern landing group, consisting of two-thirds of the 43d Division plus the 37th Division 155mm (M1918) howitzer battalion and part of the 9th Marine Defense Battalion (MDB; mainly an antiaircraft unit but including two batteries of 155mm guns and an oversized platoon of light tanks), landed at Zanama, intending to march to Munda, a little over five miles away. A northern landing group, consisting of the 1st Marine Raider Battalion and the 3d/145th and 3d/148th Infantry (37th Division) landed at Rice Anchorage, about six miles northeast of Bairoko on July 4 and 5. Marching overland they planned to reach Enogai about July 7 and then Bairoko.

The American invasion had taken the Japanese by surprise but they recovered quickly. Army and Navy personnel on Kolombangara, New Georgia, and adjacent islands totaled about 10,500. Most were evenly divided between Munda and Vila but Munda had mainly support troops and required immediate reinforcement. One battalion arrived there from Vila on July 4 and part of another two days later. Additional reinforcements were dispatched from Rabaul.

The northern landing group began its advance on July 5. The 3d/145th (minus two rifle companies) stayed behind to defend Rice Anchorage. The 3d/148th established a roadblock on the Munda–Bairoko trail on July 8. Of course the jungle prevented the 3d/148th from using its weapons carriers and the weight of its 81mm mortars and heavy machine guns greatly hampered its progress. The more lightly equipped Marine Raiders moved much faster and on July 11 they had secured a Japanese battery at Engolai Point, which they made their base. The 3d/148th roadblock repelled one attack on July 10 but the roadblock was too far from Bairoko to threaten it and Japanese reinforcements landed at Bairoko could easily reach Munda by using trails further west. On July 17 the 3d/148th moved to Triri from where it would march on Bairoko. Half of the already half-strength 1st and the newly arrived 4th Marine Raider Battalions and two 3d/145th rifle companies would attack Bairoko from Enogai along the north coast. The 3d/148th would attack from Triri to the southeast. The Americans attacked on July 20 having neither reconnoitered Bairoko nor submitted timely requests for air and naval gunfire support. The jungle canopy rendered the Raiders' 60mm mortars useless and there were no weapons to deal with the Japanese pillboxes. The attack failed and the Americans were forced to withdraw to Enogai and Triri after sustaining heavy casualties.

The southern landing group was also faring poorly. Once again, the heat and hostile terrain were as much an obstacle as the Japanese. The only "road" that the force could use was the Munda Trail (and a trail is all it was) that ran westward from a short distance north of Zanana. Upon coming ashore the 43d Division would position its 169th and 172d Regiments along line of departure on the Barike River. From there they would launch the attack on Munda.

Company "L," 27th Infantry crosses a stream as it advances along the Zieta Trail, New Georgia on August 12, 1943.

Unfortunately the reinforced 1st/172d Infantry began its move to the Barike on July 4 before the rest of the division was ready. This alerted the Japanese, who established a defense on a complex of ridges that ran northwest from the village of Ilangana on the beach to about 3,000 yards inland. They also deployed small forces to block the trail and delay the Americans.

Meanwhile, the 43d Division placed the 172d Infantry along the coast and the 169th on its right and just to the north of it. The 169th straddled the Munda Trail but a Japanese trail-block delayed its arrival at the Barike until July 8.

H-hour came one day late, on July 9 but despite heavy preparatory fire from artillery, air strikes and naval gunfire, the two regiments made almost no progress. The cause seems to have been mainly the terrain and the swollen river. The main Japanese defenses were still over 2,500 yards away. The 169th advanced along the trail in single file because movement away from the trail was so difficult. If even a squad leader tried to deploy his men in a skirmish line he would lose contact with most of them. The Japanese could stop a whole battalion with just a few men. They had been harassing the inexperienced 169th nightly since July 6. By the night before H-Hour the 169th had become so jittery that they started a major firefight among themselves. This caused a number of casualties (some fatal) and did nothing for morale.

Next day the attack made much more progress. The 169th covered 1,500 yards before hitting another trail block and the 172d covered 2,500 yards. Despite their slow advance the Americans had outrun their supply lines. The division engineers were converting Munda Trail into a road that at least jeeps could use but they had to build a couple of bridges and for several days this meant that supplies would have to be hand carried from a road terminus that was some distance from the front. This required nearly one-half of the combat troops. Although aircraft could drop supplies on the frontline there were never enough planes to deliver sufficient quantities.

To resolve the supply situation the 172d was ordered to move to Laiana Beach (only a few hundred yards from the Japanese defenses at Ilangana) and establish it as a new beachhead where supplies could be landed much closer to friendly forces. This it accomplished on July 13 despite the terrain, Japanese

(continues on page 80)

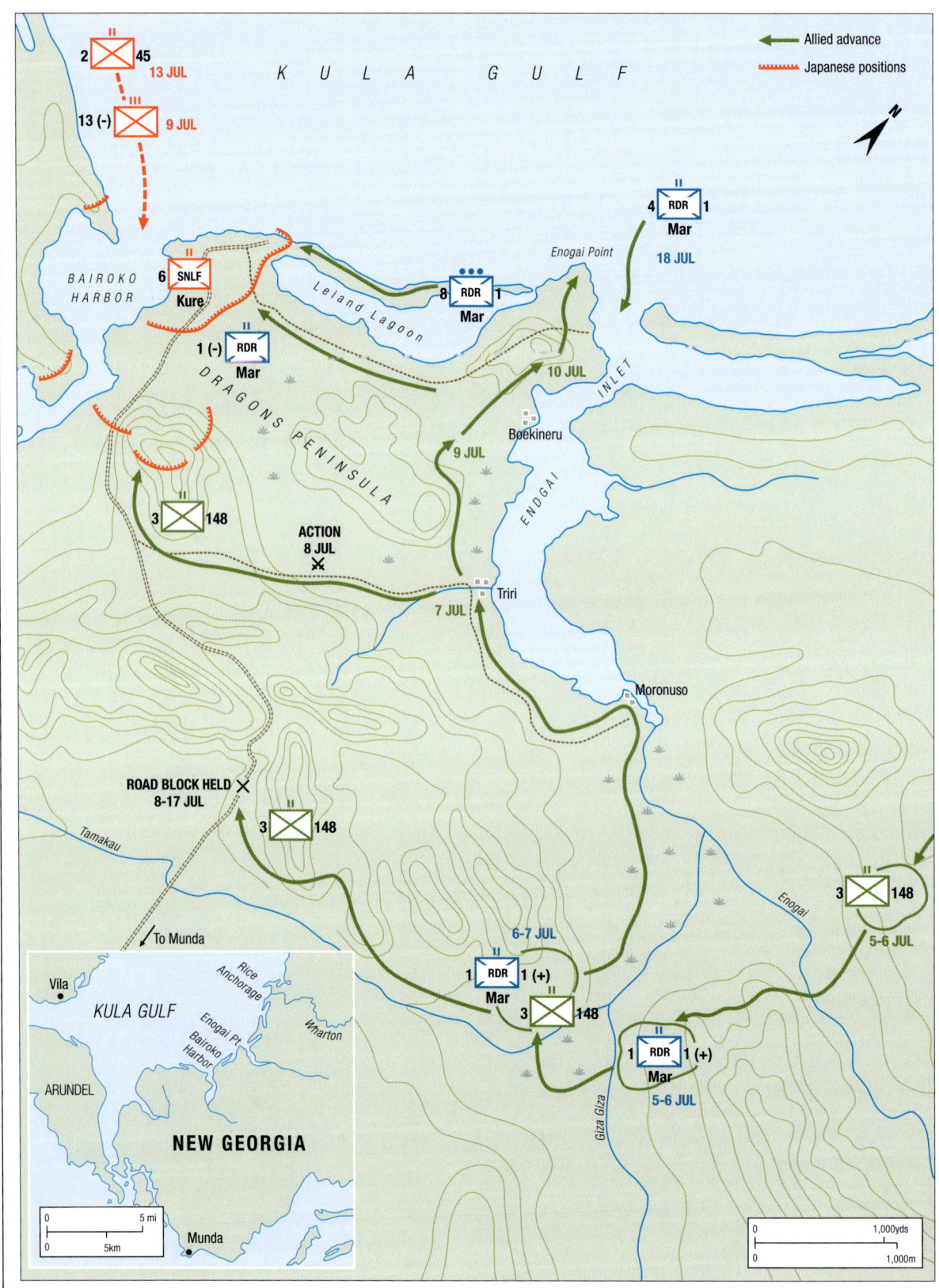

Allied advance
Japanese positions

K U L A G U L F

2 ⊠ 45 13 JUL

13 (-) ⊠ 9 JUL

4 RDR 1
Mar
18 JUL

Enogai Point

6 SNLF
Kure

8 RDR 1
Mar

B A I R O K O
H A R B O R

Leland Lagoon

1 (-) RDR
Mar

10 JUL

Boekineru

D R A G O N S   P E N I N S U L A

9 JUL

INLET

ENDGAI

3 ⊠ 148

ACTION
8 JUL

7 JUL

Triri

Moronuso

ROAD BLOCK HELD
8-17 JUL

Tamakau

3 ⊠ 148

Enogai

3 ⊠ 148

5-6 JUL

To Munda

6-7 JUL

1 RDR 1 (+)
Mar

3 ⊠ 148

1 RDR 1 (+)
Mar
5-6 JUL

Giza Giza

Vila

KULA GULF

Rice
Anchorage

Wharton

Enogai Pt

Bairoko
Harbor

ARUNDEL

NEW GEORGIA

0   5 mi
0   5km

Munda

0   1,000yds
0   1,000m

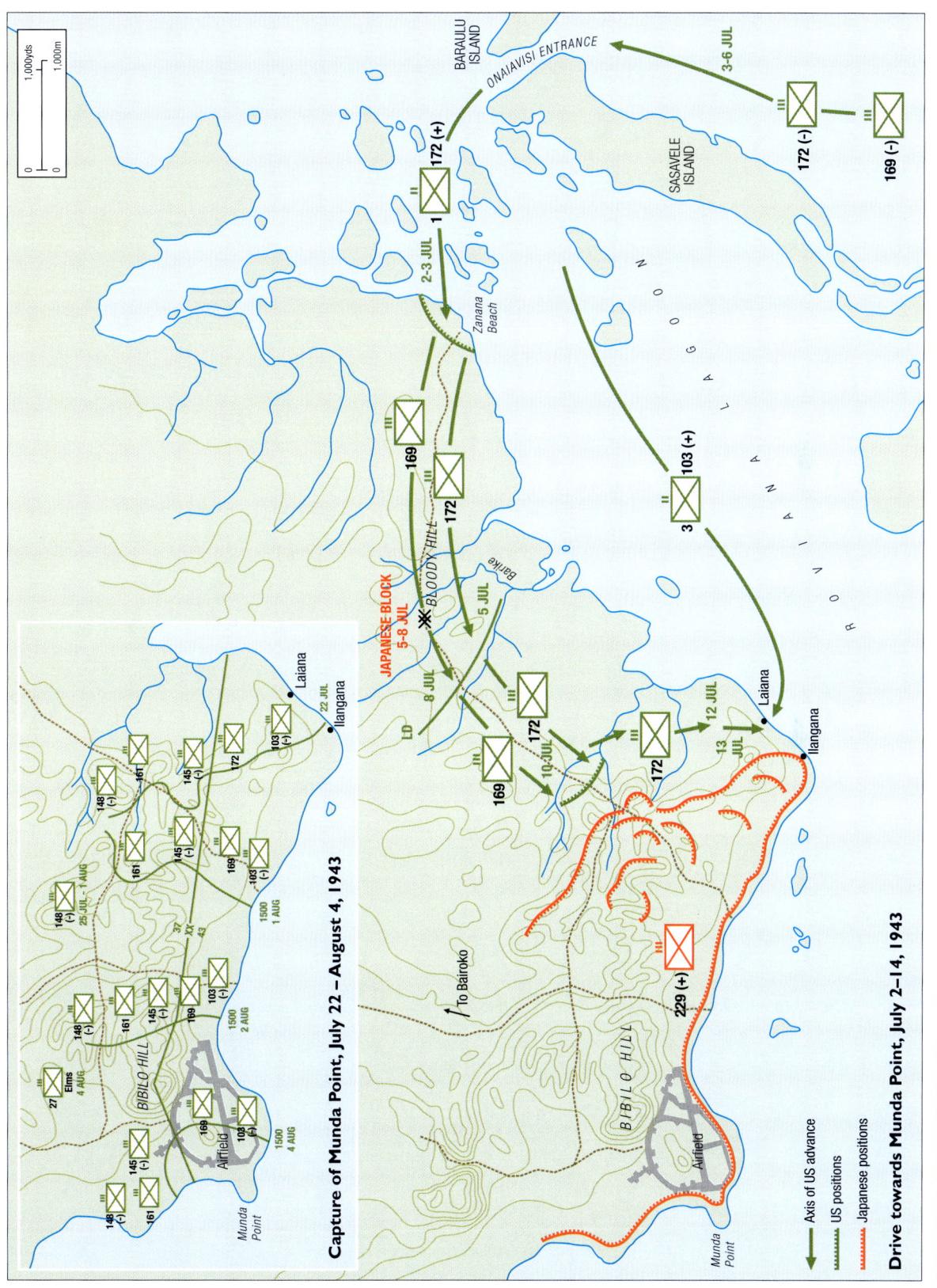

Capture of Munda Point, July 22 – August 4, 1943

Drive towards Munda Point, July 2–14, 1943

Axis of US advance
US positions
Japanese positions

The drive towards Munda Point, New Georgia, July 2–14, 1943, and its subsequent capture.

mortar and machine-gun fire, and a severe shortage of food and water. The next day, the reinforced 3d/103d Infantry landed at Laiana and re-supplied the by then starving 172d. Next day, the Americans attacked the main Japanese defenses. Members of the antitank platoon of the 3d/103d disassembled a 37mm gun, hand-carried it forward, reassembled it, and managed to destroy three Japanese pillboxes. Over the next week or so the 172d Infantry with six tanks from the 9th MDB destroyed several pillboxes near the beach and advanced about 600 yards. Though they had no antitank guns the Japanese managed to disable two tanks by using improvised weapons.

To the north, the 169th was actually making limited progress, the 3d/169th having advanced several hundred yards to seize some high ground that they called Reincke Ridge (named after the battalion commander) and Kelley Hill, which they held against Japanese counterattacks.

The supply situation was improving. The engineers had completed their bridges over the Barike and on July 14 made the Munda Trail trafficable for jeeps to within 500 yards of the 169th position. Engineers also opened a trail from Laiana to Munda Trail to motor traffic on July 20. Air-delivered supplies were no longer needed and as more trails were cut the overall logistical situation continued to improve.

The 43d Division attack was clearly failing and needed reinforcement. Between July 15 and 25 the main body of the 37th Division landed at Zanana and the headquarters of XIV Corps arrived to command both it and the 43d Division. Most of these units had reached New Georgia during the period July 15 and 25, and the 145th Infantry (37th Division) relieved the exhausted 169th. The 43d Division deployed its 103d and 172d regiments along the southern (coastal) half of the frontline while the 37th Division took over the northern (inland) half. XIV Corps brought in the 161st Infantry, 25th Division to New Georgia on July 22 to reinforce the 37th Division.

By this time the Japanese were manning their defense line with four infantry battalions (three from the 229th Infantry and one from the 230th) plus artillery and weapons units. Two battalions from Bairoko (from 13th Infantry) were to the north threatening the American right flank.

On July 25 the XIV Corps began its new offensive with the usual heavy air, artillery, and naval gunfire bombardment, but the attacks again made little progress. In the 43d Division, tanks and the first flamethrowers to be used on New Georgia spearheaded the assault. There were at first only six flamethrowers and their gunners had had only an hour of training, but together with the tanks and supporting artillery they met with great success. The 103d Infantry advanced 600 yards (on a 600-yard front) and shortened the 43d Division frontage from 1,700 yards to 1,400. Over the next four days the 43d inched forward and by July 31 had largely broken through the last real ridgeline between it and Munda. In the 37th Division sector an attempt by the 161st Infantry to pinch off an enemy salient on Bartley Ridge failed on July 25. Next day the attack was renewed, but with the support of six tanks from the newly arrived 10th MDB and a pair of newly acquired flamethrowers. This attack initially made some progress but two tanks were disabled, both flamethrower operators were killed, and the attackers withdrew to their starting positions. On July 28 an American patrol found the Japanese fortifications on Bartley Ridge mostly abandoned, but Horseshoe Hill continued to resist American attacks.

On the 37th Division right the 148th Infantry was the only regiment that was not faced with prepared enemy positions. It advanced rapidly round the Japanese north flank but it was urgently recalled when elements of the Japanese 13th Infantry from Bairoko appeared from the north and started to attack the 37th Division supply trail. The 2d/148th was further to the west and returned safely. The 1st/148th, however, was nearly cut off and only broke through to friendly lines with great difficulty, short of food and water and encumbered by 128 wounded.

The next day, the XIV Corps' advance met with little or no opposition. The Japanese had sustained heavy casualties, received few replacements, were worn out by continuous air and artillery bombardment, were very short of food and water, and they were withdrawing. The XIV Corps made rapid progress and the 169th Infantry actually reached the outer taxiway of the airfield by the end of the day. The Japanese defended Biblio and Kokengoio Hills in the middle of the base. This protected their retreat and prevented the Americans from completely securing Munda until August 4. Attempts to cut off the retreating Japanese generally failed since Bairoko was still open and in the jungle the lightly equipped Japanese found it relatively easy to evade the heavily equipped and slow-moving Americans. The 161st and newly arrived 27th Infantry marched north to help the battered northern force to take Bairoko, which they did in late August, far too late to prevent the escape of the Japanese.

Sicily and the battle for Troina

On the night of July 9–10, 1943, only two months after the end of the North African campaign, the Allies began Operation *Husky*, as their invasion of Sicily became known. The invasion force was the 15th Army Group, consisting of the British Eighth (five divisions plus reserves) and US Seventh Armies. Seventh Army included the 1st and 45th Infantry Divisions operating under II Corps and the 3d Infantry Division, 82d Airborne Division and 2d Armored Division operating separately. The 9th Infantry Division and part of 2d Armored were in reserve.

The main Allied objective was the port of Messina on the northeast corner of Sicily. Messina was and remains the primary transit point between Sicily and the mainland and in Allied hands it would ensure the elimination of all Axis forces on the island. However, the Allies chose not to attack Messina directly. The terrain around it was rugged, the beaches narrow, and the defenses appeared formidable. It was also beyond the range of Allied aircraft based in North Africa. The Allies therefore chose the more cautious strategy of landing the Eighth Army on the southeast coast between Pachino and Syracuse and then having it drive north to Messina. The Americans would land to the west at Gela and Scoglitti and protect the Eighth Army right flank. Allied airborne units would land behind the beaches to seize key terrain and block any counterattacks.

One reason behind the Allies' caution was their great overestimation of the amount of resistance that the 300,000 or so Italian soldiers on the island would make. The six Italian coastal divisions were immobile and poorly trained, armed, and led. Once the Allies were ashore most of the men in the coastal divisions who had been recruited in Sicily simply went home. The rest were glad to surrender to the first Allied soldiers they met. The four infantry

(continues on page 84)

Lieutenant General Omar H. Bradley is driven through Caltanissetta, Sicily in a ³/4-ton WC-56 C&R truck, July 18, 1943. Members of "I" Company, 157th Infantry, 45th Infantry Division rest in the shadows in the background.

GULF OF CATANIA

GULF OF NOTO

GULF OF GELA

MOUNT ETNA

CARONIE MOUNTAINS

ETNA LINE

Reggio di Calabria
Messina
Broio
Randazzo
Adrano
Catania
Augusta
Syracuse
Pachino
Noto
Gerbini
San Fratello
Troina
Santo Stefano
Nicosia
Enna
Piazza Armerina
Vizzini
Ragusa
Comiso
Scoglitti
Niscemi
Gela
Licata
Palermo
Corleone
Agrigento
Trapani
Marsala

SEVENTH XXXX BR EIGHTH

BR EIGHTH XXXX SEVENTH

8th XXXX

17 AUG
17 AUG
17 AUG
17 AUG
17 AUG Cdo
15 AUG
14 AUG
16 AUG
11 AUG
10 AUG
7 AUG
6 AUG
45 (-)
3 (-)
3 (-)
3
9
3
1
1
45
45
45
1
1
3
82
82
3
82
2
12 JUL
12 JUL
12 JUL
18 JUL
18 JUL
18 JUL
15 JUL
18 JUL
20 JUL
21 JUL
22 JUL
22 JUL
22 JUL
23 JUL
23 JUL
23 JUL
23 JUL
23 JUL
23 JUL
30 JUL
23 JUL

Frontline
Allied advance
Amphibious operations
German withdrawal
Airfield

20 mi
30km
10   20
10   20
0

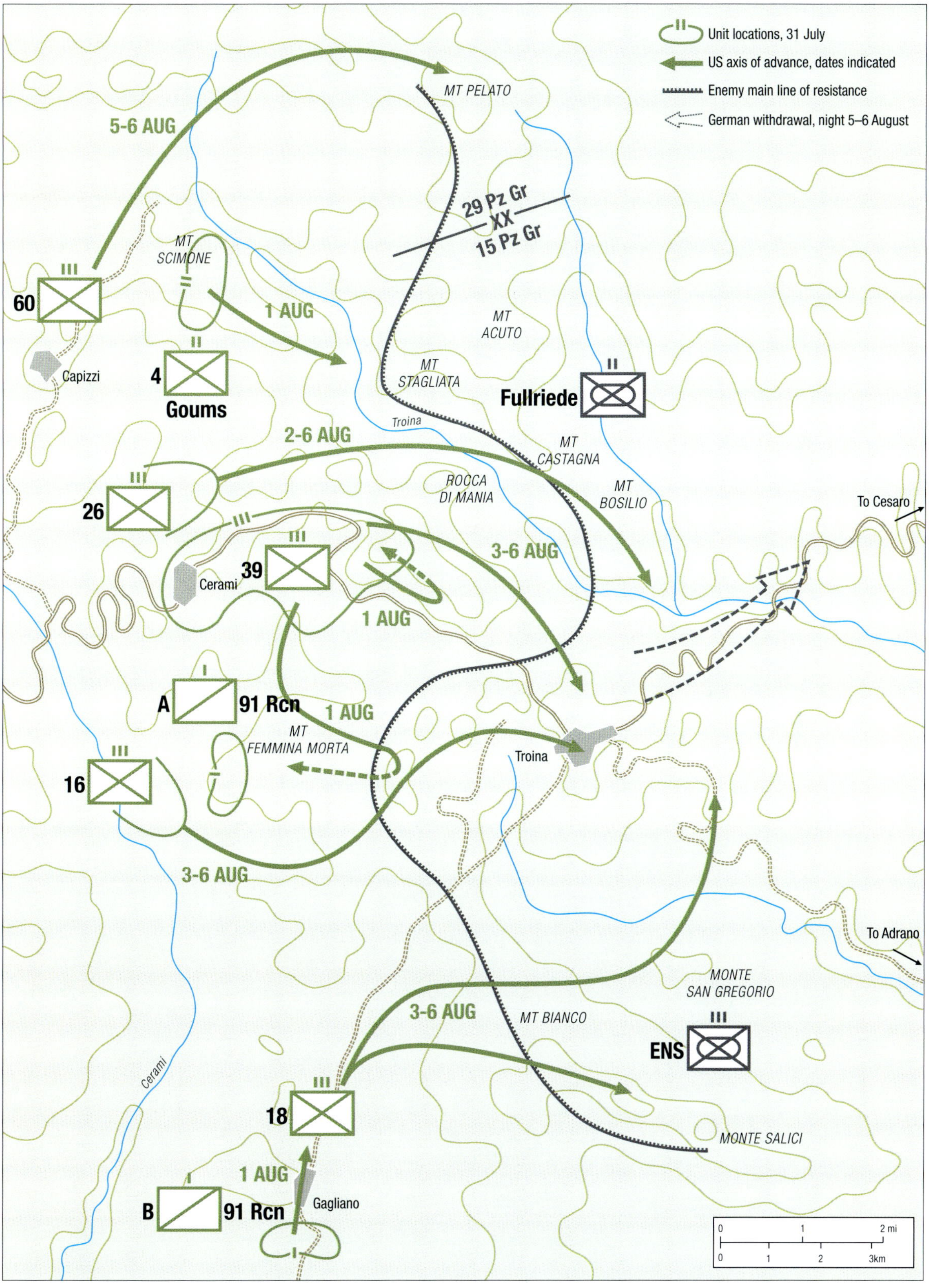
Unit locations, 31 July
US axis of advance, dates indicated
Enemy main line of resistance
German withdrawal, night 5–6 August
5-6 AUG
MT PELATO
29 Pz Gr
XX
15 Pz Gr
MT SCIMONE
60
1 AUG
Capizzi
4
Goums
MT ACUTO
MT STAGLIATA
Fullriede
Troina
2-6 AUG
MT CASTAGNA
ROCCA DI MANIA
MT BOSILIO
26
To Cesaro
39
Cerami
3-6 AUG
1 AUG
A
91 Rcn
1 AUG
MT FEMMINA MORTA
Troina
16
3-6 AUG
To Adrano
MONTE SAN GREGORIO
3-6 AUG
MT BIANCO
ENS
Cerami
18
MONTE SALICI
1 AUG
B
91 Rcn
Gagliano
0
1
2 mi
0
1
2
3km

The capture of Troina, Sicily, by 1st Infantry Division, August 1–6, 1943.

divisions were somewhat more mobile and effective but the news of the overthrow of the Italian Fascist government on July 25 caused them to fade away as well. The only serious resistance would come from the Germans, whose strength on July 10 was 33,000. Their main combat units were the 15th Panzer Grenadier and Hermann Goering Panzer Divisions (both at about half strength). Even reinforcements only brought the Germans to 60,000. Defeating them should have been easy for the more than 450,000 Allied soldiers in 15th Army Group.

Although bad weather severely disrupted the airborne landings the beach landings on July 10, 1943 encountered negligible resistance. Italian counterattacks against the Americans in and around Gela were easily defeated. Even attacks by the Hermann Goering Division were successfully thwarted although with rather more difficulty. However, elements of the German 1st Parachute Division, recently flown in from France, managed to halt the British in the vicinity of Catania. To resolve the problem Eighth Army persuaded 15th Army Group to allow it to shift its own boundaries and that of the Seventh Army to the west so that Eighth Army would have enough space to outflank the Germans themselves rather than have the Americans do it. Lieutenant General George Patton, commanding Seventh Army, although furious about these orders, did comply but he also got permission to send a "reconnaissance" westward towards Agrigento and parlayed that into a major push into western Sicily. By July 23 Patton had captured the port city and Sicilian capital of Palermo. That same day 15th Army Group ordered him to turn east and attack towards Messina along Sicily's north coast and draw away enough Axis forces to allow the still-stalled British to break through at Catania.

The campaign soon became a race to Messina between the Americans and the British, the reputations and prestige of both parties being at stake. Progress was slow. Opposition now came mostly from the German XIV Panzer Corps with the 1st Parachute, Hermann Goering and 15th Panzer Grenadier and 29th Panzer Grenadier divisions, and remnants of several Italian formations. The Germans had already decided to withdraw from Sicily and to cover that withdrawal they had established the fortified "Etna Line" across northeastern Sicily.

Though the Germans had had little time to prepare it, the Etna Line was a substantial obstacle. It ran through mountainous terrain, crossed by only four narrow roads (see map on page 82) of which only two ran all the way to Messina. The Seventh Army with several divisions organized into a provisional

A CCKW-353 (long wheel base) 2¹/₂-ton cargo truck with a G518 1-ton trailer tries to move an 81mm mortar squad to its desired firing position, Sicily, August, 10, 1943. Two jeeps are in the background.

corps would attack along Route 113 on the north coast. Eighth Army would use Route 114 on the east coast and the Adrano–Randazzo road skirting the west slope of Mount Etna. The US II Corps would use Route 120, which ran through the interior of Sicily from Nicosia to Troina and Randazzo. Stiff German resistance and the rugged terrain (that frequently required the use of pack mules rather than trucks) slowed the Allied advance to a crawl.

The 15th Panzer Grenadier Division (plus some Italian remnants) contested the advance of II Corps. Although the town of Troina was ideally suited for defense the Americans believed that the Germans at this stage would be too worn out from previous battles to fight very hard for it.

The US 1st Infantry Division led II Corps' advance. Its commander, Major General Terry Allen, was encouraged by the ease with which the 39th Infantry (attached to the 1st Division from the 9th Division) had just taken the town of Cerami (five miles east of Troina). Allen therefore ordered the 39th to attack Troina from the north, believing one regiment to be sufficient to capture the town. To ensure success he placed all the artillery belonging to the 1st and 9th Divisions plus eight battalions of corps artillery (three with 105mm howitzers, four with 155mm howitzers, and one with 155mm guns) in support of this attack. On July 31 the 39th duly attacked towards Troina but German artillery and mortar fire stopped it after it had occupied Hill 1209, about halfway to the objective. The 39th resumed its attack the next day but bad roads, German artillery fire, and even a few Luftwaffe air strikes had prevented much of their supporting artillery from reaching their firing positions. The 3d Battalion of the 39th (3d/39th), attacking north of Route 120, was soon forced back to its line of departure but south of the highway two rifle companies of the 1st/39th seized Hill 1034 against no real resistance.

Meanwhile, General Allen ordered his 26th Infantry, with a battalion of French Moroccans (the only real mountain troops available), to move round the left (north) of the 39th to seize Monte Basilio and then the hill mass overlooking Highway 120 about two miles east of Troina. Allen also ordered the 39th to continue its attack. The 2d/39th and 3d/29th moved north of the town but mortar and artillery fire soon stopped them. South of the town a 200-man German assault force pushed 1st/39th Battalion off Hill 1034, reducing its strength to about 300 men. The 26th Infantry attacks to the north on August 1–2 also went nowhere. At that point General Allen concluded that Troina would only fall to a large-scale coordinated attack. He ordered his 16th Infantry and a battalion of the 18th to take Monte Bianco, about two miles south of Troina from where they could advance to cut the road to Adrano. This was the Germans' only retreat route besides Highway 120. The attack commenced early on August 3 but German machine-gun fire halted the two lead battalions after they were halfway up the Monte Bianco ridge and ready for their final assault. Fire from six artillery battalions prevented a German counterattack from overrunning the two battalions, but by late in the day they had suffered such losses that they could no longer renew their attack. To the north, the 26th Infantry reached Monte Basilio and a battalion of the 39th had reached Monte San Silvestro. Neither had experienced much difficulty but artillery fire came down on them soon afterwards. Then the Germans attacked the battalion of the 26th on Monte Basilio, enfilading it from two sides. Despite heavy losses this battalion held on and directed artillery fire onto Highway 120 east of Troina. In response, General Allen sent two more battalions of the 18th Infantry to take positions south of the 16th with the intent of executing a pincer movement against Troina along with the 26th and 39th Regiments in the north.

Meanwhile, the 9th Infantry Division began to relieve the 1st Division as lead element of II Corps. It ordered its 60th Infantry and the French Moroccans to make a wide detour through the mountains north of Troina towards Cesarò to cut the Germans' supply and escape routes.

By late afternoon of August 5, there were two battalions of the 26th Infantry on Monte Basilio but both were in a bad way, having been cut off from supplies for three days. One company was down to 17 men. South of the 26th Infantry the 39th advanced a little further towards the highway, but south of Troina the 16th and 18th Infantry made almost no progress. However, that same day, XIV Panzer Corps decided to pull back to a much shorter defensive line a few miles to the rear. That night the 15th Panzer Grenadier slipped away to positions just west of Cesarò. It was worn out and had sustained about 1,600 casualties. Most of its heavy equipment was already heading to Messina for evacuation. Though General Allen at least partially detected the German movement he decided it was better to let the Germans go.

Thereafter the Germans continued their orderly and deliberate withdrawal with the Hermann Goering Division holding back the British in the east and the 29th Panzer Grenadier doing the same to the Provisional corps in the north. A series of small-scale landings along the north and east coasts failed to trap many Germans. On the morning of August 17 elements of the 3d Infantry Division entered Messina. They had beaten the British by a few hours but the heavily outnumbered Germans had escaped to the Italian mainland. The Allied air and naval forces did hardly anything to stop them.

Though Sicily was in many ways a flawed victory, it was still a victory. It put the Germans out of Sicily and the Italian Fascist Party out of power. An American field army had been in action for the first time. The German divisions involved had sustained significant losses, though they would soon be ready to fight again. Their successful escape had been a distinct embarrassment.

Salerno

Only three weeks after the capture of Messina the British Eighth Army crossed the straits on September 3, 1943, landed at Reggio, and began to work its way up the "toe" of the Italian "boot" against light German and Italian resistance. To support this effort a newly created Fifth Army would land on the western Italian coast further north, seize a base from which future operations could be conducted, and then move eastward to the Italian Adriatic coast to trap German forces operating further south.

The two logical localities for an Allied base on the Italian west coast were Naples and Rome. Rome was ruled out because Allied air units based in Sicily could not cover a landing in the Rome area. For Naples, there were two possible sets of landing beaches. One was at the mouth of the Volturno, about 25 miles northeast of Naples. The other was at Salerno, about 40 miles to the south. Naturally the Allies selected Salerno because their air forces could better support a landing there. The Salerno beaches themselves were excellent but the mountains behind them would hinder any movement inland.

The Fifth Army, under US Army Lieutenant General Mark Clark, would include the British Xth Corps with two infantry divisions and an armored division plus Commandos and US Army Rangers. It would also have the US VI Corps with the 3d, 34th, 36th, and 45th Divisions. The US Army 82d Airborne Division would be the Fifth Army reserve. As on Sicily, the British managed to secure for themselves the most important missions. Their Xth Corps was assigned a 25-mile sector extending from the town of Maiori to the mouth of the Sele. Its two infantry divisions would land on three beaches south of the Picento River. From there they would seize Salerno itself and Montecorvino Airfield and then, backed by the armored division, advance inland to capture the rail and highway center at Battipaglia and the bridge at Ponte Sele on Highway 19. After that they would turn north to lead the advance on Naples. The Rangers and Commandos would land on their left flank to seize the key terrain in the mountains there.

The US VI Corps had the supporting mission of landing to the right (south) of X Corps and establishing a beachhead at Paestum, south of the Sele River, and then moving inland to seize the high ground commanding the southern half of

Serre

Ponte Sele

29 Pz Gr 12 SEP

Eboli

Battipaglia

16 Pz eve, 9 SEP

169

201

167

10 BR (9 or 12 SEP)
XXX
VI

E
36

179

157 (-)

45 XX
36

Sele

2 143
Persano

3 143

3 143
1 142

3 142
Altavilla

Crotone

2 142 Rocca d'Aspide

Albanella

Calore

45
45 XX

1 142 XX 36
10 BR (9 SEP)
XXX
VI

142

143
Paestum

Solofrone

Capaccio

1 141

2 141

3 141 (-)

141 (-)
Ogliastra

Red
Green
Yellow
Blue

144
Agropoli

36

45 (-)
FLOATING RESERVE

46 XX 56

White
Red

Green

56

46

15 Pz Gr (-)
11 SEP

128

139

138

Salerno
Cdo

Vietri
sul Mare

HG Pz
11 SEP

3 Rgr

1 143 Rct

1 Rgr

Maiori

Minori

Rgr
Amalfi

3 mi
3km

The beachhead, September 9
Allied advance, 1600 September 13

Fifth Army landings, Salerno, September 9–13, 1943.

87

the Salerno plain. This would block German counterattacks against the beach areas from the east and south. The plan left a 10-mile gap between the American and British landing beaches. That gap would have to be closed as soon as possible. Initially, the VI Corps would land with only the 36th Infantry Division (a National Guard unit from Texas). One 45th Division regimental combat team (about a third of the 45th Division) would act as floating reserve. A regiment from the 82d Airborne Division stood ready on Sicily to be flown to the beaches when needed. The rest of the VI Corps would have to wait until more shipping was available. However, shortly before D-Day enough additional shipping was scraped together to carry a second 45th Division regimental combat team.

The landing began in the early hours of September 9, 1943. As expected, the beaches were only lightly held. The only large German unit in the Salerno area on D-Day was the 16th Panzer Division, a unit newly reformed in France after its destruction at Stalingrad. The division had disarmed the local Italian forces only the day before, after word of the Italian surrender had arrived, and the beach defenses in its 30-mile long sector were far from complete. The fighting elements of the division were four infantry battalions, a reconnaissance battalion, an assault gun battalion and a tank battalion with about 90 Mark IV tanks plus a separate flamethrower tank platoon with seven Mark IIIs. (The division's other tank battalion was in Germany reequipping with the new Mark V Panther.) Of these units, two infantry battalions, two tank companies (22 tanks each), and some artillery would oppose the Americans while the rest opposed the British. In addition, the 16th Panzer could rely on the support of Luftwaffe antiaircraft guns in the Salerno and Montecorvino–Battipaglia areas. A railway battery of three 132mm (5.2in.) guns was usually kept at Agropoli (at the south end of the Salerno beaches).

Before dawn on 9 September, the 36th Division boarded its landing craft and began the run to the Paestum beaches. The landing beach was divided into four color-coded "beaches." The 142d Infantry would land on "Red" and "Green" Beaches, which were furthest to the north. The 141st Infantry would land in the south at "Yellow" and "Blue" Beaches. As planned, each of the beaches varied between 500 and 1,500 yards in width but in practice they averaged about 600 yards. Each regiment would land two battalions initially while the remaining battalions came ashore in a later wave and the 143d Infantry would follow them. Once ashore they would reorganize and then advance to the high ground about 10 miles away while Army and Navy engineer groups organized the beaches for follow-on landings, communication and supply. If all went well the Americans would control the southern half of the Salerno plain by evening.

When the VI Corps landings occurred the Germans were unable to stop any of them except (temporarily) the one at Agropino. Artillery, mortar, and machine-gun fire inflicted significant losses on the unarmored wooden landing boats in the early waves. Counterattacks by German tanks caused some concern but naval gunfire proved a very effective counter to this and American tanks and artillery (including the self-propelled T-12 75mm guns of the regimental cannon companies) started to come ashore within two hours of the first wave. The German tanks were short of infantry protection, unable to concentrate into large groups and vulnerable to the new American "bazooka" antitank rocket launchers of which each rifle company had received several. By noon the Germans stopped their tank attacks and began to withdraw their troops. By nightfall, the 36th Division had seized most of its objectives, including much of the high ground.

Next day the 36th Division sought to expand and secure its beachhead. The 142d Infantry was ordered to seize key terrain in the mountains. Its 2d/142d (on the regiment's right) would move against Rocca d'Aspide across the northern slopes of Monte Soprano. The 3d/142d in the center was to attack Albanella, while the 1st/142d (on the left) was to capture the main objective, which was the Altavilla hill mass. This was a superb site for an observation post. It commanded not only much of Highway 19 but also the entire central sector of the Salerno plain. By holding Altavilla the Americans could deny Highway 19 to the Germans, prevent them from approaching the beachhead from the east and increase pressure on Highway 91, the main German escape route from the south.

The Altavilla hill mass is actually a complex of three hills. The main hill is Hill 424 (the town of Altavilla, not militarily important in itself, is on its southwest slope). A saddle joins it to Hill 315 and a smaller unnumbered hill joins the eastern part of the saddle half a mile to the south of 424. The only good way to the top of 424 was by a very steep nine-foot wide trail.

By evening the 3d/142d was in Albanella. By noon the next day the 1st/142d had occupied Hill 424, having met no real resistance. It began to prepare the hill for defense.

Meanwhile, the 179th Infantry and three artillery battalions of the 45th Division had landed on Blue Beach on September 10 (D+1) and had moved north and eastward up the valley formed by the Sele and Calore rivers with the object of protecting the left flank of the drive on Altavilla and seizing the high ground at Serre. The regiment proceeded in two columns. The southern column, consisting of the 2d/142d, a platoon of tanks, and a platoon of tank destroyers, headed up the east side of the valley, just to the left of the 142d Infantry in Altavilla. The 1st and 3d/179th and two artillery batteries formed the northern column and advanced along the southeastern bank of the Sele with the Ponte Sele (Highway 19) as its objective.

Next day (September 11), the southern column was about halfway to its objective, which was the village at Serre on Highway 19, and a little north of Altavilla when it reached a bridge over the shallow Calore River. The Germans had destroyed the bridge but the Americans managed to build a ford to get their tanks, tank destroyers, and part of their infantry across. However at that moment the 29th Pioneer Battalion (29th Panzer Grenadier Division) supported by artillery and some tanks attacked the southern column and drove it back to the south side of the Calore.

At the same time, in the northern column the 1st/179th had actually managed to get as far as some river bluffs that overlooked the Ponte Sele but resistance encountered further east had stopped the 3d/179th. Shortly after daybreak on September 12 the Germans attacked the 179th Regimental trains at the southern end of the valley and seized Persano, cutting off the 179th main body. The Germans then attacked up the valley with an infantry battalion (from the 16th Panzer Division) and eight tanks. They overran C Company of the 179th and nearly reached the regimental command post. To the south, a platoon of tanks and a company of tank destroyers tried to rescue the 179th by retaking Persano but they failed, losing one tank and seven destroyers.

By late afternoon, the main body of the 179th was hard pressed. It was out of food and water and its aid stations overflowed with casualties. Its attached artillery was down to 10 rounds per gun.

To deal with this situation it was first essential to cover the still unfilled 10-mile gap between the VI and X Corps so that the Germans could not run through it and attack US troops in the rear. To do this in part, Fifth Army shifted the VI Corps left boundary to north of the Sele and assigned the new sector to the 45th Division. The 157th Infantry of that division moved out of corps reserve up the west side of the Sele River to seize the fords north and west of Persano, thus cutting off the Germans who were besieging the 179th. The terrain west of the Sele is generally open but close to the Sele west bank was a

A jeep armed with an air-cooled M1919A4 LMG on an antiaircraft type mount is pictured in southern Italy on September 27, 1943.

A stationary armored car M8, armed with a 37mm gun, simulating its combat capabilities in the Cassino area, Italy, February 20, 1944.

tobacco factory, crowning a hill that dominated the crossing sites on the Sele River south of Ponte Sele as well as the Germans' main supply and escape route to Highway 19. A company of the 16th Panzer Pioneer Battalion (16th Panzer Division) occupied the factory and ambushed a US tank company, destroying seven tanks. Soon afterwards the 1st/157th Infantry, after having sent its C Company to block Highway 18, attacked towards the factory but was still about 500 yards short of it by dusk. The next day, the 3d Battalion, 36th Engineer General Service Regiment, temporarily acting as infantry, relieved C Company so it could rejoin its battalion.

By the evening of September 11, VI Corps still had neither rescued the 179th Infantry nor taken the tobacco factory. Allied air support was still flying from Sicily because Montecorvino Airfield was under German artillery fire. A second airfield was being built west of Highway 18 but it would not be ready until September 13. The German 29th Panzer Grenadier Division had arrived to assist the 16th Panzer. Elements of the Hermann Goering Panzer Division arrived from Naples to block any British advance northward.

On September 12, an attack by an infantry battalion of the 29th Panzer Grenadier captured Hill 424 and most of Altavilla from 1st/142d, which suffered heavily. The Hill 424 complex was too large for one battalion to defend adequately but the great shortage of trucks in VI Corps had made it impossible to bring up reinforcements. However, the Germans had weakened their forces in the west, partly to strengthen those at Altavilla. This made possible the relief of the trapped 179th and the capture of the tobacco factory. A German counterattack regained the tobacco factory but the Germans then abandoned it to avoid Allied artillery fire.

The gap between the VI and X Corps had been narrowed by the deployment of the 157th Infantry west of the Sele but what remained was still significant and held only by reconnaissance elements of the British 23rd Armoured Brigade. This situation became worse when the Germans drove the British out of Battipaglia and made the gap more vulnerable. To counter this the Americans ordered the 179th Infantry out of the Sele–Calore Valley to positions on the left of the 157th so as to extend the American line further west. Only the 2d/179th actually went into the frontline. The shattered 1st and 3d/179th were placed in reserve. The 2d/143d Infantry was brought northward to fill the gap left by the 179th.

Meanwhile, the 142d Infantry was preparing to recapture Altavilla. The 3d/142d had joined the 1st/142d (by now reduced to 260 men) from Albanella. Attached to the 142d for this attack were the 3d/143d Infantry, a company of medium tanks, and two battalions of artillery. The 3d/143d would come round to the north of Altavilla and then occupy the northern ridge. The 3d/142d would attack from the south to seize the unnumbered hill and then Hill 424.

The attack began early on September 13. The 2d/143d nearly reached the top of the unnumbered hill before German fire pinned them down and a counterattack pushed them into a defensive position at the base of the hill. When it moved up to reinforce the 3d/142d, the 1st/142d march column was raked by German artillery fire and scattered. It was nearly midnight before the remains of the battalion could be pulled together. On the opposite flank the 3d/143d managed to get a rifle company into Altavilla but was hit with a German counterattack just before it planned to attack Hill 424. The Americans held their positions for about seven hours but had to withdraw at midnight, leaving part of a rifle company still in the town.

On the same day, a heavy German counterattack by elements of the 16th Panzer and 29th Panzer Grenadier Divisions struck the 45th Division and the 2d/143d. Initially, the attack forced back the 1st/157th, driving it south and west, recapturing the tobacco factory and uncovering the Sele crossings, thus enabling one German detachment to attack the 2d/143d from the south while another attacked from the north. The 2d/143d sustained 508 casualties. The Germans continued to push south to the lower end of the Sele corridor until heavy fire from two field artillery battalions, reinforced by stragglers and self-propelled howitzers, turned them back. This was one of the rare occasions when even the artillery's 37mm antitank guns saw some action.

The result of these attacks was to cause the overextended Americans to pull back to a much shorter defensive line that, among other things, surrendered much of the high ground in the east and south. Their situation was made worse by the fact that troop buildup at the beaches had been slow (mainly due to the shipping shortage) and they had used up all their reserves. Tanks, tank destroyers, infantry cannon and antitank companies, and combat engineers all joined the infantry in the frontlines. On September 14 the Germans continued with probing attacks but gained very little. The remaining regiment of the 45th Division, the 180th Infantry, finally arrived on the morning of the 14th and the 504th Parachute arrived later that day. That night, the 505th Parachute actually parachuted behind American lines to further reinforce the beachhead while the 325th Glider Infantry came ashore in landing craft. The separate 509th Parachute Battalion parachuted behind enemy lines near Avellino, hoping to interfere with German lines of communication. Air strikes against German units in the Salerno area were greatly increased. Naval gunfire support had also been very effective. Finally, lead elements of the Eighth Army were moving to the north of the Salerno area, placing the Germans at risk of being outflanked.

Having largely accomplished their primary mission of covering the withdrawal of their forces to the south, the Germans began a phased withdrawal from Salerno to a new defensive line on the Volturno. However, they did not give up Altavilla until September 17, despite attempts by the 504th Parachute to capture it earlier. Persano and the tobacco factory did not yield until two days later. The rugged terrain, fall rains, German delaying actions, and the destruction of most of the bridges all impeded the Allied pursuit and so the German withdrawal was successful. The US 3d Infantry Division landed at Salerno on September 18 to relieve the battered 36th Division.

German losses at Salerno (including killed, wounded, and missing) totaled about 3,500 men of which 1,000 were from the Hermann Goering Division (blocking the British advance to the north), about 1,300 from the 16th Panzer Division, and the rest mostly from the 29th Panzer Grenadier since the involvement of the 26th Panzer was very slight. The Americans had about 500 killed, 1,800 wounded, and 1,200 missing (many of them captured). The British, who had faced stiffer resistance, lost about 5,500. The Fifth Army had met its minimum objectives but had failed to achieve a decisive success. The Allies still had a good deal to learn. The Germans regarded them as too cautious and over-reliant on their artillery.

Lessons learned

The major lessons that the US Army learned in the course of combat experience during the first two years after Pearl Harbor were remarkably few. The basic organization of the infantry division was shown to be sound. Given the division's conventional triangular layout, which was used by all the other belligerents, this is not surprising. However, in all the 1942–43 campaigns involving US infantry divisions, the US and its allies greatly outnumbered and outgunned their opponents. They were far better off logistically as well. Poor strategic decisions and equally poor campaign planning on the part of their enemies frequently played an important role. However, the campaigns in Sicily, New Georgia, and to a lesser extent, Salerno, demonstrated that excessive caution by American and British commanders and a slow-operating staff system could easily downgrade what should have been a decisive victory to a mere tactical success.

US divisions were sufficiently adaptable. This was especially noticeable in such places as Papua New Guinea, which was totally unlike anything that had been anticipated. Yet the infantry divisions fought successfully, despite being without their artillery and other key elements that could not adapt to the jungle. The environment was much more favorable in North Africa, Sicily, and Italy. North Africa resembled the desert areas in the United States where many divisions had trained. Even the Italian mountains had enough roads to enable supply vehicles to get fairly close to the units they supported. However, the French Moroccans, with their pack mule transport proved to be far more mobile in mountainous terrain.

Other lessons of lesser significance were that the guns in the infantry cannon companies were too heavy, while the 37mm guns in the antitank companies and artillery battalions were too light. Both had to be replaced. On the other hand, when it came to small-arms fire the combination of M1 rifle, BAR and air and water-cooled Browning machine guns had been successful enough so that the Army saw no need to change them, even though some comparable weapons in other armies were superior. Likewise the 60mm and 81mm mortars had been a complete success and were among the best of their kind, as were the M2 105mm and M1 155mm howitzers of the division artillery.

However, changes would still be needed in order to conserve an already dwindling manpower supply and limited shipping space. Additionally, these changes could not be allowed to reduce the division's fighting power.

An American .50-cal. machine gun, probably from the 41st Division, fires at Giruwa Point, New Guinea. This weapon was a decisive feature of the attack on the Point and provided excellent cover for the troops that crossed the river on January 20, 1943.

Bibliography and further research

Published books

Thomas Berndt, *Standard Catalog of US Military Vehicles 1940–65*, Krause Publications, Iola WI, 1995.

Martin Blumenson, *United States Army in World War II – The Mediterranean Theater of Operations – Salerno to Cassino*, Historical Division US Army, Washington DC, 1969.

Duncan Crowe (Ed.), *Armored Fighting Vehicles in Profile, Volume 4 – American AFVs of World War II*, Doubleday & Company, NY, 1972.

Chris Ellis and Peter Chamberlain, *American Armored Cars 1940–1945*, Almarks Publications, Edgware, Middlesex, UK, 1969.

Carlo d'Este, *Bitter Victory, the Battle for Sicily 1943*, E. P. Dutton, NY, 1988.

LTC Albert N. Garland and Harry McGaw Smith, *United States Army in World War II - The Mediterranean Theater of Operations – Sicily and the Surrender of Italy*, Historical Division US Army, Washington DC, 1965.

General Staff, Southwest Pacific Area, *Reports of General MacArthur, The Campaigns of MacArthur in the Pacific*, Volume I, and *Japanese Operations in the Southwest Pacific Area*, Volume II Part 1, US Government Printing Office, Washington DC, 1966.

G. N. Georgano, *World War II Military Vehicles, Transport and Halftracks*, Osprey Publishing, London, UK, 1994.

Kent Roberts Greenfield, Robert R. Palmer and Bell I. Wiley, *United States Army in World War II – The Army Ground Forces – The Organization of Ground Combat Troops*, Historical Division US Army, Washington DC, 1947.

Ian V. Hogg, *British and American Artillery of World War II*, Hippocrene Books, NY, 1978.

Franz Kurowski, translated by Ian McMullen, *Battleground Italy 1943–1945: the German Armed Forces in the Battle for the "Boot"*, J. J. Fedorowicz Publishing Inc. Winnipeg, Manitoba, Canada, 2003.

Dudley McCarthy, *Southwest Pacific Area – First Year Kokoda to Wau*, Australian War Memorial, Canberra, Australia, 1959.

John Miller, Jr., *United States Army in World War II - The War in the Pacific – Cartwheel: The Reduction of Rabaul*, Historical Division US Army, Washington DC, 1959.

Samuel Milner, *United States Army in World War II – The War in the Pacific – Victory in Papua*, Historical Division US Army, Washington DC, 1957.

George F. Nafziger, *The German Order of Battle, Panzers and Artillery in World War II*, Stackpole Books, Harrisburg PA & Greenhill Books, London, 1995.

Shelby L. Stanton, *Order of Battle, the US Army in World War II*, Presidio Press, Novato, California, 1984.

Articles in periodicals

Annual Report of the Chief of the National Guard Bureau 1941 (FY ending 30 June), USGPO, Washington DC, 1941.

LTC Bruce Palmer, Jr., "New Battle Lessons on Reconnaissance" *Cavalry Journal* Vol. LII No. 5, Washington DC, October 1943.

Cavalry School Staff, "Reconnaissance" *Cavalry Journal* Vol. LII No. 5, Washington DC, October 1943.

LTC Charles J. Hay, "Reconnaissance Lessons From Tunisia" *Cavalry Journal* Vol. LII No. 6, Washington DC, December 1943.

Office of the Chief of Infantry, "The Service Company" *Infantry Journal* Vol. L

No. 6, Washington DC, June 1941.

LTC William G. Livsay, "Infantry Supply in the New Regiment" *Infantry Journal* Vol. L No. 11, Washington DC, November 1941.

Office of the Chief of Infantry, "The Rifle Regiment in the Defensive" *Infantry Journal* Vol. LI No. 3, Washington DC, March 1942.

Office of the Chief of Infantry, "The Rifle Company, Condensed from FM 7-10" *Infantry Journal* Vol. LII Numbers 1, 2, 3, and 4, Washington DC, January–April 1943.

COL Mert Proctor, FA, "Notes on Liaison" *The Field Artillery Journal* Vol. 31 No. 7, Washington DC, July 1941.

MAJ John F. Bird, FA, "The Forward Observer" *The Field Artillery Journal* Vol. 31 No. 7, Washington DC, July 1941.

MAJ W. H. Bartlett, FA, "Organization of Observation" *The Field Artillery Journal* Vol. 32 No. 1, Washington DC, January 1942.

CPT J. J. Davis, FA, "Fire Direction Decentralized" *The Field Artillery Journal* Vol. 32 No. 3, Washington DC, March 1942.

LTC H. D. Kehm, FA, "Artillery Ammunition Supply" *The Field Artillery Journal* Vol. 32 No. 4, Washington DC, April 1942.

LT Angus Rutledge, FA, "What About the Service Battery?" *The Field Artillery Journal* Vol. 32 No. 4, Washington DC, April 1942.

LT W. A. Scoville, FA, "Communication Problems" *The Field Artillery Journal* Vol. 32 No. 5, Washington DC, May 1942.

Infantry School Staff, "Signal Communication—Regiment in Attack," *The Infantry School Mailing List* Vol. XXI, Fort Benning GA, February 1940.

Infantry School Staff, "Tactics of the Cavalry Reconnaissance Troop, Mechanized, Infantry Division – An Infantry School Teaching" *The Infantry School Mailing List* Vol. XXII, Fort Benning GA, July 1941.

Infantry School Staff, "Infantry School Reference Data" *The Infantry School Mailing List* Vol. XXII, Fort Benning GA, August 1941.

Infantry School Staff, "Supply—An Infantry School Teaching" *The Infantry School Mailing List* Vol. XXII, Fort Benning GA October 1941.

Infantry School Staff, "Organization and Use of the Infantry Communication System" *The Infantry School Mailing List* Vol. XXVII, Fort Benning GA, February 1944.

Infantry School Staff, "Infantry Radio Communication" *The Infantry School Mailing List* Vol. XXIX, Fort Benning GA, October 1946.

Infantry School Staff, "Engineer Combat Battalion (Infantry Division)" *The Infantry School Mailing List* Vol. XXIX, Fort Benning GA, October 1946.

Infantry School Staff, "Infantry Weapons" *The Infantry School Mailing List* Vol. XXX, Fort Benning GA, April 1947.

Websites

www.gordon.army.mil/ocos/museum – Official US Army Signal Corps website.

www.greenradio.de/e_bc222.htm – Describes the SCR-194/195.

www.greenradio.de/e_bc611.htm – Describes the SCR-536.

www.greenradio.de/e_bc728.htm – Describes the SCR-543/593.

www.kpjung.de/e_kplc.htm – Describes WWII-era vehicle-mounted radios.

www.kpjung.de/e_pogo.htm – Describes the SCR-511 man-pack radio.

www.vectorsite.net/ttwizb.html – An essay on WWII radio communication technology.

www.associated-ind.com/pdf/FIELD_WIRE.pdf – A PDF download covering field telephones and associated equipment.

www.labradorman.com/Reenacting/Research/WW2_Communications.htm – Excellent site covering a wide range of US WWII radios.

Index